POEMS

Also available from Bloodaxe Books

J.H. Prynne: *The Oval Window* (2018)

J.H. Prynne: *Poems 2016–2024* (2024)

POEMS

J. H. PRYNNE

BLOODAXE BOOKS
2015

ISBN: 978 1 78037 154 2 paperback edition

First published 2015 by
Bloodaxe Books Ltd,
Eastburn,
South Park,
Hexham,
Northumberland NE46 1BS.

www.bloodaxebooks.com

Supported using public funding by
ARTS COUNCIL
ENGLAND

The cover image is reproduced from a photograph of a specimen of native crystalline sulphur (S_8), in the orthorhombic system, bipyramidal in formation, found in frequent co-occurrence with gypsum along the outer arc of the Apennines; this example from Sicily, maximum vertical dimension 37mm. The photograph, by Sig. Carlo Bevilaqua of Milan, was published in Vincenzo de Michele (ed.), *Il Mondo dei Cristalli* (Istituto Geografico de Agostini, Novara; Novara, 1967), plate 65 (p. 48), presented here with kind permission. The bright filmaments detected in the polar region of the planet Venus are probably composed of sulphuric acid droplets.

Digital reprint of the 2015 Bloodaxe Books edition printed by Lightning Source at the printing works identified by the code inside the back cover.

For the Future

Author's Note

This book is a newly expanded edition of *Poems* (Fremantle Arts Centre Press, South Fremantle, W.A., & Bloodaxe Books Ltd, Tarset, Northumberland), 2005, including (except for minor corrections) the unchanged contents of five separate volumes published between 2006 and 2014 and seven uncollected poems ('Refuse Collection', 2004, and six additional poems). Four collections republished in America under the interim title *Furtherance* (The Figures, 2004) are fully included in the present volume. For the first publication of the collections newly reprinted here the author expresses his grateful thanks to Keston Sutherland and Andrea Brady (of Barque Press, London and Brighton), to Justin Katko (of Critical Documents, Cambridge), and to Ian Heames (of Face Press, Cambridge). For the present republication the author expresses his grateful thanks for the use of text-setting from earlier 1999 and 2005 editions to Clive Newman and Cate Sutherland (of Fremantle Arts Centre Press), and to Kevin Taylor.

Contents

KITCHEN POEMS

(1968)

The Numbers

The whole thing it is, the difficult
matter: to shrink the confines
down. To signals, so that I come
back to this, we are
small / in the rain,
open or without it,
the light in de-
light, as with pleasure amongst not merely
the word, one amongst them; but the
skin over the points, of the bone.
That's where we have it & should
diminish: I am no
more, than custom,
which is the vital
& signal, again, as if we tie into
so many voices. Wish for them:
elect the principal, we must take
aim. *That* now is the life, which
is diffused, out of
how we are too
surrounded, unhopeful.
The politics, therefore, is for one man,
a question of skin, that he ask
of his national point no more, in
this instance, than brevity. The
rest follows: so long regardful
of the rule, the decision
as knowledge and
above all, trust.
All too easy it seems with this slip
into trust if it weren't that silver
is another brightness, & we know it.
I must stand off from the warm
decay, invoke
some Danish insistence,
it doesn't concern any
of us, the risk
of exception
but we must each have, more

than, the place defined by what
we *owe* (in the weak sense,
what we too warmly
desire.
                    Only watch the weather
                    as the sky does change,
                    or the seasons in
                    quick-slip succession,
                    see it, as
walking is a white charge
in the bones we look at, constantly. Or
*in*constantly, without even a shred of desire
like maps at our feet. We want
                    too much for the others.
                    We must shrink / we
                    are small with it,
                    our pains are too earnest.
And the plain is wide: we are so
far, we should conserve
by election, which means at least
being less than so apt & so reasonable.
                    Able with reason, the light
                    isn't there, but down, in the
                    mines, for silver.
That's where the state is, where we should
recognise the renewed fact: William Smith
or suchlike could be the founder
if we needed that. Which I suspect myself
                    isn't so, as we have no
                    need of the star uppermost
                    in anyone's mind.
We *are* alive, the esteem already is
there in potential. It is
a firm question, of election,
the elect angels. Signs or array,
we should take this, we should
really do so. There is no other
                    beginning on power.
                    Such is to elect terms,
                    to be the ground for names.

We should come to the other thing, the in-
fluence of terminal systems, from there.
In the air, but first,
before that other thing
in the air.

One is each; and in
succession / or by elect
thus, there will be the
new wandering
star, in
the heavens, the
state of our own

coherence. These are the ligatures to
revise governance,
of the local disposing, the
quality as firstly position.
Here is the elect, the
folds of our intimate surface.

They call it peace
or history. Give it
nothing: to them
it is the elect,
the principal,
the voice.

Die A Millionaire

(pronounced "diamonds in the air")

The first essential is to take knowledge
back to the springs, because despite
everything and especially the recent
events carried under that flag, there is
specific power in the *idea* of it
                                        that
what is known can be used to pick up
or more usually to hold on and develop
as what for the econometrist is
"profitable speculation"–the intellect
on the trigger once more, as those
poor seventh century Irish monks (being
sentimentalists) would have believed
if they could.
                    If there's any need
for proof & it can be kept from
running to violence (to which ex-
tremity it should anyway perhaps
be swooping homewards) the twist-point
is "purchase"–what the mind
bites on is yours
                        the prime joy of
control engineering is what they please
to denote (through the quartzite window) "self-
optimising systems", which they like
to consider as a plan for the basic
living unit. And thus "accelerating the con-
vergence of function", we come to our
maximal stance.
                        Imperialism was just
an old, very old name for that
idea, that what you want, you by
historic process or just readiness
to travel, also "need"–and
need is of course the sacred daughter
through which you improve, by
becoming more extensive. Competitive
expansion: if you can designate a

prime direction, as Drang nach Osten
or the Western Frontier, that's to
purify the idea by recourse to History

before it happens. Envisaging the chapter-
head in the historical outline as "the
spirit (need) of the age"–its primary
greed, shielded from ignominy by the
like practice of too many others.
That
of course is *not* expansion but acquisition
(as to purchase the Suez Canal was merely
a blatant example): the true expansion
is probably drift, as the Scythians
being nomadic anyway for the most part
slipped sideways right across the Russian
steppes, from China by molecular friction
through to the Polish border.
Otherwise it's
purchase, of a natural course, the alteration
or storage of current like dams in the
river: what starts as irrigation ends up
selling the megawattage across the grid.

The grid is another sign, is knowledge
in appliqué-work actually strangled & latticed
across the land; like the intangible consumer
networks, as the market defines wants from
single reckoning into a social need, graphed
for instance as "contour tangent elimination".
And the drift of that is again to divert the
currency (as now in England
to the north-
east). As, it was actually losing its grip
on the *population*: real people, slipping off
the face of that lovely ground, leaving the
green & pleasant lands of Northumberland
to be nearer the belly & catch scraps
with the shit we set out so grudgingly
on plates for the blind to eat in gratitude.

The grip is *purchase* again, and the current
chic of information theory will tell you how

many bits of that commodity it takes to
lift one foot/lb. of shit to a starving mouth,
or not starving actually, but just rather
unthinkingly hungry.
                                        And don't let some
wise and quick-faced historical rat tell us about
the industrial north and its misery, since every
songbird since then (& with *no* honourable
exception for D. H. Lawrence) has carolled about
that beautiful black colour as if
this were the great rot in the heart.

It was not and it is not. The twist-point
of this is again power by the grid, putting
lives into strings of consequence into
molecular chains like the pit-ponies we love
to cry over. Coal is so beautiful as I
could weep over the carbon it shines with:
what is scattered over those colliery towns
is not soot or sulphur or coal or foaming
detergent but the waste produced by
mass-conversion of *want* (sectional) into
need (social & then total). All this by
purchase on the twist-point, the system gone
social to disguise
                                    the greed of ambition
swimming in great seismic shocks through
the beds of our condition. All the needles are
twitching frantically across their smoky paper,
but society is "predictably" as we know "in
a state of ferment"—as if that could ever turn
to *wine* or raise *bread*, from the sad shit it
is, to that crispy crunchy loaf we shall all
eat only in heaven.
                                        The fact is that right
from the *springs* this water is no longer fit
for the stones it washes: the water of life
is all in bottles & ready for invoice. To draw
from that well we must put on some
other garment. Do what one can, that's
the gas-and-water talk, which is "do
what *we* can" and *we* are the social strand
which is *already* past the twist-point &

into the furnace. We don't burn only
because
we are invisible to each other,
our shoulders no longer so hopeless and
beautiful as they meet at the spine rising
up the dorsal rift: lovely and lonely, until
the whole spread squints into the neck and
vanishes, into the *head*.
And unlike Cerberus
we all share the same head, our shoulders
are denied by the nuptial joys of television,
so that what *I am* is a special case of
what *we want*, the twist-point missed exactly
at the nation's scrawny neck.
What runs
back, or could be traced upstream by simply
denying that conspiracy of "cause", is the
question of names & the seven tribes,
which are not "predictions" and socially can
be grouped only by the thinnest of
generalising systems. As these are not
economically self-centring, they *can*not be
used as designations for targets (like
the gun-sight on what "we *want*").

And the back mutation is *knowledge* and
has always been so in the richest tradition
of the trust it is possible to have, to repose
in the mysteries. The perversions which
thrust it *forward*, as a new feed into the
same vicious grid of expanding prospects
(profits) are let through by the weakness, now,
of names.
There is no other break in the
descent, since without that it's all break
anyway. The purity is a question of
names. We are here to utter them. This is
a prayer. I have it now between my
teeth and my eyes, on my forehead. Know
the names. It is as simple as the purity
of sentiment: it is as simple
as that.

Numbers in Time of Trouble

Whichever time standard we're on, the question
of how fast and whether it's worth it, we are
underlaid by drift in the form of *mantle*, and
that should at least be a start. If the woman
gets up in the morning you could say it
was to be anointed, if that (in this time)
weren't so puny and obsequious. The wrong
standard makes it so, and the brutal fact
is, that there's no simple difference of opinion
involved: the wrong is an *entailment*, and
follows into the glowing tail of "history" as
for example the Marxist comet burns with
such lovely, flaring destruction.

That we could come off the time standard is
a first (and preliminary) proposal; having
nothing to do with some zeal about traverse
or the synchronous double twist of a minor
protein. We could come off all that, to-
gether, into the nearest city of numbers
(of which there are four, & could be five). This
is just a proposal, set on the table to move
right out of range of those sickening and
greasy sureties–like "back to our proper
homes" (or look after the Golden Rose).

The homing instinct of a great deal
else might then be cracked up: the loving
magnetism by which consequence springs
to attentive display in the field of roses.
That, say, and the justice of what we
are said to deserve when so hopelessly
we want so much more. We do *not*
get what we deserve, *ever*, since we have
proper claim by the limits of hope and
however far a given desire has within range.

So, we could come off that standard, and
"possessive individualism" would be *who we
are*–the first city. Break the charter, lift
the harlot's curse, the revolted abstraction

of "populism" by which the dark is so feared. Holding hands is a disgusting trick, and is augmented by the expectation of plenty.

Which would set out our past as gained *into* the territory of fortune, and dispose of that lumpy yarn running back into the trees. Again, what we recall is the *choice*, of our prevalence, the rich garden of the climatic terrain. And choice is not then one *from* "the rest"–the élitist dream of the crown donned in the Castle of Gold–but an inclusion *within* that measure, of choice, the second city of this middle earth.

And the question of "exchange" is thereby also dismantled. The dispute, over how far the values are trimmed, is strictly a consequent disturbance, since "fair price" is only the extent of our fears in the chest, of whatever sundry moth & rust we see in our age. "*Our* age"–at it again, the credible is what we aptly wear in our timid & tender years. The standard is a *fear index*, a measure of what (for example) "*natural* gas" will do to a precarious economy. Whoever in some sheltered domain called that vapour "natural" deserves to laugh right into the desert. These are the arid displacements beyond which lies in its state the third city, or the jewel of the air.

Further than this, up to our necks in our polluted history, the fourth city is not yet known. Going off the standard is thus far only a proposal: the mantle is warm and in constant flow, but no man has yet crossed the plains. No trumpets in any case for such *banal* folly: the modest hatred of our condition and the competition which we therefore call time. They will not sound, as we cannot yet see the other side. But we deserve to, and if we can see thus far, these are the few outer lights of the city, burning on the horizon.

Sketch for a Financial Theory of the Self

1. The qualities as they continue are the silk
under the hand; because their celestial
progress, across the sky, is so hopeless & so
to be hoped for. I hope for silk, always, and
the strands are not pure though the name
is so. The name is the sidereal display, it
is what we *know* we cannot now have.
The last light is the name it carries,
it is this binds us to our unbroken trust.

2. So then, we should not trust the hope
that is merely a name for silk, for
purity untouched by any Italian hand.
The celestial routine is begging, & a nasty
toy at that; the stars are names and the
names are *necessarily* false. We choose
to believe in the flotsam, the light glance
passing & innocent because unpriced.

3. Which is grossly untrue, because we
pay for it well enough, I have squandered
so much life & good nature I could hardly
guess the account.
The numbers are out
there in the human
sky, the pure margin
which *are* the trust we
deserve.
And we should
have what the city does need,
the sky, if we did not so
want the need.

4. The name of that is of course money, and
the absurd trust in value is the pattern of
bond and contract and interest–just where
the names are exactly equivalent to the trust
given to them.
Here then is the purity of
pragmatic function:

we give the name of
our selves to our needs.
We want what we are.

5. And not silk, except for ties, or the sky
as even for exchange, the coin of the
face we look up to as a vault ready
for trust. That much
is trickery,
but the *names*,
do you not
see, are just
the tricks we
trust, which
we choose.
The qualities then are a name, corporately,
for the hope that they will return to us. The
virtue in whose exercise we retain the fiction
of air, silence, fluid round the hub of the week.

6. How could this be clearer? The items are,
that we are bribed and that silk is a random but
by tradition a costly gift. Quality is habit.

7. What follows is where we are now, or where
I am. The old cry about chastity, that we are
bound by the parts of our unnatural frames.
The median condition is the city and not the travel
or the remoteness of travel, in sound. Music,
travel, habit and silence are all *money*; purity
is a glissade into the last, most beautiful return.

8. And how much we hope for it is the primacy
of *count*. This is the shining grudge of numbers,
the name we will not lose to any possible stranger:
the star & silk of my eye, that will not return.

A Gold Ring Called Reluctance

As you drag your feet or simply being
tired, the ground is suddenly interesting;
not as metaphysic but the grave maybe,
that area which claims its place like
a shoe. This idea of the end is a neat
but mostly dull falsity, since the
biologic collapse is violence reversed,
like untying a knot.
                                        And so slowness is
interesting and the dust, in cracks between
boards. The old ones have their senses
in the elegant droop they sometimes con-
trive, the knowing falter that makes it
all like some trick. Fluff, grit, various
discarded bits & pieces: these are the
genetic patrons of our so-called condition.

No resolve about places, the latch-key to
our drifting lives, seems relevant without
this smallest notion of dust. How to
purge the dismal objection to this, remains
a question. Not to be answered, but used,
as a metabolic regulator: pulse rate, place
rate, dust. If you lie on your back the
literalness of that position is a complete
                        transfer. Thus I
                        dream about courage
                        but love chiefly
                        several friends
                        and one woman
                        who is the Lady
                        of wherever we
                        may go.

The evident shift of pronoun (what I
now mean by "we") is a clear question
about place. We eat to live. We afford
this; the genetic links are everywhere claimed,
and you could say speech was the domin-
ating discretion. All discretion is a private
matter, all changes of pace and childhood.

And as I emerge from feeling some lingering
sense of beginning, that privacy (having
all the time some *start* in view), this is another
and perhaps my greatest transfer. The public
is no more than a sign on the outside of the
shopping-bag; we are what it entails and
we remain its precondition. Even the most
modern shops, if you work at them, will
resolve into streets or thoroughfares; their
potential for transfer has simply been absorbed,
by trade.
                    The confinement of that is no option:
the public assertion of "value" does not over-run the
channels, seeping into our discretion. Whom
we love is a tangled issue, much shared; but
at least we are neither of us *worth* it,
                    though we transfer
                    it into all other
                    matters; that
                    discretion is
                    our one place.

So that the dead are a necessity to us,
keeping our interest from being too much
about birth. The end is a carpet on
which we walk: they are our most formal
pursuit and we have our private matters
by this allowance.
                              I don't refuse the sign
in whom I know, because that's not a re-
striction. Who that is concerns
the question of who *there* is, i.e., being
in place to the hopes they are met by. The
English condition is now so abstract that
it sounds like an old record; the hiss and
crackle suborns the music, so that the
true literal has very few names. And we
too are remote within this, like the noble
gases, since it's our discretion that
is affected. Sedately torpid, we inquire
into our questions, the "burning issues"
that "face us on all sides".

The private
recourse that might also *reclaim* the transfer
is our hesitancy. Whenever we
find our unwillingness a form on which to pause.
The white pills have no mark on them &
the box extols three times daily, before meals.
But the meals are discretion. We can eat
slowly. We know all about the dead ones,
choosing to consider only the approach. Have
you had enough? Do have a little more?
It's very good but, no, perhaps I won't.

What dignity we avoid, as we
commit ourselves thankfully to these needs.
How definitely glad I am that greed is
an alternative to hunger. The few friends
are the genetic patrons, the Lady is
thankfully no
lady, I don't
owe anyone
that assurance.

And as the age or condition of this
fact we call place grows daily more remote,
the literalness thrives unchecked. The
imbalance is frightening; the splintered
naming of wares creates targets for want
like a glandular riot, and thus want
is *the* most urgent condition (e.g. not
enough credit).
I am interested instead in
discretion: what I love and also the spread
of indifferent qualities. Dust, objects of use
broken by wear, by simply slowing too much
to be retrieved as agents. Scrap; the old ones,
the dead who sit daily at the feast. Each
time I hesitate I think of them, loving what
I know. The ground on which we pass,
moving our feet, less excited by travel.

DAY LIGHT SONGS

(1968)

Inhale breathe deeply and
  there the mountain
    is there are
  flowers streams flow
simple bright goods clutter
    the ravines the
air is thin & heady
  the mountain
respires, is equal to
    the whole

So much, is just
    by pulse then
  the sky clears, again
love is a term
    of shadow and
  the shade flickers
    here, too

Since otherwise snap &
        a false a hope
less polythene lung
    when so easily the
        town fits to
    the stride, we look
at pots of jam we
        look upward

And so when it does
    rain & will glide
down our necks like
    glances into
        the soul, drop
    lets work their
way forward the sinus
    is truly the scent
of the earth, upraised

Who shall make the
sigh, of the
waters, sign of
rain & coming down
over the ridge
the entire air a nod
to for
tune, who else

The leaves make drops, drop
down the great
tent of falling, the
twigs are inside
us, we the
branches beyond which
by which through which
ever the
entire brightness ex
tends

Do not deny this halo
          the shouts are
against nothing we all
          stand at variance
we walk slowly if it
          hurts we rant it
is not less than true oh
          love I tell you so

As now, a term less than
          misty forewarnings
less ready in simple
     motions of cloud
          we breathe the
same motions of habit
     some part of the sky
is constant, that old
          tune, Sonny Boy

Foot, how you press
me to keep that
old contact alive
the repeated daily sentiment
of pace so
grim, always that
untrusting silence

And the hill is a
figure, dust in the
throat
did you say that
or was
it merely spoken
as love a thirst for
this and both together the
morning

The whole cloud is bright
    & assembled now
we are drawn by simple
        plea, over
    the membrane and its
        folded parts
into the point, and touch the
    air streaming away

VOLL VERDIENST

Follow the line the same
way down and
pale in the sky

Leave in disgrace with
fortune in
her face & eye

You cannot know
under the
brow of the hill

What she will say or do
inclining to let
ages go by.

Light in the forearm it
    lies in the
crook you can feel
    it like quick
silver where is she now.

I had a key upon a ring
    it was a pretty
thing I held it in my hand
    lest the heart grow
fond & as I watch'd it climb
    about my wrist in
time it reach'd my heart & stopp'd
    dead in the vein.

Go home said the
  stranger to the
boy's mother he's too
  weak & she
cried bitterly & led
  him to the door.

There was a maid her
  name was Jim
they always took her
  name for him.

THE WHITE STONES

(1969)

Airport Poem: Ethics of Survival

The century roar is a desert carrying
too much away; the plane skids off
with an easy hopeless departure.
        The music, that it should
        leave, is far down
        in the mind
just as if the years were part of the
same sound, prolonged into the latent
                action of the heart.
                That is more: there
        affection will shoot it up
        like a crazed pilot. The desert
is a social and undedicated expanse, since
what else there is counts as merest propaganda.
                The heart is a changed
                petromorph, making
                pressure a social
intelligence: essential news
or present fact
over the whole distance back
and further, away.
        Or could be thus, as water
        is the first social fluency
        in any desert: the cistern
comes later and is an inducement of false power.
Which makes the thinning sorrow of flight
the last disjunction, of the heart: that
        news is the person, and love
        the shape of his compulsion
                in the musical phrase,
                nearly but not
        yet back, into
        the remotest
        past.
Of which the heart is capable and will journey
over any desert and through the air, making
the turn and stop undreamed of:
        love is, always, the
        flight back
        to where
        we are.

A Figure of Mercy, of Speech

On the hilt of fortune: so that he
asks the time and it's grey, with
almost solemn insistence. Yes it is, so
that perhaps only the smell of resin

holds him to a single
hopefulness. She knows
that, there is an oblique
incitement, between them.

The branches dissolve upwards, into slivers
of the horizon: for each, the fear of this, or too
far into the side. The rift that she loves
to play, as forward, the sound of his breathing kind.

In the light, that each
might, running from both
in reach to the distance
that is unspoken, in the eye

where love is, and the sound of water, euterpe
shall it be called. They will play over
the slip, making the flesh and nails on the
handsome fingers, to the action of the light,

will play the open palm
hoping to keep to it, the fearful
exaction of love: in grey light
and hope in columns, by the river side.

The Stranger, Instantly

The tie only: how I want so much
to allow for it, the wish to know
where, in that face
                                        which is an absent
match, to the spirit.
                    So that a restless time
                    prevails; my spine arches
with the wish that's here
                                        as itself a note a sign
                                        of who they are.
And are, sitting in all the hours
of love I must translate, out
                                        back to the place
                    where I feel it, as a local thing
                    and want now
                    to allow for:
to manage between the hands and hope
of the voice, that's it, there must be
                                        a voice here also, lent
                                        to but not taken–
since even from the edge the resting
                                        waiting inshore is
travel as knowing, the quick
                    placement of love as
                    trust: at the source.
And so here, it is the others I most
                                        take to, like stones
                                        in the mist, in
                                        the voice.

Living In History

Walk by the shore, it is
a cool image, of water
    a bearing into certain
    distinctions, as
    the stretch, out there
the temple of which way
he goes; and cannot shake
    the haze, from
    a list of small
    flames.
        He wants
only the patient ebb, as
following the shore: that's
    not honest, but where
    his foot prints and
    marks his track
        in the fact of
        the evening
the path where he grabs at
motion, like a moist plant
    or the worth, of
    hearing the tide come in.
Walk on it, being a line, of rest
and distinction, a hope now lived up
    to, a coast in awkward
    singular desires
        thigh-bone of the
        world

On the Anvil

Finely, brush the
sound from your
eyes: it rests
in the hollow

as looking in
the shops at both
reflections, in
the glass

                how
to move and the
sun slanting over
the streets: shielded
from the market

in the public
domain, as
taking the pace
of movement

in the hollow
furnished with that
tacit gleam, the
cavernous heart

The Holy City

Come up to it, as you stand there
that the wind is quite warm on the sides
of the face. That it is so, felt
    as a matter of practice, or
    not to agree. And the span,
to walk over the rough grass–all of this
is that we do, quite within acceptance
    and not to press
    the warm alarm
    but a light
    surface, a day
    lifted from high
    thick roots, upwards.
Where we go is a loved side of the temple,
a place for repose, a concrete path.
There's no mystic moment involved: just
    that we are
    is how, each
    severally, we're
    carried into
the wind which makes no decision and is
a tide, not taken. I saw it
    and love is
    when, how &
    because we
    do: you
could call it Ierusalem or feel it
as you walk, even quite jauntily, over the grass.

How It's Done

Always who turns is more than
the same, being in desire the pivot
of what he would most want: or
          in point of fact, they say,
          driving through the
          early morning, to go to it.
And this is true, therefore, in such sense
as the light will allow. We take leave
of it, in the prospect of being allowed, on
          as the rocks are, the folds
          let into the saddle, cut down
          to any hope, acquired.
All the rage of the heart reaches this lifted
point, then: a fashion of spirit, a made thing.
For this there is no name but the event,
          of its leaving. There is no
          lattice, we don't sit by
          the traffic lights bathing
the soul in the links of time. The place
rises, as a point of change. There are
rocks and trees as part of it, none in
          forms of evidence. Within
          limits this arena is
          where each one is allowed
to be: the movement to be found, in the
distance is the sound that I too hope for,
here at the rock point, of the world.

If There is a Stationmaster at Stamford S.D. Hardly So

A matter of certain
essential oils
volatile
in the prolonged evening
nor would he allow
as the light stemmed
back
boarded up in the face of
that the line ran swiftly
and skimming the
crests only
into the hills of Vietnam

With so little water
the land creates a curved &
muted extension
the whole power is
just that, fantasy of control
the dispersion, in such
level sky
of each pulse the sliding
fade-through of hills
"a noble evasion of privacy"

This is parkland for
watered souls, the final
policeman's dream
that the quanta of wish
and desire, too, can be marched
off to some goal so distant
where in the hermitage
of our last days the
handcuffs would seem
an entirely proper
abstraction:
the dry and
arid gentleness, to the eye
with its own confidence
in the deep wells
of the spirit

All no more than
a land in drift
curled over and dry, but
buried way under the ice
and as spillway for these
glacial waters the
scented air
runs easily into the
night and while
the public hope is as
always the
darkened ward
the icecap will
never melt
again why
should it

In the Long Run, to be Stranded

Finally it's trade that the deep changes
work with, so that the lives are heavier,
less to be moved from or blunted. The city
is the language of transfer
        to the human account. Here
        the phrases shift, the years
        are an acquiescence.
This isn't a wild comment: there's no
good in the brittle effort, to snap the pace
into some more sudden glitter of light:
        hold to this city or the slightly pale
        walking, to a set rhythm of
        the very slight hopefulness. That
is less than patience, it's time or more clearly
the sequence of years; a thickening in the words
as the coins themselves wear thin and could
        almost balance on the quick
        ideal edge. The stirring is so
        slight, the talk so stunned, the
city warm in the air, it is a
too steady shift and life as
it's called is age and the merest impulse,
        called the city and the deep
        blunting damage of hope.
        That's where it is, now
as the place to be left and the last
change still in return: down there
in the snow, too, the loyal city of man.

The Western Gate

Too far up, into the sky, so that
the hills slip with the wash of
the quick brightness. What could the weather
shift, by those changes of place?
          Manganese on the brow;
          the rich ore, clouds over
          the stars, coming inshore–
all the power of our sentiment, what we
do feel, wanting the inclusion, the shade.
Watch any road as it lies on the
seam of the earth, with that partly
          turning & falling metaphysic:
          we believe it even despite
          the engineers. The power
is the wish to move, to recognise a
concealed flame in the evening
or dawn or whatever. The gleam
is history, desire for a night sky
          during the day too, since
          the stars circle the hills &
          our motives without reproach.
The formal circuit is inclusion. The line runs
inflected but the shapes are blue & shining.
It is the orbit, tides, the fluctual spread,
we shiver with reason and with love:
          the hills are omens, & the
          weather how long, with
          the stars, we can wait.
Or, it rains and the camber of the road
slips into it too–it's all there, as
the brickwork or hope for advice.
Write a letter, walk across the wet pavement,
          the lines are taut with
          strain, maybe they'll
          snap soon. The explosion
is for all of us and I dedicate the results
to the fish of the sea and the purity of
language: the truth is sadder but who
would ask me to hope only for that?

Lashed to the Mast

9th Nov 65:
Thus you have everything, at this
moment, that I could ever
command or (the quaint word)
dispose; rising now
in the east or wherever
damn well else
it's yours but the old
weather must be (must still
be watched, thunder
is a natural phenomenon
the entire sequence
is holy, inviting no
sympathy: who should dare
let that out, towards
what there is
anyway
love the set, tight, the life
the land lie & fall, between
also the teeth, love the
forgetfulness of man which
is our prime notion of praise
the whole need is a due thing
a light, I say this in
danger aboard our dauncing boat
hope is a stern purpose &
no play save the final lightness
the needful things are a sacral
convergence, the grove on
a hill we know too much of–
this with no name & place
is us / you, I, the whole other

image of man

Fri 13

no one thing
to say, leaving
nothing but
all that smell of
        the sea
        (private
& the gulls, squawking
in the knowledge
of time, of nothing
        at all, here
        on the rim.
Viz, the shelf out
as a pillar to fortune
        the shoals a
        quick draw
or longer, which is
a width to be gauged
        by the most
        specific &
        hopeful
        eye

Break It

And again it finishes, as we should
say it's over, some completeness numbs me
with the final touch
                                        we are sealed, thus
and why it should be so, well, that's life
not well, you see you see or we
do, we touch that, and
                                              it's the last time or
thing or some edge. Like cliffs, the de-
parture is overwhelming as a casual
thread, leading into this, that, the
gray darkness.
                              Call it evening the days
are no shorter but ah how they do
foreclose, that the tide turns and
the wick burns and curls and all

the acrid wavering of language, so full
of convenient turns of extinction. Phrase
falls, we call it an ancient city, as
we look down from
                                        the heights, hugging
the only mountain for many miles.
Blessed, as we leave: that we do, how
we do what there is these are
                                                        the one thing:
where are you   I drift into what it
should be or have you do you have, would
you. Would you. Life is a gay bargain.

How could I say, where you are among
the mountains of the city in their midst.
Turn to the east, the west, the torque
at the waist running round
                                                  the ribs, and
settling there. The end of that is a
sorry thing, how much more
beautiful is the city than
                                                the abrupt cliffs, the
                                                end, of that?

Against Hurt

Endowed with so much
suffering, they should be / and that
they are so–the pain in the head
which applies to me
and the clouds low over
the horizon: soon it
will be dark
We love the brief night, for its
quick passing, the relative ease as
we slide into comfort and
the trees grow and
grow. I can hear
every smallest growth
the expanse is grinding with it,
out on the flats beyond, down by
the sodium street-lights, in the head:
pain, the hurt to these who are all
companions. Serenity
is their slender means.
There is not much time
left. I love them all, severally and in
the largest honour that there is.
Now and with the least hurt, this
is for you.

Moon Poem

The night is already quiet and I am
bound in the rise and fall: learning
to wish always for more. This is the
means, the extension to keep very steady
            so that the culmination
            will be silent too and flow
            with no trace of devoutness.
Since I must hold to the gradual in
this, as no revolution but a slow change
like the image of snow. The challenge is
not a moral excitement, but the expanse,
            the continuing patience
            dilating into forms so
            much more than compact.
I would probably not even choose to inhabit the
wish as delay: it really is dark and the knowledge
of the unseen is a warmth which spreads into
the level ceremony of diffusion. The quiet
            suggests that the act taken
            extends so much further, there
            is this insurgence of form:
we *are* more pliant than the mercantile notion
of choice will determine–we go in this way
on and on and the unceasing image of hope
is our place in the world. We live there and now
            at night I recognise the signs
            of this, the calm is a
            modesty about conduct in
the most ethical sense. We disperse into the ether
as waves, we slant down into a precluded notion
of choice which becomes the unlearned habit of
wish: where we live, as we more often are than
            we know. If we expand
            into this wide personal vacancy
            we could become the extent
of all the wishes that are now too far beyond
us. A community of wish, as the steppe
on which the extension would sprinkle out
the ethic density, the compact modern home.
            The consequence of this

pastoral desire is prolonged
as our condition, but
I know there is more than the mere wish to
wander at large, since the wish itself diffuses
beyond this and will never end: these are songs
in the night under no affliction, knowing that
the wish is gift to the
spirit, is where we may
dwell as we would
go over and over within the life of the heart
and the grace which is open to both east and west.
These are psalms for the harp and the shining
stone: the negligence and still passion of night.

Love in the Air

We are easily disloyal, again, and the light
touch is so quickly for us, it does permit
what each one would give in the royal
use of that term. Given, settled and
broken, under the day's sun: that's the pur-
pose of the gleam from my eyes, cloud from
the base of the spine. Whose silent
watching was all spent, all foregone–
the silver and wastage could have told you
and allowed the touch to pass. Over the
brow, over the lifting feature of how
slant in the night.
                                        That's how we
are disloyal, without constancy to the little
play and hurt in the soul. Being less than
strict in our gaze; the day flickers and
thins and contracts, oh yes and thus does
get smaller, and smaller: the northern
winter is an age for us and the owl of
my right hand is ready for flight. I have
already seen its beating search in the sky,
hateful, I will not look. By our lights
we stand to the sudden pleasure of how
the colour is skimmed to the world, and our
life does lie as a fallen and slanted thing.

If he gives, the even tenor of his open
hands, this is display, the way and through
to a life of soft invasion. Is constancy
such a disloyal thing. With the hurt wish
torn by sentiment and how very gross our
threshold for pain has become. And the
green tufted sight that we pass, to and
from, trees or the grass and so much, still
permitted by how much we ask.
                                                            I ask
                        for all of it, being
                        ready to break
                        every constant thing.
                        We are bound and

we break, we let loose
what we nakedly hold
thus, he turns
she watches, the
hills slip, time
changes hands.

I ask for it all, and the press is the sea
running back up all the conduits, each
door fronting on to the street. What you can
afford is *nothing*: the sediment on which we stand
was *too much*, and unasked for. Who is the
light linked to the forearm, in which play
and raised, up off the ground. I carry you for-
ward, the motion is not constant but may
in this once have been so, loyalty is
regret spread into time, the hurt of how
steadily and where
it goes. She feels
the glimpse over
the skin. She is
honest: she loves
the steady
fear. The
durable fire.

And what you own, in this erotic furtherance,
is nothing to do with response or that
times do change: the matter is not to go
across, ever, making the royal deceit de nos jours.
As each one slips and descends, you could call
it coming down to the streets and the seedy
broken outskirts
of the town.

Bronze : Fish

We are at the edge of all that and
can reach back to another
matter, only it's not back but
down rather, or in some involved
sense of further off. The virtues
of prudence, the rich arable soil:
but why should ever the whole
mercantile harvest run to form
again? The social cohesion
of towns is our newer ligature,
and the binding, you must see, is
the rule for connection, where we
are licensed to expect. That's
the human city, & we are
now at the edge of it. Which way
are we facing. Burn the great sphere:
count them, days of the week.

For a Quiet Day

There are some men that focus
on the true intentness, as I know
and wouldn't argue with: it is
violent, the harp–I will not do it
            though, and the time is
            so gentle, in the shadow
            that any youth might
            sleep. But I will
not do it, with the gilded harp
and of all things, its pedals, for
the nice touch. As the curves too
are sometimes gentle, where we shall be
            in the succession of
            light, hope, the
            evening
distracts: and it is always too
fine, too hopeless and will not let
the gentle course–by the chance
rise of a voice.
            And if the intentness
            is the more true, then
            I want the gentler
            course, where
the evening is more of what we are:
or the day as well–moist, casual,
broken by inflictions of touch. This
is the resting-place, out in the street.
            That we are so, and
            for the other thing
            I will not do it, will
            not; this is a quiet day.

Just So

How long they ask, we ask, it
is the question. So much time to
travel or stop and yet the heart
is so slow & reluctant
        leave it, that's one
        way–there, on the
        ground: I love you
so, here but how long again, the
history of what we allow, are per-
mitted to have. A life for this
branch, dividing in the headlights
        waiting, the beam in
        prism, play or the sound
        in a great arc for the
world, it is an open fire, a hearth
stone for the condition of trust.
Don't ever wait for that. Twist it
out, in ply and then run, for
        the door: we must
        have the divine sense,
        of entrance. The way
in as what it is, not which then, or
how long as the question. Such things
are, the world is that fire, it burns
along all the horizons. It is
        the heart, where we
        are. I love you, so
        much. As this, as
this, which is for even more than I
could tell. The night flickers and
the day comes; has, will come. That's
the question, the mark strapped to
        the hands; not the
        eyes. Trust them, the
        fire of the mind, lust
of the pure citizen, on every path
of the earth. The soil, tarmac, grass,

remorse, the sea, love in the air
we breathe. Fire on the hearth. The life
    in what I now have
    and listen to, just so
    long, as we are.

Mouth Open

To set a name to it, hold them
down and ask merely
are they shouting, with both feet
planted and leaning towards me

    the note forming no con-
    sequence, they gulp the
    landscape before them

Alert, to the name of an occasion
which is theirs as I take
it from them, the offered gift
met by the purest sound

    I cannot hold this
    it is a name: shouting
    or leaning, on the single

earth which is below them, each one

From End to End

Length is now quite another thing; that is,
waiting or coming right up slap into the sun,
spreading into the land to cross, the smell of
diesel oil on the road. The friends there are,
as if residing in what instantly goes with it,
as if longer than the infinite desire, longer
and across into some other thing. Keeping
the line, running back up into the mountains,
denied. And so, in the actual moment dis-
honest, actually refusing the breakage, and
your instinct for the whole purpose
                    again shows
        how gently it is all broken
        and how lightly, as you
                    would say, to come in.
All the milky quartz of that sky, pink and
retained, into the sun. See such a thing climb
out of the haze, making the bridge straight
down into the face–which way, this way,
length beyond this, crossed. The dawn thing
suddenly isn't tenuous, and the reach back to
the strand is now some odd kind of debris:
                    how strange to
        say this, which abandons of
        course all the joy of not
                    quite going, so far.
I would not have recognised it if the sun
hadn't unexpectedly snapped the usual ride,
and with you a real ironist, your length
run off out into some other place. Not the
mountains, nothing to do with the sacred child.
The continued quality I know is turned down,
pointed into the earth: love is a tremor, in
this respect, this for the world without length.
Desire is the turn to a virtue, of extent
                    without length. How
        I feel is still along this path,
        down the cancelled line and
                    even in the dawn
as almost a last evening, coming back the

day before. Where they all live, and to say
such a thing is as you say it, promptly no
clouds but the sun. How else, in the face
of so much prudence, as the total staff of life;
as the friends, glittering (who would ever have
been ready for that? The sun, the red
                    shift; your hair
          is at the moment copper, a
          bronze mark, and the absurd
                    gift is just some
allowance, a generous move. How would that
ever have been so, the length taken down and
my nervous rental displayed. Not just holding
or drawing the part. You are too ready, since I
know you still want what we've now lost, into
the sun. Without either, the mark of our light
and the shade as you walk without touching
the ground. Lost it, by our joint throw,
and the pleasure, the breakage is no longer, no
more length in which we quickly say
good-bye, each to each at the meridian. As now
each to each good-bye I love you so.

The Wound, Day and Night

Age by default: in some way this must
be solved. The covenants that bind
into the rock, each to the other
are for this, for the argon dating
        by song as echo of the world.
        O it runs sweetly by, and prints over
        the heart; I am supremely happy,
the whole order set in this, the
proper guise, of a song. You can hear
the strains from so far off: withdrawn
        from every haunted place
        in its graveness, the responsive
        shift into the millions of years.
I am born back there, the plaintive chanting
under the Atlantic and the unison of forms.
It *may* all flow again if we suppress the
        breaks, as I long to do,
        at the far end of that distance
        and tidings of the land;
if we dissolve the bars to it and let run
the hopes, that preserve the holy fruit on the tree,
casting the moist honey, curing the poppy of sleep.
        "And in variety of aspects
        the sum remains the same,
        one family"–
that it be too much with us, again as
beyond that enfeebled history: that we be
born at long last into the image   of love

The Glacial Question, Unsolved

In the matter of ice, the invasions
were partial, so that the frost
was a beautiful head
                                        the sky cloudy
and the day packed into the crystal
as the thrust slowed and we come to
a stand, along the coast of Norfolk.
That is a relative point, and since
the relation was part to part, the
gliding was cursive; a retreat, followed
by advance, right to north London. The
moraine runs axial to the Finchley Road
including hippopotamus, which isn't a
joke any more than the present fringe
of intellectual habit. They did live as
the evidence is ready, for the successive
drift.
            Hunstanton to Wells is the clear
margin, from which hills rise into
the "interior"; the stages broken through
by the lobe bent south-west into the Wash
and that sudden warmth which took
birch trees up into Scotland. As
the 50° isotherm retreats there is
that secular weather laid down in pollen
and the separable advances on Cromer (easterly)
and on Gipping (mostly to the south).
The striations are part of the heart's
desire, the parkland of what is coast
inwards from which, rather than the reverse.
And as the caps melted, the eustatic rise
in the sea-level curls round the clay, the
basal rise, what we hope to call "land".

And the curving spine of the cretaceous
ridge, masked as it is by the drift, is
wedged up to the thrust: the ice fronting
the earlier marine, so that the sentiment
of "cliffs" is the weathered stump of a feeling
into the worst climate of all.

Or if that's
too violent, then it's the closest balance that
holds the tilt: land/sea to icecap from
parkland, not more than 2°–3° F. The
oscillation must have been so delicate, almost
each contour on the rock spine is a weather
limit
the ice smoothing the humps off,
filling the hollows with sandy clay
as the litter of "surface". As the roads
run dripping across this, the rhythm
is the declension of history, the facts
in succession, they *are* succession, and
the limits are not time but ridges
and thermal delays, plus or minus whatever
carbon dates we have.
We are rocked
in this hollow, in the ladle by which
the sky, less cloudy now, rests on our
foreheads. Our climate is maritime, and
"it is questionable whether there has yet been
sufficient change in the marine faunas
to justify a claim that
the Pleistocene Epoch itself
has come to an end." We live in that
question, it is a condition of fact: as we
move it adjusts the horizon: belts of forest,
the Chilterns, up into the Wolds of Yorkshire.
The falling movement, the light cloud
blowing in from the ice of Norfolk
thrust. As the dew recedes from the grass
towards noon the line of recession
slips back. We know where the north
is, the ice is an evening whiteness.
We know this, we are what it leaves:
the Pleistocene is our current sense, and
what in sentiment we are, we
are, the coast, a line or sequence, the
cut back down, to the shore.

References

Ordnance Survey Limestone Map, Sheets 1 and 2 (1955 edition), with Explanatory Text (1957)

K. W. Butzer, *Environment and Archaeology; An Introduction to Pleistocene Geography* (London, 1965), especially chapters 18, 21, 22, 28

W. B. R. King, "The Pleistocene Epoch in England," *Quart. Journ. Geol. Soc.*, CXI (1955), 187-208

R. P. Suggate and R. G. West, "On the Extent of the Last Glaciation in Eastern England," *Proc. Roy. Soc.* B, 150 (1959), 263-283

G. Manley, "The Range of Variation of the British Climate," *Geogr. Journ.*, CXVII (1951), 43-65

R. G. West and J. J. Donner, "The Glaciations of East Anglia and the East Midlands: a differentiation based on stone-orientation measurements of the tills," *Quart. Journ. Geol. Soc.*, CXII (1956), 69-87

Charm Against Too Many Apples

Still there is much to be done, on the
way into the city, and the sky as yet
only partly written over; we take all
our time and the road is lined with apple trees.
That's where we go, then, and if this sounds
too obviously prolonged, remember that
the ice was our prime matter. Flame is only
just invisible in sunlight
                                                  and the smoke goes
wavering into the atmosphere with all the
uncertainty of numbers. And so we can't
continue with things like this, we can't simply
go on. In this way through the forest, we
lose too much and too quickly: we have
too much to lose. How can anyone hope,
to accomplish what he wants so much not
finally to part with. We even pick up
the fallen fruit on the road
                                                       frightened by the
layout of so much *fallen*, the chances we know
strewn on the warm gravel. Knowing that
warmth is not a permanence, ah we count
on what is still to be done and the keen
little joys of leaves & fruit still hanging up
on their trees.
                                  Whereas I wish that it would
all drop, or hang in some other way suspended;
that we should not be so bribed, by incom-
pletion. The ransom is never worth it and
we never get it anyway. No one can eat so
many apples, or remember so much ice. I

wish instead that the whole federate agency
would turn out into and across the land.
With any circling motion it could be so easily
for them, theirs as a form of knowledge, and we
would rest in it: the knowledge that *nothing*
remains to be done. What we bring off is
ours by a slip of excitement: the sky is our eternal
city and the whole beautiful & luminous trance
of it is the smoke spreading
                                                          across into the upper air.

First Notes on Daylight

Patience is truly my device, as we wait
for the past to happen, which is to come into
the open. As I expect it to, daily & the ques-
tion is really what *size* we're in, how much of
it is the measure, at one time. Patience is
the sum of my inertia, by which the base-line
lays itself out to the touch
                    like the flower in
                    heaven, each pebble
                    graded in ochre. How
to extend, anyway to decline the rhetoric
of *occasion*, by which the sequence back
from some end is clearly predictive. We
owe that in theory to the history of person
as an entire condition of landscape–*that*
kind of extension, for a start. The open
fields we cross, we carry ourselves by ritual
observance, even sleeping in the library.
                    The laggard, that is,
                    whose patience
                    is the protective
                    shield, of the true
                    limit to *size*.
"The ceremonial use of the things described",
the *cinar* trees or the white-metal mirror, forms
of patience, oh yes, and each time I even
move, the strophic muscular pattern is *use*, in
no other sense. The common world, how far we
go, the practical limits of daylight. And as I
even think of the base-line the vibration is
strong, the whole sequence of person as his
own history is no *more* than ceremonial,
                    the concentration
                    of intersect: dis-
                    covery back to
                    the way over, the
entire crossing an open fabric, which we wear
stand on or carry in the hand. That this could
really be so & of use is my present politics,
burning like smoke, before the setting of fire.

Frost and Snow, Falling

That is, a quality of man and his becoming,
beautiful, or the decoration of some light and
fixed decision, no less fluent than the river
which guards its name. The preservative
of advice, keeping to some kind of order,
within the divine family of ends. The snow
level is where it fell and the limit thus
of a long cadence, the steppe whitening
in the distance and the winter climate.
The fall of snow, as of man in the ice block
and its great cracking roar, is a courtesy;
we don't require the black spiral, being gentle
and of our own kind. We run deeper, cancel
the flood, take to the road or what was before
known as champaign. We stand off the shore
even when turning to our best and most serious
portions of time. I judge that, as a snow level
but equally in seasonal pasture, pleasure or
as the rival comes, with clay on his shoes.
How far have you come and how long was your
journey? Such persons are hungry; the rival
ventures his life in deep water, the reddish gold
glints in the shadows of our lustful solitude.

So that when the snow falls again the earth
becomes lighter and lighter. The surface con-
spires with us, we are its first-born. Even
in this modern age we leave tracks, as we
go. And as we go, walk, stride or climb
out of it, we leave that behind, our own
level contemplation of the world. The monk
Dicuil records that at the summer solstice
in Iceland a man could see right through the
night, as of course he could. That too is a
quality, some generous lightness which we
give to the rival when he comes in. The tracks
are beaten off, all the other things underground.

On 9th May 1247 they set out on the return
journey. "We travelled throughout the winter, often

sleeping in the desert on the snow except when
we were able to clear a place with our feet.
When there were no trees but only open country
we found ourselves many a time completely
covered with snow driven by the wind." That
sounds to me a rare privilege, watching
the descent down over the rim. Each man
has his own corner, that question which
he turns. It's his nature, the quality he
extends into the world, just as his stature is
his "royal dignity". And yet Gregory did not
believe in the pilgrimage of place: Jerusalem,
he says, is too full of rapine and lust to be
a direction of the spirit. The rest is some kind
of flame, the pilgrim is again quality, and
his extension is the way he goes across the crust
that will bear him. The wanderer with his
thick staff: who cares whether he's an illiterate
scrounger–he is our only rival. Without this
the divine family is a simple mockery, the
whole pleistocene exchange will come to
melt like the snow, driven into the ground.

For This, For This

The next stave we come to is the mansion
or house, wondering about the roof and the
set, as it were, back into the silence which
is the social division, split into quietness.
Why are we so tensed as we prepare to make
some side step, into the house and thus, you
would say, out of the world. Off the planet
even, while the amber glow of Mercury shines
from the flashing shield? Oh no it's not this,
any more than we deny the sound its direction,
choosing to "hear" the splinter and splash
of some ordinary thing.

I will not listen, or claim
to, that ignoble worship of
the wrong road. They are
too clean, always, they
fall in part to part, this knife
will go straight into
the fire if that's the heart.

And þerto when þou seest þat alle soche werkes in þeire
use mow be boþe good & iuel, I preie þee leue hem boþe,
for þat is þe most ese for þee for to doo if þou wilt
be meek.

Watch the colour run up the blade; watch the
house held off, we live so much in this way.
How does he know when to "speak his mind"
and come back in through some pattern of
misery? Buying his way in through this price
making the doorway, and now even current coin
is frozen in the banks; some weird puritan
stringency that believes cold to be bracing.

All the quick motions
as we nip upstairs, turn
to steps we take: leading
to the moral exits

which we see enjoined. Some idea of
completeness; protection
is wretched and what we pay for.

And leue þe corious beholdyng & seching in þi wittes to loke wheþer is betir.

Yet some soft stirring to speak is in the air,
the casual motion flirts with us. We are
less sombre now, slipping out at the door
and into some silent affair through which
we hear everything. All of that, without
name, not with regret, as a musical turn.
The importance is complete, the sequence
is urban, needful; she comes like some
obvious choice, picking her way. I see
this, you see the world in her wide sails,

the knife is not playful
or an agent of just
device. It comes from
the kitchen, I'm not
going to tell you that; you know
how outside the door too
we are ready in one.

Bot do þou þus: sette þe tone on þe to honde and þe toþer on þe toþer, and chese þee a þing þe whiche is hid bitwix hem, þe whiche þing when it is had, ȝeueþ þee leue, in fredom of spirite, to beginne and to seese in holding any of þe oþer at þin owne ful list, wiþouten any blame.

In Cimmerian Darkness

When the faint star does take
us into the deeper parts
of the night there *is*
that sudden dip
and we swing across into
some other version of this
present age, where any curving
trust is set into
the nature of man, the green raw and fabulous
love of it, where every star that shines,
as he said, exists
in love, the *brother*
dipping into the equal limit,
help as the ready art, condition of the
normal
since no more simple
presence will fade, as the dawn does, over
water, the colonies of feeling like stacks
of banknotes waiting to be counted.
Anyone waits, the brother is a section of
the waiting art, whereby and
through which agency the whole
cosmic vibrations disport their limbs, their
hopes, the distant repose.
We dip into the ready world
which waits for us: the
name of it is our brother and we must pro-
tect what we want of it,
as we need more than I personally
can ever admit. Or now do so
admit, the title to this going into the sky
is the trust of the lighted brother in the
first sense, the *standard*.
Stand there, I implore you, the trust *is* an agency
of surrender, I give it all up, the star
is yielded. No part of this dipping
coil shall be withheld; no
light further than the figure of some complete
fortune, making and made weak
by affection and the promise of it.

Led to the star, trusting to rotten planks,
the equal limit, we must have it, I ask only
in sequence, in this parity of
art ready with its own motion. It swings out
and we are quickly cruel, the brother reforms
his wish to roam the streets, he
should refuse as much as he can.
Nor is the divine in any sense
full, the vacancy stretches away
to the standard out on the plain; the cups
of our radio telescopes stand openly
braced to catch the recoil. Focus, the
hearth is again warm, again the human patch
waits, glows in the slight wind.
And we *are* ready for this, the array *is* there in
the figure we name brother, the
fortune we wish for, devoutly, as the dip
turns us to the face we have
so long ignored; so fervently refused.

Song in Sight of the World

In sight of the world they are
heavy with this, the sea
thrown up, the shore and all
the lamps out on the road–
        but where are they, will
        they go to: why do
        not love and instruction
        come swiftly to the places
where they stand? Who are the muses
in this windblown instalment–as
if there is much uncertainty
about that. We are a land
        hammered by restraint, into
        a too cycladic past. It is
        the battle of Maldon binds
        our feet: we tread
only with that weight & the empire
of love, in the mist. The name of this
land, unknown, is that. Heavy with sweat
we long for the green hills, pleasant with
        waters running to the sea
        but no greater love. The politics
        of this will bear inspection. They are
        the loss of our each motion, to history.
Which is where the several lost stand
at their various distance from the shore
on gneiss or the bones of a chemical plan
for the world's end. This is it, Thule,
        the glyptic note that we carry
        with every unacted desire felt
        in the continent of Europe. Lot's
        wife, the foreshore of the world.
And the weight? Still with us, the hold
is a knowing one. The night is beautiful
with stars: we do not consider the end
which is a myth so powerful, as to throw
        flames down every railway line
        from London to the furthest tip
        cape and foreland left by the axe.
        Apollo it is that I love, that

shall be swallowed by the great wolf and be
reborn as a butterfly in the hair of a goddess.
We are poor in this, but I love
and will persist in it, the equity
          of longing. The same is not true
          but desired: I desire it and shall
          encircle the need with bands of iron,
          this is the wedge of my great hope.
All the shores are a single peak. All the
sea a great road, the shore a land in
the mist. The tears of the world are spread
over it, and into the night you can hear
          how the trees burn with foreknowledge.
          As before, I am the great lover
          and do honour to Don Juan, & sharpen
          his knife on the flat of my foot.
The forest, of stars. The roads, some grey
people walking towards the restaurant.
The headlights, as a lantern; now they are
in the restaurant. See, we shall eat them.
          The light will do all this, to
          love is the last resort, you
          must know, I will tell
          you, this, love, is
                              the world.

Quality in that Case as Pressure

Presence in this condition is quality
which can be transformed & is subject
even to paroxysm—but it is not
lapse: that is the chief point. As I
move with my weight there is collusion,
with the sight of how we would rise
or fall or on the level. How *much* we
see is how far we desire change, which
is transformation from the ridge and fore-
land *inverted*—with all the clouds
over the shore.
                    The sun lies on the
                    matching of the ridge, &
                    passing is what you
                    cannot have, it is
                              the force, where
                              else to see
                              how in, this
                              is, the oblique
turned into a great torque which is
pleasure as a name for each part:
no nearer than
                    the ridge, or side
                    slope end time so
                    much but not *how*
much. My own satisfaction in this
mild weather is violent; I am moved
by the *condition* of knowledge, as the
dispersion of form. Even, tenuous, gorged
in the transgressions of folding
                    the orogeny of passion the
                    invasion of ancient
                    seas
                              the neutral
                              condition of
                              that
                    the heart/heartland, prize
                    of the person who can be
seen to stumble & who falls with joy, unhurt.
Or who hurries, on some pavement, the

sublate crystal locked for each step.
They aim their faces but also bear them
and have cloth next to most of their skin.
They are the children of proof.
The proof is a *feature*, how the
spine is set. The invasion
of fluid, where the
action of money
is at least tem-
porarily displaced.
By seepage or transgression, the mineral salts
"found their way" into the Zechstein Sea. The
reciprocation of fault and inversion,
poverty the condition, of which I am so clearly
guilty I can touch the pleasure involved.

For such guilt is the agency of ethical fact:
we feel shame at the mild weather too and
when the National Plan settles comfortably
like a Grail in some sculpted precinct
I am transported
with angelic
nonchalance.
The quantities of demand are the measure
of want–of lack or even (as we are told)
sheer grinding starvation. *How much* to
eat is the city in ethical frenzy
the allowances set against
tax the deductions in respect
of unearned income
the wholly sensuous & mercantile matter
of *count*. As I move through the bright
bones of their hands & faces
shattered by the exact
brimming of love &
pleasure, the force
is a condition
released in the
presence
that
this is the chosen remnant, of a plan
now turned on its axis, east-west into the
wind. I am bound to it, by an aggressive
honour, and
in this the peace of the city does now reside.

Oil

In the year; intact in the cycle of days
passing over him like the damp air
he is back on the first level,
some floating completeness
has assailed him. He
is perfect. In the sight of his eye the
wind dripping with rain
has come so far, round over the crests
and fields, the cornea moist the
lymph draining and curled
down to rest. This level sequence of history
is his total and our total
also, is
the certain angular sustenance
of the world. So I walk over the
top of the steady and beating level of his
eye; he has so much to bestow, he is
generous. What he has is our
shout, the sound of the pathway, going down into
the breathing touch of the air, the rain
which soaks into our clothes. At last
we are wet,
wet through with what we have
in his eye, in our time, in the ribs in-
flated with it, the
last few days of the year

Shadow Songs

1

The glorious dead, walking
barefoot on the earth.
Treat them with all you
have: on the black marble
and let Nightingale come
down from the hills.
Only the procession is halted
as this spills down into
the current of the river:
their glorious death, if
such on earth were found.

2

And if the dead know this,
coming down into the dark, why should
they be stopped? We are too gentle
for the blind to see or be heard.
All the force of the spirit lies open
in the day, praise in the clock face
or age: the years, with their most
lovely harm. Leading the gentle
out into the wilds, you know they
are children, the blind ones, and
the dead know this, too.

Concerning Quality, Again

So that I could mark it; the continuance of
quality could in some way be that, the time
of accord. For us, as beneath the falling water
          we draw breath,
          look at the sky.
Talking to the man hitching a lift back
from the hospital, I was incautious in sympathy:
will she be back soon I was wishing to
encourage his will to suppose. I can hardly
expect her back he said and the water
fell again, there was this sheet, as the time
          lag yawned, and quality
          became the name you have,
like some anthem to the absent forces of nature.
Ethnic loyalty, breathe as you like we in fact
draw it out differently, our breath is gas
in the mind. That awful image of choking.

We *have* no mark for our dependence, I would
not want to add a little red spot to the wrist of
the man in the newsreel, the car passing the lights.
I draw blood whenever I open my stupid mouth,
          and the mark is on *my* hand, I
          can hardly even feel the brass wire
          nailed down into the head.
Paranoid, like the influencing machines; but who
they are, while their needs shine out like flares,
that quality *is* their presence outward to the night
sky: they do ask for that casual aid. The re-
cognition is accident, is an intolerable fall like
water. We whizz on towards the blatant home
and the armies of open practice. His affairs are
electric; they cancel the quality of the air;
          the names are a blankness as
          there are no marks but the wounds.

Even the accord, the current back (for him as for
me outward) has an electric tangent. He could
have flown off just there as he was. Simply
moved sideways, in his sitting posture, across the

next hedge and into a field I know but could
not recognise. The mark is Abel's price, the
breath is blood in the ears as I even dare to think
of those instruments. The sky is out there with
the quality of its pathic glow, there is a bright
thread of colour across the dashboard; the accord
　　　　is that cheap and we live
　　　　with sounds in the ear
　　　　which we shall never know.

On the Matter of Thermal Packing

In the days of time now what I have
is the meltwater constantly round my feet
and ankles. There the ice is glory to the
past and the eloquence, the gentility of
the world's being; I have known this
as a competence for so long that the
start is buried in light

usual as the warm grass and shrubbery
which should have been ancestral
or still but was, then, bound like crystal
into the last war. There was a low
drywall, formal steps

down I now see to the frozen water, with
whitened streaks and bands in it;
the same which, in New England, caused
a total passion for skating, and how still
it all was

the gentility of a shell, so
fragile, so beautifully
shallow in the past; I
hardly remember
the case hardened
but brittle

constant to the eighteenth century or the
strictly English localism of moral candour,
disposed in the copses of those fields
which bespoke easily that same vague lightness,
that any motion could be so much

borne over the
top, skimming
not knowing the flicker
that joins
I too

never knew who had lived there. It was then
a school of sorts, we were out of the bombs
I now do, I think, know that. But the flow
so eloquently stopped, walking by the Golden
Fleece and the bus time-table

("It is difficult
to say pre-
cisely what
constitutes
a habitable
country"—A
Theory of the Earth

the days a nuclear part
gently holding the skull or
head, the skin porous to the
eloquence of

where this was so far! so ice-encased like
resin that whiteness seemed no more, than
cloudy at that time. The water-pattern is
highly asymmetric, bonding hardly as proof
against wealth, stability, the much-loved ice.

Which I did love, if
light in the field
was frozen
by wire
ploughed up, I
did not know, that
was the gentle
reach of ignorance
the waves, the
ice

the forms frozen in familiar remoteness—
they were then, and are closer now, as
they melt and rush into the spill-
ways: "one critical axis of the crystal
structure of ice remains dominant after
the melt"—believe that?

or live there, they would say in
the shade I am now competent
for, the shell still furled but
some nuclear stream

melted from it.
The air plays
on its crown, the
prince of life
or its
patent, its
price. The absent
sun (on the
trees of the field) now does strike
so gently
on the whitened and uneven ice
sweet day so calm
the glitter is the war now released,
I hear the guns for the first time

Or maybe think so; the eloquence of melt
is however upon me, the path become a
stream, and I lay that down
trusting the ice to withstand the heat; with
that warmth / ah some modest & gentle
competence a man could live
with so little
more.

Price Tag Song

OK and relevant to the
cosmos, scarce of
air said
aunt Theoria, the scar
city is not for
resale or photograph
ic repro
duct
ion I mean at
least you can't look all
the time out
of sight or mind the
choice is
sheer care
less debauchery I count, as
three two one &
scarce
the part healed city
where we start
led in
sects live

The Common Gain, Reverted

The street is a void in the sequence of man,
as he sleeps by its side, in rows that house
his dreams. Where he lives, which is the
light from windows, all the Victorian grandeur
of steam from a kitchen range. The street
is a void, its surface slips, shines and is
marked with nameless thoughts. If we could
level down into the street! Run across by
the morning traffic, spread like shadows, the
commingling of thoughts with the defeat we
cannot love
                                        Those who walk heavily
                                        carry their needs, or lack
                                        of them, by keeping their
                                        eyes directed at the ground
                                        before their feet. They are
said to trudge when in fact their empty thoughts
unroll like a crimson carpet before their
gentle & delicate pace. In any street the pattern
of inheritance is laid down, the truth is for our
time in cats-eyes, white markings, gravel
left from the last fall of snow. We proceed
down it in dreams, from house to house which
spill nothing on to the track, only light on the
edge of the garden. The way is of course speech
and a tectonic emplacement, as gradient it
moves easily, like a void
                                        It is now at this
                                        time the one presence
                                        of fact, our maze
                                        through which we
                                        tread the shadow or
                                        at mid-day pace
level beneath our own. And in whichever form
we are possessed the surface is sleep again and
we should be thankful. By whatever movement,
I share the anonymous gift, the connivance
in where to go as what I now find myself
to have in the hand. The nomad is perfect
but the pure motion which has no track is

utterly lost; even the Esquimaux look for sled
markings, though on meeting they may not speak.
The street that is the
sequence of man
is the light of his
most familiar need,
to love without being stopped for some im-
mediate bargain, to be warm and tired
without some impossible flame in the heart.
As I walked up the hill this evening and felt
the rise bend up gently against me I knew
that the void was gripped with concentration.
Not mine indeed but the sequence of fact,
the lives spread out, it is a very wild and
distant resort that keeps a man, wandering
at night, more or less in his place.

Aristeas, in Seven Years

Gathering the heat to himself, in one thermic
hazard, he took himself out: to catch up with
the tree, the river, the forms of alien vantage
1 *and hence the first way*
by theft into the upper world–"a
natural development from the mixed
economy in the drier or bleaker
regions, where more movement was
necessary"–and thus the
floodloam, the deposit, borrowed for
the removal. Call it inland, his
nose filled with steam & his brief cries.
Aristeas took up it
seems with the
singular as the larch
tree, the
Greek sufficient
for that. From Marmora

And sprang with that double twist into the
middle world and thence took flight over the
Scythian hordes and to the Hyperborean,
touch of the north wind
carrying with him Apollo. Song
his transport but this divine
insistence the *pastural clan*:
sheep, elk, the wild deer. In each case
the presence in embryo, god of the shep-
herd and fixed in the movement of flock.
Wrung over the real tracts. If he was
frozen like the felted eagle of Pazyryk,
he too had the impossible lower twist,
the spring into the middle, the air.
From here comes
the north wind, the
remote animal
gold–how did
he, do we, know
or trust, this?
Following the raven and

sniffing hemp as the
other air, it was
himself as the singular that he knew and
could outlast in the long walk by the
underground sea. Where he was as
the singular
location so completely portable
that with the merest black
wings he could survey the
stones and rills in their
complete mountain courses,
2 *in name the displacement*
Scythic.
And his songs were invocations in no frenzy
of spirit, but clear and spirituous tones from the
pure base of his mind; he heard the small
currents in the air & they were truly his aid.
In breath he could speak out into the northern
air and the phrasing curved from his mouth
and nose, into the cold mountain levels. It
was the professed Apollo, free of the festive line,
powdered with light snow.

And looking down, then, it is no outlay
to be seen in
the forests, or
scattered rising
of ground. No
cheap cigarettes nothing
with the god in this
climate is free of duty
moss, wormwood as the cold
star, the dwarf Siberian pine
as from the morainal deposits
of the last deglaciation.
Down there instead the long flowing hair,
of great herds of sheep and cattle, the
drivers of these, their feet more richly
thickened in use than
any slant of their
mongoloid face or
long, ruched garments.

With his staff, the larch-pole, that again the
singular and one axis of the errant world.

Prior to the pattern of settlement then, which
is the passing flocks fixed into wherever
they happened to stop,
the spirit demanded the orphic metaphor
3 *as fact*
that they did migrate and the spirit excursion
was no more than the need and will of the
flesh. The term, as has been pointed out,
is bone, the
flesh burned or rotted off but the
branch calcined like what
it was: like that: as itself
the skeleton of the possible
in a heap and covered with
stones or a barrow.
Leaving the flesh vacant then, in a fuller's shop,
Aristeas removed himself for seven years
into the steppes, preparing his skeleton and the
song of his departure, his flesh anyway touched
by the in-
vading Cimmerian
twilight: "ruinous"
as the old woman's
prophecy.
And who he was took the
collection of seven
years to thin out, to the
fume laid across where
he went, direction north,
4 *no longer settled*
but settled now into length; he wore that
as risk. The garment of birds' feathers,
while he watched the crows fighting the
owls with the curling tongues
of flame proper to the Altaic
hillside, as he was himself
more than this. The
spread is more, the
vantage is singular
as the clan is without centre.

Each where as
the extent of day deter-
mines, where the
sky holds (the brightness
dependent on that).
And Apollo is in any case seasonal, the
divine "used only of a particular god,
never as a general term." The Hyper-
borean paradise was likewise no general
term but the mythic duration of
spirit into the bone
laid out in patterns
on the ground
"the skulls are sent on hunting
journeys, the foot-prints alongside;
that towards which they journey
they turn them towards, so that
they will follow behind."
From the fuller's shop as from
the camp of the seal hunter,
5 *some part of the bone must be twisted*
& must twist, as the stages of Cimmerian
wandering, viz:
1. 1800–13th Century B.C., north
of the Caucasus, then
2. 13th–8th Centuries, invaded
by the Scythians and deflected
southwards & to the west. And
3. after that, once more displaced
(8th Century to maybe 500 B.C.),
the invasion of Asia Minor,
"ruinous", as any settled and complaisant fixture
on the shoreline would regard the movement of
pressure irreducible by trade or bribery. Hence
the need to catch up, as a response to cheap money
and how all that huddle could
be drawn out
into the tenuous upper
reach, the fine chatter
of small birds under the
head of the sky
(sub divo columine)
on the western slope of the Urals and the scatter

of lightning, now out of doors & into
the eagle span,
6 *the true condition of bone*
which is no more singular or settled or the
entitled guardian even, but the land of the
dead. Why are they lost, why do they
always wander, as if seeking
their end and drawing after them
the trail and fume of burning hemp?
Or they are not lost but
passing: "If thoughtless abandonment
to the moment were really a blessing, I
had actually been in 'the Land of the
Blessed'."
But it was not blessing, rather a fact so
hard-won that only the twist in middle
air would do it anyway, so even he be wise
or with any recourse to the darkness of
his tent. The sequence of issue is no
more than this,
Apollo's price, staff
leaning into the
ground and out
through the smoke-hole.
It is the spirit which dies
as the figure of change, which
is the myth and fact of extent,
which thus does start from
Marmora, or Aklavik, right
out of the air.
No one harms these people: they
are sacred and have no
weapons. They sit or pass, in
the form of divine song,
they are free in the apt form of
displacement. They change
their shape, being of the essence as
a figure of extent. Which
for the power in rhyme
7 *is gold, in this northern clime*
which the Greeks so held to themselves and
which in the steppe was no more
than the royal figment.

This movement was of
course cruel beyond belief, as this
was the risk Aristeas took
with him. The conquests were for the motive of
sway, involving massive slaughter as the
obverse politics of claim. That is, slaves and
animals, *life* and not value: "the western Sar-
matian tribes lived side by side not in a loose
tribal configuration, but had been welded
into an organised imperium
under the leadership of one
royal tribe." Royalty
as *plural*. Hence the calendar as taking of
life, which left gold as the side-issue, pure
figure.

Guarded by the griffins, which lived close to the
mines, the gold reposed as the divine brilliance,
petrology of the sea air, so far from the shore.
The beasts dug the metal out with
their eagle beaks, rending in the
cruel frost of that earth, and
yet they were the guardians, the figure of flight
and heat and the northern twist of the axis.
His name Aristeas, absent for
these seven years: we should
pay them or steal, it is no
more than the question they ask.

References

A. P. Vaskovskiy, "A Brief Outline of the Vegetation, Climate, and Chronology of the Quaternary Period in the Upper Reaches of the Kolyma and Indigirka Rivers and on the Northern Coast of the Sea of Okhotsk" (1959), in H. N. Michael (ed.), *The Archaeology and Geomorphology of Northern Asia: Selected Works* (Arctic Institute of North America, Anthropology of the North: Translations from Russian Sources, 5; Toronto, 1964)

J. Harmatta, *Studies on the History of the Sarmatians* (Magyar-Görög Tanulmányok, 30; Budapest, 1950)

Herodotus, *History*, 4; Longinus, *On the Sublime*, 10

T. Sulimirski, "The Cimmerian Problem," *Bulletin of the Institute of Archaeology* (University of London), 2 (1959), 45-64

G. S. Hopkins, "Indo-European **Deiwos* and Related Words," *Language Dissertations Published by the Linguistic Society of America* (Supplement to *Language*), XII (1932)

K. Rasmussen, *The Netsilik Eskimos; Social Life and Spiritual Culture* (Report of the Fifth Thule Expedition, 1921-24, Vol. VIII, Nos. 1-2; Copenhagen, 1931)

E. D. Phillips, "The Legend of Aristeas: Fact and Fancy in Early Greek Notions of East Russia, Siberia, and Inner Asia," *Artibus Asiae*, XVIII, 2 (1955), 161-177

E. D. Phillips, "A Further Note on Aristeas," *Artibus Asiae*, XX, 2-3 (1957), 159-162

J. Partanen, "A Description of Buriat Shamanism," *Journal de la Société Finno-Ougrienne*, LI (1941-42), 1-34

H. N. Michael (ed.), *Studies in Siberian Shamanism* (Arctic Institute of North America, Anthropology of the North: Translations from Russian Sources, 4; Toronto, 1963), especially the two papers by A. F. Anisimov: "The Shaman's Tent of the Evenks and the Origin of the Shamanistic Rite" (1952) and "Cosmological Concepts of the Peoples of the North" (1959)

J. Duchemin, *La Houlette et la Lyre: Recherche sur les Origines Pastorales de la Poésie*, Vol. 1: *Hermès et Apollon* (Paris, 1960)

M. S. Ipşiroğlu, *Malerei der Mongolen* (München, 1965)

Señor Vázquez Speaking and Further Soft Music to Eat By

So today it is quite hot again and the
erotic throb of mere air replaces the traffic;
we (the warmed-up) are not separate
from the body flowing into and just being
with air. So delectable, another sense for
presence, glandular pressure; so all
            the dark air comes running
            up like some woven thing,
            soft like our own possessions.
We read about that in cheap paperbacks–maybe
today it's the turn of the scarlet athlete.
Anyway, the angelic hosts were undisturbed
in their eminence of domain, not caring
at all for charter or land reform. In that
sense mostly far distant from the Colombian
peasants whose current leader is so
evidently named by a small promethean gesture.
            To return, this is an
            intimately physical place,
            picked out of the air like
forbidden fruit. So much air and so close I
can feel the lunar caustic I once used in
a lab note-book headed "analysis". Now
it's Laforgue again, the evening a deep city
of velvet and the Parisian nitrates washed off
into the gutters with the storm-water. In the
more entire flarings of sheet lightning the
rain-drops glittered violently in their
descent, like a dream of snake's eyes.
            All this the static and
            final saturation of air:
            the physical world in
which, somewhere out in the Andes or in
the jungle valleys the same bitter spasm
is fought, for life and traffic: it is the

air, we breathe and if
now it
trembles like some satiric
sexual excitement we
are no more than the air we
now are, baffled. The angels have
no reason to worry, about that.

Thoughts on the Esterházy Court Uniform

I walk on up the hill, in the warm
sun and we do not return, the place is
entirely musical. No person can live there
& what is similar is the deeper resource, the
now hidden purpose. I refer directly to my
own need, since to advance in the now fresh &
sprouting world must take on some musical
sense. Literally, the grace & hesitation of
modal descent, the rhyme unbearable, the
coming down through the prepared delay and
once again we are there, beholding the
complete elation of our end.
                                        Each move
into the home world is that same loss; we
do mimic the return and the pulse very
slightly quickens, as our motives flare in
the warm hearth. What I have is then already
lost, is so much there I can only come down
to it again, my life slips into music &
increasingly I cannot take much more of this.
The end cadence deferred like breathing, the
birthplace of the poet: all put out their lights
and take their instruments away with them.

How can we sustain such constant loss.
I ask myself this, knowing that the world
is my pretext for this return through it, and
that we go more slowly as we come back
more often to the feeling that rejoins the whole.
Soon one would live in a sovereign point and
still we don't return, not really, we look back
and our motives have more courage in
structure than in what we take them to be.
The sun makes it easier & worse, like the
music late in the evening, but should it start
to rain–the world converges on the idea
of return. To our unspeakable loss; we make
sacred what we cannot see without coming
back to where we were.

Again is the sacred
word, the profane sequence suddenly graced, by
coming back. More & more as we go deeper
I realise this aspect of hope, in the sense of
the future cashed in, the letter returned to sender.
How can I straighten the sure fact that
we do *not* do it, as we regret, trust, look
forward to, etc? Since each time what
we have is increasingly the recall, not
the subject to which we come. Our chief
loss is ourselves; that's where I am, the
sacral link in a profane world, we each do
this by the pantheon of hallowed times.
Our music the past tense:
if it would only
level out into some complete migration of
sound. I could then leave unnoticed, bring nothing
with me, allow the world free of its displace-
ment. Then I myself would be the
complete stranger, not watching jealously
over names. And yet home is easily our
idea of it, the music of decent and proper
order, it's this we must leave in some quite
specific place if we are not to carry it
everywhere with us.
I know I will go back
down & that it will not be the same though
I shall be sure it is so. And I shall be even
deeper by rhyme and cadence, more held
to what isn't mine. Music is truly the
sound of our time, since it is how we most
deeply recognise the home we may not
have: the loss is trust and you could
reverse that without change.
With such
patience maybe we can listen to the rain
without always thinking about rain, we
trifle with rhyme and again is the
sound of immortality. We think we have
it & we must, for the sacred resides in this;
once more falling into the hour of my birth, going
down the hill and then in at the back door.

A Sonnet to Famous Hopes

Then the mind fills with snow the
free, open syllables of reward. All the
limbs respond, to this my eyes see, there
the sense of an immense patch–the north
atlantic wake. A line of scrubby trees, those
fields still not ready but the snow, is still
the physical rain. Also hopeless, as if dead
with strain and every nerve, in the dismal
cathedral a grey waste. But the freedom plant
springs alert, in its curious way and reserved
in guesswork, now in biblical sequence. O
Jerusalem you are no less than this, Cairo
and Massachusetts, trust your eyes only
when they fill with more than, the price of
what you see. As what I feel about it &
meanwhile, the retinal muscle is bound to
another world, the banks of snow are
immense. The patch of salvation, so we are
too late not paranoid or jewish yet but
the snow fills, me with reward & with me, the
road is the tariff: above all then great
banks of cloud tether my elate muscle, to
nothing less & its fields–still fresh & green.

Whose Dust Did You Say

How old how far & how much the
years tear at us the shreds of cloth as
I think of them and the great palaces
with courts & the sounds of mirth
merriment in the darkness within the
great dream of the night. I live still
with the bitter habits of that fire &
disdain I live in it surrounded by
little else who can impair or bound
that empire of destined habitation
or go off into that coyly drab town
by slow stages or by any other damn
thing else who can who would waste
his time who would fritter his time
away how the years now do encircle
the season and when is a wage a
salary by dead reckoning from the
merest centre of the earth the
mere & lovely centre, of the earth.

A Dream of Retained Colour

We take up with the black branch
in the street, it is our support and
control, what we do with life in
the phase now running on. From here
each time the glitter does settle out,
around some lamp, some fried-up
commercial scene we live in
support of and for. Who is this
that may just do the expected
thing; not the magic silence
of the inward eye you may be quite
positive. TV beams romantically into
the biosphere, plant food is our
daily misery. Mine: light & easy,
the victim-path is so absurd.

Misery is that support & control: the
force of sympathy is a claim no one
can pay for. We are indeed supplanted
and I know the light is all bribery,
daylight, electric, the matching stroke.

Uncertain whether the stars of my
inner canopy are part of this
brittle crust I watch them often.
The moon is still silent, I count that
a favour unpurchased, but the
scintillant clusters are the true test:
                    how much then *are*
                    we run, managed by
                    the biograph & pre-
                    dictive incision, it
must be possible to set the question
up & have it operational, in time
to restore the eye of fate: Lucifer, with-
out any street lamps or TV. The
branch is rained on, it does nothing,
the event is unresponsive / & attending

to such infantile purchase is the
murderous daily income of sympathy.

                    The stars then being
                    ideas without win-
                    dows, *what* should we
                    do by watching, is
it true: is it true? Starlight is the
new torture, seraphic host, punishment
of the visionary excess. What else, they
glide with their income intact, how often
they travel. What they do in this
social favour, that and how with, is
                    it true. The prism
                    of mere life is un-
                    bearable, plants and
                    animals in their
sæcular changes, eaten up with will-power.
Who would believe in the victim, as, in
such general diversion, who would need to.
O you who drive past in my dream-car
of the century, lead me by no still waters,
don't touch me with the needle. I'm watch-
ing no one, the torture is immaculate and
conserved, I'd love to go so much it
                    isn't true it
                    really isn't true.

3 Sentimental Tales

one

further towards the
sky now well don't
be such a damn
nuisance you'll break
the cord what of
that it's nearly time
for supper we must
eat the clouds range
in their places the
tide's up the other
waits for him

two

that's wormwood we'll
pick some we'll
hang it up the line
holds back a tidal
point eastwards it's
nice there anyway
why take the
trouble the lines
dip lean & famous

three

you could say it
was the water the
birds often come
here a nice glide
before dark I
must say the
salt thickens mere
prospects and any
way they could hardly
get better now
could they as
the wind freshens they
do so slowly

Foot and Mouth

Every little shift towards comfort is a manoeuvre
of capital loaned off into the jungle of interest: see
how the banks celebrate their private season, with
brilliant swaps across the Atlantic trapeze. Such del-
icate abandon: we hold ourselves comfortingly braced
beneath, a safety-net of several millions & in what
we shall here call north Essex the trend is certainly
towards ease, time off to review those delicious values
traced in frost on the window or which wage-labour
used to force to the Friday market. Actually as I look
out the silly snow is collapsing into its dirty self
again, though I don't feel the cold as I have thought-
fully taped out the draughts with Pressure Sensitive
Tape (also known as RUBAN ADHESIF and NASTRO AD-
HESIVO). Thus my own sphere of interest, based on a
quite sharp fahrenheit differential, contains no trace
of antique posture; I'm waiting for the soup to boil
and even the slow, pure, infinitely protracted recall
of a train-ride in northern Ontario (the Essex of north
America) can't fully divert me from the near prospect
of Campbell's Cream of Tomato Soup, made I see at
King's Lynn, Norfolk. Another fine local craft, you
don't need to believe all you read about the New York
art industry: "the transfer of capitalistic production
to the foreign market frees the latter completely from
the limitations imposed by its own consumer capacity."
And note that *completely* here, as I do while looking at
this dirty cold patch of road and suchlike, thinking
of cree indians and their high-bevelled cheeks &
almost ready for my skilfully seasoned 10½oz. treat.
No one in Minnesota would believe, surely, that the dollar
could *still* be whipping up tension about this? I am
assured by this thought and by the freedom it brings,
& by the garishly French gold medal won by my soup in 1900.

Star Damage at Home

The draft runs deeper now & the motion
relaxes its hold, so that I pass freely from
habit to form and to the sign complete
without unfolding–the bright shoots in the
night sky or the quick local tremor of leaves.
Where this goes is a scattered circle, each
house set on a level and related by time
to the persons whose lives now openly
have them in train. Each one drawn in
by promise recalled, just as the day itself
unlocks the white stone. Rain as it
falls down turns to the level of name, the
table slanting off with its concealed glint.
And what is the chance for survival, in this
fertile calm, that we could mean what
we say, and hold to it? That some star
not included in the middle heavens should
pine in earth, not shine above the skies and
those cloudy vapours? That it really should
burn with fierce heat, explode its fierce &
unbearable song, blacken the calm it comes
near. A song like a glowing rivet strikes
out of the circle, we must make room for
the celestial victim; it is amongst us and
fallen with hissing fury into the ground. Too
lovely the ground and my confidence as I
walk so evenly above it: we must mean the
entire force of what we shall come to say.
I cannot run with these deeply implicit
motions, the person is nothing, there should be
torture in our midst. Some coarsely exploited
money-making trick, fast & destructive, shrill
havoc to the murmur of names. The
blaze of violent purpose at least, struck
through : light : we desire what we mean
& we must mean that & consume to

ash any simple deflection:
I will not be led
by the mean-
ing of my
tinsel past or
this fecund hint
I merely live in. Destruction is too
good for it, like Cassius I flaunt the path
of some cosmic disaster. Fix the eye on
the feast of hatred forcing the civil war
in the U.S., the smoke towering above the
mere words splitting like glass into the
air. The divinity of light spread through
the day, the mortal cloud like no more than
heat haze, that thing is the idea of blood
raised to a final snow-capped abstraction. I
mean what the name has in its charge,
being not deceived by the dispersal which
sets it down. We live in compulsion, no
less, we must have the damage by which
the stars burn in their courses, we take/
set/twist/dispose of the rest. There is
no pause, no mild admixture. This is to
crush it to the centre, the angelic song shines
with embittered passion; there is no price
too high for the force running uncontrolled
into the cloud nearest the earth. We live here
and must mean it, the last person we are.

One Way At Any Time

Through the steamed-up windows it says
"Thermal Insulation Products" I can't see
where it's come from, as the warm steamy
sound puffs out from the jukebox. The girl
leans over to clear off my plate, hey I've not
finished yet, the man opposite without think-
ing says must be on piecework and his
regular false teeth gleam like sardines. But
the twist here is that it's all in that yokel
talk they have for the rustics and this man
is in overalls, his boy about nine silent
beside him. The driver opposite looks as
if from some official car, he carries unworn
black leather gloves & wears a black cap,
with a plastic vizor. He has a watch-
chain across his waistcoat and a very
metallic watch on his wrist–he is not
functional in anything but the obvious
way but how will he too speak? Mc-
Cormick International rumbles past
in truly common dialect, diesel in low
gear but the boy is still quiet. His teeth are
the real thing, crooked incisors as he
bites into B & B his father's mate sways
with natural endorsement back and forward
in his chair left by six he says and I don't
know whether a.m. or p.m. The girl shouts
and the young driver in uniform gives
an urban, movie-style flick of a nod as
he pushes back his chair it is Bristol it
is raining I wish I were Greek and could
trust all I hear but suppose anyway
that one of them turned out to be Irish?

Acquisition of Love

The children rise and fall as they
watch, they burn in the sun's coronal
display, each child is the fringe
and he advances at just that blinding
gradient. As I try to mend the broken
mower, its ratchet jammed somewhere
inside the crank-case, I feel the
blood all rush in a separate spiral,
each genetically confirmed in the
young heartlands beyond. The curious
ones have their courses set towards
fear and collapse, faces switch on and
off, it is not any image of learning
but the gene pool itself defines these
lively feelings. I get the casing off,
sitting on the flat stone slab by the
front door, you would think fortunes
could be born here and you would
be wrong. Their childish assertion is
bleeding into the centre, we are determined
that they shall do this: they look outwards
to our idea of the planet. Their blood
is battered by this idea, the rules for
the replication of pattern guide their dreams
safely into our dreams. The two ratchets
are both rusted in; I file out their
slots and brush out the corroded
flakes with oil. They watch, and
what they watch has nothing to do
with anything. What they do is an
inherited print, I lend it to them
just by looking & only their blood
seems to hold out against the complete
neuro-chemical entail. I guess their
capacity in pints, the dream-like membranes
which keep their faces ready to see. The
mower works now, related to nothing
but the hand and purpose, the fear of
collapse is pumped round by each linked
system & the borrowed warmth of the heart.

Questions for the Time Being

All right then *no* stoic composure as the
self-styled masters of language queue up to
apply for their permits. That they own and
control the means of production (or at least
the monopoly of its more dangerous aspects)
seems not to have struck home. But it
must, or hysterical boredom will result and
we shall all think that creative paranoia
has now finally reached these shores–and as
if we didn't invent it anyway, as Wyndham
Lewis tried so fiercely to explain. And in the
face of the "new frankness" in immaculate
display in the highest places, why should
the direct question not be put: if any discrete
class with an envisaged part in the social process
is not creating its own history, then who is doing
it for them? Namely, what is anyone waiting
for, either resigned or nervous or frantic from
time to time? Various forms dodge through
the margins of a livelihood, but so much talk
about the underground is silly when it would re-
quire a constant effort to keep below the surface,
when almost everything is exactly that, the
mirror of a would-be alien who won't see how
much he is at home. In consequence also the
idea of change is briskly seasonal, it's too cold
& thus the scout-camp idea of revolution stands
in temporary composure, waiting for spring. All
forms of delay help this farce, that our restrictions
are temporary & that the noble fiction is to have
a few good moments, which represent what we know
ought to be ours. Ought to be, that makes me
wince with facetiousness: we/you/they, all the
pronouns by now know how to make a sentence
work with *ought to*, and the stoic at least saves
himself that extremity of false vigilance.

Yet living in hope is so silly when our desires
are so separate, not part of any mode or con-
dition except language & there they rest on

the false mantelpiece, like ornaments of style.
And expectancy is equally silly when what we think
of is delay, or gangsterism of the moment, some
Micawberish fantasy that we can snatch the controls
when the really crucial moment turns up. Not with-
out asbestos gloves we can't, the wheel is permanently
red-hot, no one on a new course sits back and
switches on the automatic pilot. Revisionist plots
are everywhere and our pronouns haven't even
drawn up plans for the first coup. Really it's
laughable & folks talk of discontent or waiting
to see what they can make of it. How much
cash in simple gross terms went through the
merger banks in the last three months? Buy one
another or die; but the cultured élite, our squad
of pronouns with their lingual backs to the wall,
prefer to keep everything in the family. The up-
shot is simple & as follows: 1. No one has any right
to mere idle discontent, even in conditions of most
extreme privation, since such a state of arrested
insight is actively counter-productive; 2. Con-
tentment or sceptical calm will produce
instant death at the next jolt & intending
suicides should carry a card at least exonerating
the eventual bystanders; 3. What goes on in a
language is the corporate & prolonged action
of worked self-transcendence–other minor verbal
delays have their uses but the scheme of such
motives is at best ambiguous; 4. Luminous
take-off shows through in language forced into any
compact with the historic shift, but in a given con-
dition such as now not even elegance will come
of the temporary nothing in which life goes on.

Starvation / Dream

The fire still glides down
in the hearth, the pale season
and the leaky boat drops
slowly downstream. Like emeralds
the remote figure of a
remote capital gain: the case
of fire rests in a flicker, just
short of silence. So the dream
still curls in its horizon of
total theft, cooled by the misty
involvement of dew, and at once
it is clear, finally, that this
is not our planet: we have come
to the wrong place. We steal
everything we have–why else
are we driven by starved passion
to the dishonour of force? The
Russian trick was to burn up
wads of banknotes, so as to
clear the imperial stain, the hedged
& tree-lined avenues of our desires.
And what we dream we want is
the whole computed sum of plants and
animals of this middle world, the
black lands called up by our
patient & careful visits. By any
ritual of purpose we extend the idea
of loan and we dream of it, the
payment of all our debts. But we
never shall, we have no single gain
apart from the disguise of how far
we say we earn. The ground out-
side mistily involves itself with its
contour, the leaky boat glides down
the morning flood, in this rival
dream all our enemies are with us
and the animals & plants shall
take nourishment from the same
silent and passionless table.

Smaller than the Radius of the Planet

There is a patch like ice in the sky this
evening & the wind tacks about, we are
both stopped/fingered by it. I lay out my
unrest like white lines on the slope, so that
something out of broken sleep will land
there. Look up, a vale of sorrow opened by
eyes anywhere above us, the child spread out
in his memory of darkness. And so, then, the
magnetic influence of Venus sweeps its
shiver into the heart/brain or hypothalamus,
we are still here, I look steadily at nothing.
"The gradient of the decrease may be de-
termined by the spread in intrinsic lumin-
osities"–the ethereal language of love in
brilliant suspense between us and the
hesitant arc. Yet I need it too and keep
one hand in my pocket & one in yours,
waiting for the first snow of the year.

Crown

The hours are taken slowly out of the
city and its upturned faces–a rising fountain
quite slim and unflowering as it
is drawn off. The arrangements of work
swell obscurely round the base of the
Interior Mountain, in the pale house with
its parody of stairs. The air is cold; a
pale sunlight is nothing within the con-
strictions of trust in the throat, in
the market-place. Or the silver police
station, the golden shops, all holy in this
place where the sound of false shouts too
much does reconcile the face and hands.
Yet the feet tread about in the dust, cash slides
& crashes into the registers, the slopes
rise unseen with the week and can still
burn a man up. Each face a purging
of venom, an absent coin, oh why as the
hours pass and are drawn off do the
shoulders break, down to their possessions,
when at moments and for days the city
is achieved as a glance–inwards, across,
the Interior Mountain with its cliffs
pale under frost. And the question rises
like helium in its lightness, not held down
by any hands, followed by the faces dis-
owned by the shoes & overcoat settling in
behind the wheel and pulling the door shut.

Thus the soul's discursive fire
veers with the wind; the love
of any man is turned
by the mere and cunning front:

No hand then but to coin, no
face further than
needs be, the sounds fall
quickly into the gutters:

And from this the waters thin into their
ascendant vapour, the pillar of cloud; it
stands over the afternoon already half-
dark. No one is fearful, I see them all
stop to look into the sky and my famished
avowals cast the final petals. It is the
Arabian flower of the century, the question
returned upon itself; the action of month and
hour is warm with cinnamon & clear water,
the first slopes rise gently at our feet.

Love

Noble in the sound which
marks the pale ease
of their dreams, they ride
the bel canto of our
time: the patient en-
circlement of Narcissus &
as he pines I too
am wan with fever,
have fears which set
the vanished child above
reproach. Cry as you
will, take what you
need, the night is young
and limitless our greed.

Night Song

The white rose trembles by the step   it is
uncalled for in the fading daylight and
tiny plants sprout from between the stones

Soon Mizar will take the tawny sky
into protection   they will soon be calling
for the sick ones and all our passing

sounds will rise into the horn and be
cast outwards   scattered   the scale rises
like a tide and the frail craft is afloat

Who would believe it   yet the waters are
rough and the seabirds fly unblinking as
if wind were the ointment they wished for

Come back to the step I call as the house
turns and it is almost night   but there is
no end to the peace claimed by the sick

body and no relief for the mere lack of
fever by which now I lean from the step
and touch at the bare twigs with my wrist

A Stone Called Nothing

Match the stone, the milk running in the
middle sea, take your way with them. The way
is the course as you speak, gentle chatter:
the lights dip as the driver presses the
starter & the bus pulls away to leave
for the moonstruck fields of the lower paid.
Gentle chatter, match the stone, we are
running into the sea. Pay your fare, have
the road beamed out:
                                        nay, eat as much
bread as you find, and leave the wide earth
to pursue its way; go to the brink of the
river, and drink as much as you need, and
pass on, and seek not to know whence
it comes, or how it flows.
                                                A good course
in the middle sea, we swing into a
long rising bend. The equinox is our line for
the present, who is to love that: the thought
dries off into the arch ready for it. Faintest
of stellar objects, I defy you and yet this
devastation curls on, out over the road. Are
we so in the black frost, is this what we pay
for as the ruined names fade into Wilkes Land,
its "purity of heart"?
                                        Do your best to have your
foot cured, or the disease of your eye, that you
may see the light of the sun, but do not enquire
how much light the sun has, or how high it
rises.
            The devastation is aimless; folded with-
out recompense, change down to third do any
scandalous thing, the gutters run with milk.
The child of any house by the way is something
to love, I devise that as an appeal to Vulcan, to
open the pit we cannot fall into. Failure
without falling, the air is a frozen passage,
the way bleached out, we are silent now. The
child is the merest bent stick; I cannot move.
There should be tongues of fire & yet now

the wipers are going, at once a thin rain is
sucked into the glass, oh I'll trust anything.

The babe, when it comes to its mother's breast,
takes the milk and thrives, it does not search
for the root and well-spring from which it
flows so. It sucks the milk and empties
the whole measure
                                        : listen to the sound yet
we go on moving, the air is dry, I seem
to hear nothing. It is for the time an aimless
purchase, where are we now you say I
think or not /go on/get off/quiet/ match the stone.

John in the Blooded Phoenix

Days are uncertain now and move by
flux gradients laid by the rare min-
erals, sodium in dreams of all the body
drawn into one transcendent muscle:
the dark shopfront at 3 a.m. But
we are close to the ancient summits
of a figure cast for the age, the gas-
fire we sit by, the sharp smell of burning
orange-peel. The axis of landform runs
through each muted interchange, the
tilt is a plausible deflexion of energy / now
we are not at the side of anything.
In the vision made by memories of metal
we walk freely as if by omen over an
open terrace, of land like chalky
sediment in soft water. It is the gas-fire
that does it, I despise nothing which
comes near a skyline as old as this.
We could pace in our own fluids, we speak
in celestial parlance, our chemistry is
reduced to transfusion. Who would for-
bid fair Cleopatra smiling / on his poor
soul, for her sweet sake still dying? If
he were he is, the condition of prompt
dilatancy is exactly this: the palest
single spark in all the Pleiades.

Chemins de Fer

It is a forest of young pines and now we
are eating snow in handfuls, looking at the
towers which when the light topsoil is warm
again will carry the firewatchers. From here there
is no simple question of *preparing to leave*, or
making our way. Even the thinnest breath of
wind wraps round the intense lassitude, that
an undeniably political centre keeps watch; the
switch of light and shadow is packed with
foreign tongues. I shall not know my own
conjecture. The plants stare at my ankles in
stiffness, they carry names I cannot recognise.
Yet in the air, still
now, I am claimed
by the memory of
how the join, the
incessant *lapping*, is
already reported in
talk to a human figure. Again he is
watchful, the dream slides right up to the
true Adam and he keeps silent among the
branches. The approach, here, of streamy recall
seems like the touch of Europe, an invert logic
brought in with too vivid a pastoral sense,
too certain for Alsace, the double eagle or the
Gulf of Lions. He is a dark outline, already
struck by sacred
emptiness. He goes
slowly, her body
fades into reason,
the memory ever-
green and planted,
like the lost child.
And so slowly, still, draining gradually into
the Rhine, the huge barges freeze in the heat
of trade. How much power, the machine gun in
a Polish scenario, black and white fade into those
passionless excursions of childhood. The small
copse, water rusted in, an adventure! With which
the flimsy self pivots in wilful envy and lusts
after its strange body, its limbs gorged & inert.

As It Were An Attendant

Proceeding still in the westward face, and like
a life underwater: that facade
                                        sheer and abrupt,
the face in all that shot towards venus, march
on the pentagon, all the prodigious cycle of ages.
Going on then any person still frequent, fixed by
the sun in that euclidean concept of "day", takes
a pause and at once is the face
                                        or some account
of it: *mostly* we are so rushed. Harassment is
not on the switch, playback of the perfect
                                                  darling
and late again–we can begin with the warmup
about the politics of melody / that one, and
please you say at once, not *again*.
                                             By the face
we converse about stars, starlight & their twinkle,
since sweetly it subsides and by proceeding,
a long file above water, single
        laced after this
        jabber we keep it
        all going, at one time
        it is just that,
                    gone; the
                    rest is some
                    pale & cheshire
                    face. Conspicuous
        by its rays & terrible and grand this
                    is not our feeling
        as blindly I tread to find myself
                    out of it, running
        on before them, accompanying them and
                    going with them,
        there, as I have not known for months,
                    standing by a hedge: "I
love the shipwrecked man who was betrayed
by misfortune." As a cork rammed in the
century's neck, I see at once the faces who have
unsuccessfully dogged my path–the procession

headed by the old woman who walks & does other
things
maybe she
sings, this is
her song:
Blackie, she
calls (her cat free
of sparks), she
treads with her
face, the grave
carried away
she has stringy hair
water flows at her feet
it is often dark there
nor quick nor neat nor
any thing / along the path leading
up to the Congregational Chapel at
Linton the sepulchral urns mourn
their loss of protein & like its
beautifully fishy stare the frontage
outfaces the morning, the star at evening, like
milk. *Mostly* this is the
end of it, through into some-
thing else, as, statement:
the child is so quiet now
he has stopped screaming
the scarlet drains from
his cheeks he is pale and
beautiful he will soon be
asleep I hope he will
not thus too quickly die
in the sky the face Blackie she calls
him & he is there & without passion.

The Corn Burned by Syrius

Leave it with the slender distraction, again this
is the city shaken down to its weakness. Washed-out
green so close to virtue in the early morning,
than which for the curving round to home this
is the fervent companion. The raised bank by
the river, maximum veritas, now we have no
other thing. A small red disc quivers in the street,
we watch our conscious needs swing into this point
and vanish; that it is more cannot be found, no
feature, where else could we go. The distraction
is almost empty, taken up with nothing; if the two
notes sounded together could possess themselves, be
ready in their own maximum: "O how farre
art thou gone from thy Country, not being
driven away, but wandring of thine owne accord."
On the bank an increase of sounds, and walk through
the sky the grass, that any motion is the first
settlement. We plant and put down cryptic slopes
to the damp grass, this passion fading off to the
intensely beaten path: that it should be possessed
of need & desire coiled into the sky, and then dis-
membered into the prairie twitching with herbs,
pale, that it is the city run out and retained
for the thousands of miles allowed, claimed to be so.

A NOTE ON METAL

[1968]

The early Bronze Age would, I suppose, locate the beginnings of Western alchemy, the theory of quality as *essential*. The emergence of metal technologies (smelting & beating, followed by knowledge of alloys) was clearly a new way with the magical forms through which property resided in substance. Until this stage, weight was the most specific carrier for the inherence of power, and weight was and is a mixed condition, related locally to exertion. The focus of this condition is typically stone; and though this seems most obviously to insist on the compact outer surface, in fact it provides the most important practical & cultic *inside*: the cave. The privilege of that ambiguity about surface gives the painted rock-shelter and the megalithic chamber-tomb the power of formal change, and in this way substance can be extended, by incorporation, to allow the magical and political/social presences their due place.

Whereas with copper, tin (and perhaps antimony), weight coincides with other possible conditions which are less mixed and specific: brightness, hardness, ductility and general ease of working. And further, the abstraction of *property* (characterised as formal rather than substantive) makes the production of alloys a question of technique in the most theoretical sense.[1] Bronze may have been known to the Sumerians at a very early stage, and yet tin is rare in the Near East and must have been imported over considerable distances. The difference between the kinds of intent supporting the movement of bluestones from Pembrokeshire to Wessex, and the Sumerian acquisition of tin from Cornwall or Bohemia, must be obvious.

And through the agency of the most ostensive control of force, namely fire, sword-blades or spear-heads could be forged into a strength infinitely more abstract than the flaking of high-quality flint or the hardening of wooden points. The new quality thus gained was sharp and killed with new speed and power, from a long range. Animal hides could be sewn up with metal bodkins and fish taken with fine wire hooks; the metal ploughshare could cut deeper into the soil and with less effort.[2] The new quality of spiritual transfer was concentrated in these most durable forms of leading edge, seen especially in the flattened motive of ornament, and the history of substance (stone) shifts with complex social implication into the theory of power (metal).

That's a deliberately simplified sketch, because it may well be that this theorising of quality, with its control over weaponry and tillage and hence over life, induced a deeper cultural adherence to substance as the zone of being in which the condition was also limit: the interior knowledge of dying. By death I mean here in particular those forms of life and ritual, the extension of body, in which persistence through material transmutation was an ego-term (even when socialised) rather than one concerned chiefly with the outer world (enemies or animals hunted for food, flesh as object). So that stone becomes the power-substance marking the incorporated extensions of dying, and is still so as a headstone is the vulgar or common correlative of a hope for the after-life.

And in parallel with this reactive development (maybe, an exilic theory of substance) comes the rapid advance of metallurgy, shifting from the transfer of life as power (hunting) into the more settled expectation of reaping what you have already sown; this itself produces the idea of *place* as the chief local fact, which makes mining and the whole extractive industry possible from then on. The threshing of millet or barley must bring a 'purer' and more abstract theory of value; the mixed relativism of substance leads, by varied but in outline predictable stages, to value as a specialised function and hence as dependent on the rate of exchange. The Sumerian settlement was founded on the innovations of metallurgy, and these abstractions of substance were in turn the basis for a politics of *wealth*: the concentration of theoretic power by iconic displacement of substance. The unit of exchange was still the ingot by weight and not yet coins by number, but we are already in what Childe called a 'money economy' as opposed to a 'natural economy': there is already a code of practice for capital loaned out on interest.[3]

For a long time the magical implications of transfer in any shape must have given a muted and perhaps not initially debased sacrality to objects of currency-status, just as fish-hooks and bullets became strongly magical objects in the societies formed around their use. But gradually the item-form becomes iconized, in transitions like that from *aes rude* (irregular bits of bronze), through *aes signatum* (cast ingots or bars) to *aes grave* (the circular stamped coin). The metonymic unit is established, and number replaces strength or power as the chief assertion of presence. In consequence, trade-routes undergo a dramatic expansion, since mercantile theory operates with the most conspicuous success when employed over large inter-cultural distances: "In the Early Bronze Age peninsular Italy, Central Europe, the West Baltic Coastlands, and the British Isles were united by a single system for the distribution of metalware, rooted in the Aegean market."[4]

The clearest instance of this type of change arises probably where a more 'sophisticated' and 'progressive' economy meets an idiom of change and value less efficiently abstracted. The mercantile contact between the sea-borne traders of the Eastern Mediterranean and the peoples of the Anatolian hinterland can show this interaction already by the late Bronze Age (for this region, c.1600 B.C.). On the great alluvial plains of Asia the condition was one of power rather than value; that is, substance, and not (in the first instance) transfer as exchange. Flocks and herds can be stolen, bartered, given in gift or tribute, so that wealth for the most part is the power of a technique to hold all that, again the politics of limit. Whereas the Greek traders were already middlemen with no political standing, Sardis no city but a commercial centre working on the trick of abstract distance between real supply and real demand. Lydia, as Childe again said, was "a frontier kingdom owing its prosperity to transit trade."[5]

Here finally, and for the first time (according to tradition) arises sheer mercantile distance in the form of *coin*, where the magical resonance of transfer is virtually extinct: "That coined money should have been evolved here [the Eastern Mediterranean] is not surprising, for it was an area of intense commercial activity, encouraged and fostered by natural advantages. The Lydians, 'the first shopkeepers' as Herodotus called them, as well as the neighbouring Ionians, received goods from the caravan routes and river communications across Asia. They had access to safe and sheltered harbours for easy coastwise trade. They exported their famous Chian wines, their purple dye which gave its name to Erythrae, and their Samian pots, but above all they were renowned for their gold, which provided the fabulous wealth of Croesus, and still more fabulous wealth of Midas."[6] And Croesus, the first recorded millionaire, is also the first to devise a bimetallic currency, where even the *theoretic* properties of metal are further displaced, into the stratified functionalism of a monetary system. We are almost completely removed from presence as weight, and at this point the emergence of a complete middle class based on the technique of this removal becomes a real possibility. So that by this stage there *is* the possible contrast of an exilic (left-wing) history of substance.

And yet the shifts are off-set and multiple, and in the earlier stages are accompanied by extensions of awareness newly sharpened by exactly that risk. The literal is *not* magic, for the most part, and it's how the power of displacement side-slipped into some entirely other interest which is difficult, not a simple decision that any one movement is towards ruin. Stone is already the abstraction of standing, of balance; and dying is still the end of a man's self-enrichment, the 'reason' why he does it. The North American Indians developed no real metallurgy at all, at any stage of their history.[7] The whole shift and turn is *not* direct (as Childe, too insistently, would have us believe), but rather the increasing speed of displacement which culminates only later in a critical overbalance of intent.[8] If we are confident over the more developed consequences, at the unrecognised turn we are still at a loss to say where or why.

Notes

[1] Some of the earliest British metal-technologies have been held to include techniques of "smelting, alloying, casting, hammering, grinding and polishing, work in repoussé with punches, traced ornament, perforation with a punch and perhaps also by drilling, riveting, probably the use of a mandrel, and most likely an empirical skill in the exploitation of work-hardening and annealing" (D. Britton, "Traditions of Metal-Working in the Later Neolithic and Early Bronze Age of Britain," *Proceedings of the Prehistoric Society*, N. S. XXIX [1963], p. 279).

[2] On the technology of this, see G. E. Fussell, "Ploughs and Ploughing before 1800," *Agricultural History*, XL (1966), 177-186.

[3] See also Marc Bloch, "Natural Economy or Money Economy" (1933), in J. E. Anderson (trans.), *Land and Work in Medieval Europe; Selected Papers by Marc Bloch* (London, 1967). Even in the case of early Greek coinage it has been argued that the original intention was not so much in the first place to facilitate trade (external or internal), but rather to establish a system of centralised national wealth which could support a professional military caste; see C. M. Kraay, "Hoards, Small Change and the Origin of Coinage," *Journal of Hellenic Studies*, LXXXIV (1964), 76-91.

[4] V. G. Childe, *The Prehistory of European Society* (London, 1962), p. 166.

[5] On the overland trade-routes in Asia Minor and traffic in metals (especially copper) see R. Dussaud, "La Lydie et ses voisins aux hautes époques," *Babyloniaca*, XI (1930), and in particular the tentative route-map included as plate 1. There is reason to consider this hypothesis of overland trade with the interior as conjectural, but there is little evidence which would refute it. See G. M. A. Hanfmann, "Prehistoric Sardis," in G. E. Mylonas (ed.), *Studies Presented to David Moore Robinson* (Saint Louis, 1951-3), Vol. I, pp. 160-183, and J. M. Birmingham, "The Overland Route across Anatolia in the Eighth and Seventh Centuries B.C.," *Anatolian Studies*, XI (1961), 185-195. On specifically Lydian trade and the monopoly structure of the Lydian mining industry, see C. Roebuck, *Ionian Trade and Colonization* (New York, 1959), Chap. III and especially note 83 (p. 59) on *kapelos*.

[6] A. H. Quiggin, *A Survey of Primitive Money; The Beginnings of Currency* (London, 1949), p. 282. Concerning Midas (briefly) see J. M. Cook, *Greek Settlement in the Eastern Aegean and Asia Minor* (Vol. II, Chap. XXXVIII of the revised *Cambridge Ancient History*, issued in fascicle, Cambridge, 1961), pp. 26-27.

[7] Although the almost pure native copper from the Lake Superior region was being hammered into various points, blades and ornaments as early as 2000–1000 B.C. But the forms are in most cases copied directly from earlier types in flint or bone, and none of the smelting or alloy processes was involved. See J. B. Griffin, "Late Quaternary Prehistory in the Northeastern Woodlands," in H. E. Wright Jr., and D. G. Frey (eds.), *The Quaternary of the United States* (Princeton, 1965), p. 663.

[8] Urban totalitarianism, for example, as Childe argued in "The Bronze Age," *Past and Present*, 12 (1957), 2-15.

5 UNCOLLECTED POEMS

And Only Fortune Shines

We are not the person for this as we
do make away / over to the / side I
            tell you oh love the ones
            we are the touch of, as
            going in the dark, why
should it be less. I will keep down
to the damp ground, splayed in the
faint hope it is love when in this last
passion I see we are then who we
            love, in the open. Cheeks
            ever puffed with hollow
            pieties, the wild flames
                        feeding from the
star in the forehead. Each while he
hurts, where the brief turn & coil
of the chin, eyes for me the
                        other, the mild
            trust. She stands
            swaying as I know her
            in the beauty of that,
one voice containing the other.
I will go on with this: daylight slides
into the bloodstream, how can we
            hold what we are
                        So I see the
            other come in, the
                        slight figure
buckled in close and pale oh lady
be the present figure of what I
do feel & will go to, over the
            glance in the dark
            the passage, foot-
            fall as she stands
or runs now, up the steps. They breathe
the air there is, we are not short
of any thing. We love what we
trust it is the coming age of
            the face, oh please do
            set this in the sight
            I must have. The per-

son we now / are not I / will wait
for you as we both stand, so here
far from the star the needful
            life of the cheek
            the rise of,
            the heart.

Poem in Time to This

At that moment the tone of the
first sound came to me, walking
under the changing cloud cover,
up past the place of rise and turn I
know so well. Like water it is
the continuance of opinion; if the
green comes on again or we fall as
we pass through what we know
already, this is truly our pace
for the joy of season. In my own time
I too choose to defer and expand,
my limbs loose like the gradual
& cancelled reason: call it "the
purpose of the self". So chastely
the sound ministers to the ease
of motion, I walk knowing the
whole past like a single brown shell.
If it is the absent sea, I have never
seen that, I am at this present
time in no rage for the real noise,
clatter of shingle etc. The first
sound is enough, I do nothing but
know as I walk, past the new
green and rise to the fertile crest,
that my feelings are all given away,
the murmur lost to the ear.

East-South-East

And so it is the figure, gleaming on the path,
the person who shines in the torrents of fresh
rain. That rushing sound is already lifted
as if being carried over, taken so slowly that

    the rate is birth. Struck into
    birth, into lightning and so
    slow the touch not at all wild.

The *slowness* is what's strange, as if the
washing *were* a coin ready for the soul,
the shining road just a surface to years,
to the years & their raiment kept out

    and folded. The light pleating
    the rain. Coming from Hitchin
    the way twisted under some

trees & I met there the Shining One. No
conversation or investment followed, the
rain was incessant; there was a completely
steady flow of change. The damp was ionised,

    with charges slipping down quite
    unmatched paths, it was a most
    beautiful and painless night.

And there is nothing to rescue, where the figure
may stay & receive wine with the blood of a white
hind, on the A 602 and the shelter of
the journey. Nothing to save, we shine, we also

    shine in our neglect.

Hey Oswald

He wanders in-
ertly, with a shrewd
unattending absence,
his being on a thin
stalk: he twists
from reluctance to
keep to the one plane
when his name comes
in sound, to him

The light bracing
of muscle confronts
him, already he
has that instinct:
connected to the
shadow, draw what
is yours into the
evidence, of person

But the sun most
marks it, by a
sudden flashing on
and off, going black
from the centre like
a flower rotting: this
is the stable sign
by which the world
insists in the one
ecliptic

He is there
at loss, knowing the
world to be so: his
youth now the
sentiment drawn off
by his being
so, by his first
name: by his
owning his thought
(his coming end)

How Many There Are: A Letter

Even to wait slowly, as with the one word 'far'
is the reach of a number theory, the art attached to
that extension of the holy war. As I walk down
the fold in the banks, following the water is an
axis, the flow brushes the leaves and houses
into the channel, the progress of relevance; which is,
I know about that, more familiar in these parts.
But where, in some
sense I might *other-*
wise be is the
number I live with,
who is the three in
my hand, always so
hungry for it
at the break; or even the pure form of change.
The greedy halo is the enlargement of similar
things (included in likeness). There are five, the
air is moist round the just visible moon, you
could double and split the very birds of the field.
Three is the means
of survival and five
is its consort; it arises
as a permission from
who one is, a non-
finite proliferation
of tireless limbs.
If the road be crossed (or traversed), the break so
caused is a fault in creation. We must move
carefully again & magic is the presence of form
without number. As if that weren't as old-fashioned
as exactly it sounds. Each time I go the same
way the file of occasion increases: perhaps we
should just grow more
solemn. Yet I know
you are there, finding
the five steps of my
entire life, we stay in
the figure & can af-
ford to count nothing else.

P.S. This may be just sentiment. But if we think so, the term is still our claim, the form of water & I do hope at least very much, for that.

FIRE LIZARD

(1970)

Come and tell me. The draw
of the beetle, making the lane
of water, the fire lizard.
I hear the front of your
visited wish, I am
inside it now.

I hear where you go to. My
love of the corners. If your
scarf is deeper blue, come
past the bridle,
the bodiless parterre
shakes the sleeve. There
I believe what you say.

Oh small lamp of the
scarlet, tell me: the front
rests by the sky. We too
seek perfect pitch.
Cracking nuts, leaning
either way you say so.

Bright shadows point
under the snow. The
intelligence is not even
held under. The new
thing cries like a cat.
Shew me sweet with
the fingers

for that's enough.
The proem strides off
as breakfast by the
plate washed over;
oiling the shell,
ringing the bell.

I cannot part you, try
as I often do. The hour
snaps up my tinder bank
and where will be
the last of her
time to go with it;
which is the step.

As you say so he
takes his flit, over
the water creamy
toes, envy with coins
right by the phone box.
We are the recession
of blue-green.

The broken dangerous cup
is not mended.
The point of sky has
all that in sight but
optics apart. Parsecs
fiddle the onion,
don't you know?

Or care what the cave
says, who said it.
Burning the gum while
the bird made solemn mock.
He says balsam in
defence, warningly on.

Are you hurt now,
scalded anywhere on
the arm. I take your
part my Russian winter,
ice on the stream. On
the formal disclaimer,

that's so too. Banded opal
in the mouth of June, why
not. I know why. The fish
delays, that's why, scale
rattles over the crossing.

Still I love you.
That's the reason too.

BRASS

(1971)

On eût crié *bravo! Ouvrage bien moral!* Nous étions sauvés

The Bee Target on his Shoulder

Gratefully they evade the halflight
rising for me, on the frosty abyss.
Rub your fingers with chalk and
grass, linctus over the ankle, now TV with
the sound off & frame hold in
reason beyond that. Paste. Thereby take
the foretaste of style, going naked
wherever commanded, by
                    the father struck
                    in the plain. His
                    wavy boots glow
                    as he matches
                    the headboard.
Do not love this man. He makes
Fridays unbearable, with the
ominous dullness of the gateway
to the Spanish garden. His
herb-set teeth are impossible,
tropic to R.E.M. and the white doll.
It's all so prognostic: he wakes in-
clined to say just that. But then he
stretches / beyond / the
                                silent floating torpor of
                                stupefaction, flesh
                                pierced & stripped like
                                comb honey.
                                                Water the
                                ground with song, aria
                                with cloud, *that's* his
aunt with the brown teapot jammed
into edible, macerated crumpet. So you
shrilled unwittingly in the 3rd chorus.

Oh he wants no more but bright
honour sparkling in his eye, he
flies into pungent happiness.
He insists, rather grandly, that this
is "right" for him. The greedy mule
recoils from Salamanca, still won't eat.
                    And after rain the

mild rushes shoot
for you and com-
mand the house
to be built at once.
Red and grey as
they come. In the sheen
of dew his socks are wet and the
tincture stains his instep indeed.
The head film matches the conduit
with banal migraine. Father pokes
about for the gay snuff of Algiers.
Together we love him limb from
limb, walking in the moonlight;
moderate SW gales do nothing but
blandish the same story.
Which is
spelled from birdsong anyway,
say indeed under cumin,
fetlock, going out and
gentle with the
prime order
of frost and reason, reason and frost,
the same stormy inconsequence. A patch
of wanting is not singing successfully,
the adverbs of a spate are too like, well,
écriture fatale. The ring is on the other
wall of the shop.
The plaster ceiling is
clear and true.
Say so, as a median
nature, up the sad trellis.
Say you do, lighting the
"sacred squadron",
flat on their faces.
The wall
of the shop has a blue tablet, in
memory of ATV Channel Nine. On this
bonny bank father pauses, to empty
his boots of seedlings and filthy change.
A rash of invasion follows, in
strict order of love; first the new
non-vintage, then casually sitting
out in the garden atop the grass.

Be gentle with his streamy locks until he gets the wrapper off.
Strip pieces of flesh from the animals lying dead in the streets.

Love him, in *le silence des nuits, l'horreur des cimetieres*;

otherwise the trendy book will slide
into the bath & linger there,
avec le savon
and the Rose of Texas, toasted marine-style.
"If he eats the flesh of his hand: his
daughter will die"—that too
is costly, like rime. I mean, day after day
is sunk into the river & washed
like palest blue *Reinheit* into the last
droplet of Kümmel. So
wolf-tallow is
smeared on his
lower lip. It is
dear to be left
calm in face of the house and the night. If
it is dark and cloudless, without stars, some
friendly woman will blunder with the tap.
No news can be less valued, by
derisive acts
of mercy nonetheless; don't come
while I'm away with the sad
touches of sulphur. Rain.

The water is rose-blue also and gentle while
mist curls into his daughter and she
receives it pleasantly, muting the comic scowl.
Bravely she traces
the path of father's boots
on the lawn—little
sister we sob merrily & settle down
by the newest grave: fresh
earth as the clay to see with,
standing by the head,
making the song with shadows set
over the reed-bed. That's
what they're for, seasons and for days and years in
the circle of teeth by the cosy fire. You know if you ask
that the air terminal
is not yet rebuilt.

Sun Set 4·56

Small flares skip
down the coal
face   how can I
refuse them
the
warm indolence
of fancy the
solace of wheels
muffled in sheep-
skin
then Bruckner
on the radio & how
easily I am taken
from the hearth &
returned
changed
& unnoticed   it
is the pulse of
birch tar &
molten amber
the
estranged blood
in the vein

Viva Ken

Euphoric gloom writes itself off into
the air: some views are quite terrific but
really I don't give a damn and
flimsy scorn-like sails scatter all
over the lake. It's like stencilled
cardboard again, ascending to its
lumpy clouds and the snow creeps into
meek sexy puffs, ready for morning.
And there
is this much more, as the march of
literary lancers pales in the mirror:
sweet nothing for lunch this time, yet another
talk about diamonds. What is this
glittery filth; not the factual remains
of desire, not refinements all over
again? Comic disbelief fractures
the glottis, glottal pauses, nothing
is in high season &
your tender looks are
frankly incredible
here
the prevailing sense of
occasion minces feelingly
to the meter and pops in another ketchup insult, beneath
which the spirit
labours uncontaminated by
you me or anyone but
the old man caressed by his
sweating animal chair. Here
zooms into view the new floor, spinning down
ready-dirtied with vengeance and catastrophe:
fate strikes! fainting members compose
"hope" and "trembling", mere watchers burst
into pieces!
That's what happens at the
harbour, that too is
rabid for traffic
in
hilarious absolute daybreak or drop
at the very first call.

The Kirghiz Disasters

1. The news comes in from the Tarim Basin, that
the passes are blocked by fresh falls. Ice forms
upwards from the floors of gravel & inwards
from the sides, the train is halted by needs quite
unforeseen in its schedule. Rock tumbles in
pretty cascades. The base-line of the 'time is
money' quadrant shifts to take up new stress;
only the line of major ripple still twists
free, trapping air under the crystal. The muse
in reckless theophany gives a familiar yell:
juniper, moss agate, jurassic boredom glows in
the empty waiting-room. The fire is an unreal
mixture of smoke & damp; the reason for
this is unmusical, in stoic silence by the door.

2. Readable at Easter, the arrows flash to the lonely
mark and spell ruin quite quickly, in fact make
up the letters in triple nourishing layers. Beyond
this, light and some kind of extraction, the heart-
felt sighs drawn off like grass–there's nothing in
the way of dawn with its bald patches, why don't the
men on the other side get up & do it? The heart
has its excuses, no friend waits who has not met
the postman half-way down the beach, calmly in-
different. Wake up wake up he shouts through the
open window and you reach for the time, feeling
the warm air & its wax. Otherwise the rest is just
absolute; right down at the foot of the buttress a mark
of wasted affection lies awry, all falling apart.

3. Come on in then, goes up a general shout, there's
still room & there is, who would trouble with the
freedom to dissent when there would be so much
respect to put up with–oh/oh/oh and off out into
the etc. Better far a lizard, an excursion special,
attracting the lowest rate of tax compatible with
unnoticed grace. Can smoke freeze? Without
warning the ice emits its periodic crackle, jumping
upwards like wall-paper, and searching the band
for another station reveals new liassic beds near
the previous shelf. So without tooting we depart, she
knowing all the while that freedom would just
leave her stranded again. The continent will of
course embrace us: we wound only, reluctant to kill.

4. The rider touches his hopeful cabin, in the form
of a child aged about seven months; the circle of
knowledge is unbroken. There is even price in
the air, its upward lift near to the limit.
The driver peers from his screen at the circle,
now leafy and flashing, the sign of the imposed
progress by late evening. Only the decision is
stopped: "the idea expressed is for any
of the three persons to deeply desire or hope
to do a difficult thing"–and they do, they always
run to the gate with news or make wide grabs
at the leaves as they whizz past the window.
What else is there: the captain orders the sight
of land to be erased from the log, as well he might.

5. Hell, not water creeping like afflicted soup into
the park, no prospects for renewing our tickets. The choice
commissar lifts his glove by the thumb and returns it to
the very short lady at the desk, legs deep in turbid
current: she can't stir yet either, she flips up
an eye in each socket. She is quite disdainful. The flocks
of songsters translate the old films into dirty little
blocks each time round, they "never think of removing a
single stone." They are zealots in the park all over,
they pick away his glove more than they watch for
the morning rush. And at that the fringes wither
with tight credal echoes, bringing fear into the homely
recital. Swear at the leather by the knee-joint
shouts Jerome, crumbs ready as a favoured bribe.

6. Then I eat a care-
ful selection of food.
My fork skims thought-
fully from side to
side. I keep up a
steady munch, al-
most like a heart-
beat you could say only
slower by a certain
amount. I am pre-
pared to discuss it
with anyone. The
tribe inflates and
each muscle shuts.

7. He now drops the heavenly coin in the doorway; under the
autumn heaps the battalion choir make twits and observe
the coin's unblemished descent. A flashing silver rivet
slips into the anthill on the bend. Conclusive appetite
is in that chorus of disaster, we shall call him me-me &
have done with it, crippled stick. And while replies
sprout between the bricks the hired contra-basso feels his
cheek with another finger, thinks of a note falling into
his auntie's purse. The choir is widely aroused, rises in
respectful attention. And the pain runs down his right
side, making him gasp: the traffic goes into twinges,
everything does this, flicking through knots, but the
really first question is still not warm. How could it be
as we turn quickly round and look at what you see.

8. So that Jerome springs back into place, your friendly
dental technician trailing his new bridge-work. He is
esteemed always, loved to distraction, the first principles
of life must be "tender and ductile"; strip off, and
that too is rotten. The redeemed corset strains into view
again and we perk up finally by the counter. Tip tip
tip as the band refuses to watch, we don't like to
fix it so close to the keel. What to prune, come down
into the store-room. Or not this time, they all stroll in
from the drill and its wreckage: they are all here.
All disgustingly crouched along the spinet, they
spin, they catch at enamel, they gasp at the
pollen count. She next stuffs her little crown into a
bag and runs daintily upstairs, she nauseates everyone.

Royal Fern

1

By the beads you sleep, laden with scrip.
How can you love me in dream,
always walking from field to field.
You sleep on, seeded by snowy drift.

2

In strings it bales from the crest.
And singing with it I run, half
fearingly, out of the hot shade.
Love holds me to the mallet path.

3

In his youth he walked much.
Tears streamed down his unlined face,
damping his shirt. Sleep glows
in its beads, staring the wing blind.

4

Still the snow hums, fetching my life:
the pain to come, still the key
takes cover in the chamois case.
The key is the edge of our day.

5

So the fiat parks by the kerb.
We hear him switch off, he is
dreaming of the void. In time,
soup for the father in open green.

6

Now the family is rejoined. In a
gold circlet they weep of old fears.
It is warm here, the sycamore
pales at last. His to keep. Amass.

L'Extase de M. Poher

Why do we ask that, as if wind in the
telegraph wires were nailed up in some
kind of answer, formal derangement of
the species. Days and weeks spin by in
theatres, gardens laid out in rubbish, this
is the free hand to refuse everything.
                              No
question provokes the alpha rhythm by
the tree in our sky turned over; certain
things follow:
                  who is the occasion
                      now   what
                  is the question in
                      which   she
                  what for is a version
                      of when, i.e.
some payment about time again and how
"can sequence conduce" to order as more
than the question: more gardens: list
                  the plants as distinct
                      from   lateral
                  front to back or not
                      grass   "the most
                  successful plant on our
                      heart-lung by-
pass and into passion sliced into bright
slivers, the yellow wrapping of what we do.
Who is it: what person could be generalised
on a basis of "specifically" sexual damage,
the townscape of that question.
                              Weather
of the wanton elegy, take a chip out of
your right thumb. Freudian history again makes
                  the thermal bank: here
                      credit   92°
                  a/c payee only, reduce to
                      now   what
                  laid out in the body
                      sub-normal
or grass etc, hay as a touch of the

social self put on a traffic island. Tie
that up, over for next time, otherwise there
is a kind of visual concurrence;
yet
the immediate body of wealth is not
history, body-fluid not dynastic. No
poetic gabble will survive which fails
to collide head-on with the unwitty circus:
no history running
with the french horn into
the alley-way, no
manifest emergence
of valued instinct, no growth
of meaning & stated order:
we are too kissed & fondled,
no longer instrumental
to culture in "this" sense or
any free-range system of time:
1. Steroid metaphrast
2. Hyper-bonding of the insect
3. 6% memory, etc
any other rubbish is mere political rhapsody, the
gallant lyricism of the select, breasts & elbows,
what
else is allowed by the verbal smash-up piled
under foot. Crush tread trample distinguish
put your choice in the hands of the town
clerk, the army stuffing its drum. Rubbish is
pertinent; essential; the
most intricate presence in
our entire culture; the
ultimate sexual point of the whole place turned
into a model question.

The Five Hindrances

His canopy makes a new pallor; the crescent
strikes a high whistle as from the bridge over
the gap. How it displays itself, eating the
seed like cough sweets. Listen under the wheel,
from Mannheim to Trieste, what you hear is
wide air in chaos, dusted over and softened
like flesh. That's how we part, not caring, in
a blood spot absolute for destruction. We rise
and fall with hedge-trimmer's finesse, when
the step veers round to the east:
        take what you hear slowly,
        as water makes the sun
        pale again, near the
        scabious pinned out for
        rescue. It cannot turn
back now in the room smelling of damp wood,
it is so far outreached, cross-bred with the future.

His former self wastes on the stair, putting oil
to each hinge in turn. Now we come through
the air we breathe bemused by the week: the fire
of heaven, gentle, very light. The brilliant patch
(thorium) where the pilot touches the web and
"intersects the gross national product", undeserved
incest with the soft light of the planet. What is
this high street at night, in every direction the
same as itself? As it will not change but
pleads for its topical centre, rising to the cone
        of wind and ash: fields of
        pure inertia. He folds the
        stem of his two cheeks to
        this, he fans the servant with
        scented leaves. The two friends
walk down the sandy track and we hold back
the ends of the crescent. The future history of the
air is glowing, with amity beyond the path itself;
touched gently and brought to this stubborn wreck.

Wood Limit Refined

Looking out on to
was his bet devised for
the blotched appearance
of a stain, high in the
parlour
again again we want it more
terribly faster, why are we
blamed for
eating the whole west bank
of the town, pleasure gardens, pair
of pliers, salad oil
remorse floods in natal reflex, life in
the ear is marked
by this throbbing uncertainty
winding up
water for a ridiculous fountain, a
jet called Gaspard
give him his snack stained
into the plate
again
again
how can his leg reach
the shelf in (under) such
"thirst"
for the train of events
for the brushed-up dinner
for the sea of aral
& nothing else, actually.

The Ideal Star-Fighter

I

Now a slight meniscus floats on the moral
    pigment of these times, producing
displacement of the body image, the politic
    albino. The faded bird droops in his
cage called fear and yet flight into
    his pectoral shed makes for comic
hysteria, visible hope converted to the
    switchboard of organic providence
at the tiny rate of say 0.25 per cent
    "for the earth as a whole". And why
go on reducing and failing like metal: the
    condition is man and the total crop yield
of fear, from the fixation of danger; in
    how we are gripped in the dark, the
flashes of where we are. It pays to be
    simple, for screaming out, the eye
converts the news image to fear enzyme,
    we are immune to disbelief. "If there
is danger there ought to be fear", trans-
    location of the self to focal alert, "but
if fear is an evil why should there be
    danger?" The meniscus tilts the
water table, the stable end-product is dark
    motion, glints of terror the final inert
residue. Oriental human beings throw off
    their leafy canopies, expire; it is
the unpastured sea hungering for calm.

II

And so we hear daily of the backward
    glance at the planet, the reaction of
sentiment. Exhaust washes tidal flux
    at the crust, the fierce acceleration
of mawkish regard. To be perceived with
    such bounty! To put the ring-main of
fear into printed circuit, so that from the
    distant loop of the hate system the
whole object is lovable, delicious, ingested
    by heroic absorption! We should
shrink from that lethal cupidity; moral
    stand-by is no substitute for 24-inch
reinforced concrete, for the blind certain
    backlash. Yet how can we dream of
the hope to continue, how can the vectors
    of digression not swing into that curve
bounding the translocal, and slip over, so
    that the image of suffered love is
scaled off, shattered to a granulated pathos
    like the dotted pigments of cygnus?

III

What more can be done. We walk
    in beauty down the street, we tread
the dust of our wasted fields. The
    photochemical dispatch is im-
minent, order-paper prepared. We
    cannot support that total of dis-
placed fear, we have already induced
    moral mutation in the species. The
permeated spectra of hatred dominate
    all the wavebands, algal to hominid.
Do not take this as metaphor; thinking to
    finish off the last half-pint of milk,
look at the plants, the entire dark dream outside.

Nothing Like Examples

With its threatened yellow tag on the chain
we were ready again in the evening. Pallor from
the week was intense, as a flame in some
weir or wicker basket; marks on the brickwork
destroy pain. Its yield is so tight and graceful,
you see it passing under the lower shutters and
through the arch into the yard. Failure like
the frantic lark has no place by the lock.

Please invent the change to advance, gripping
the rail by the chapel door. Had you a sister I
could have thought longer and down the slope
where water ran out over the limestone sill.
The full moon flashes its Roman tinge and
prepares for new decimal butter. But none of
the smaller plants had been returned, it was
a betrayal of sorts in a rather uncertain mile.

She is racked by desires so foolish, such a
lombardy storm in the small park where the
children play with gravel. By the stream all
the glass is coarse and twisted and yet this is
more and more a peaceful universe. He will cut
off his thumb to please a select crowd but it
is a trick of course; death hovers because of
the dove's lamentation, his part of the soul.

Why don't you go down the street, why not
believe this? As a slip of praise to the glory
of an old building, its stones delicious in
metal foil. Then his spirits declined, he gave
his time to listless staring; the child sang
to his brother notable for black looks. Vacant
and possessed the hours stepped by in the
heat, the glutted alcove swarming with ants.

By the clock he turns again in her
shadowy arm. Hem-stitched to fate she
is still the fountain, giving him her
                sweep of
hopeful grins: home like the bell & laid
in earth, in the shipwright's flower.

Ash surmounts the town on the hill.
The wharf has some glint in it, his
hands drip with syrup. Warm air flies
                among her
thoughts, the razorbill swerves past the
obelisk and such a delicate yarn also.

What he would say if he could. And why don't
you just drop it anyway, on some bridge where
envy curdles the strange visit. Chiffon ahoy is
beamed out to the dog, a yapping mongrel whose
plate in the Dutch tavern is thick with flies.
Love is all you need to start with, then the porcelain
stove will gobble up anything there is around,
including the lesser-used faggots of the brain.

And who would drown under the noetic shower,
not her sister, mimic benediction. But this is
more and more a peaceful universe, it turns on
this mossy pivot. Who does not feel the new
petrel under his scapula, which is the tremor of
fortitude as it subsides. The question unasked
is too flushed and hazy for the bayonet in
the guard of honour, the water in the ground.

Es Lebe der König

(for Paul Celan, 1920–1970)

Fire and honey oozes from cracks in the earth;
the cloud eases up the Richter scale. Sky divides
as the flag once more becomes technical, the print
divides also: starlight becomes negative. If you
are born to peaks in the wire, purple layers in the
glass format, re-enter the small house with
animals too delicate and cruel. Their throats fur
with human warmth, we too are numbered like
prints in the new snow.

It is not possible to
drink this again, the beloved enters the small house.
The house becomes technical, the pool has
copper sides, evaporating by the grassy slopes.
The avenues slant back through the trees; the
double music strokes my hand. Give back the
fringe to the sky now hot with its glare, turning
russet and madder, going over and over to
the landing-stage, where we are. We stand
just long enough to see you,

we hear your
fearful groan and choose not to think of it. We
deny the consequence but the outset surrounds us,
we are trustful because only thus is the flame's
abstract review the real poison, oh true the
fish dying in great flashes, the smell comes from
shrivelled hair on my wrist. That silly talk is
our recklessly long absence: the plum exudes its
fanatic resin and is at once forced in, pressed
down and by exotic motive this means the rest,
the respite, we have this long.

Only
the alder thrown over the cranial push, the
waged incompleteness, comes with the animals
and their watchful calm. The long-tailed bird
is total awareness, a forced lust, it is that

absolutely. Give us this love of murder and
sacred boredom, you walk in the shade of
the technical house. Take it away and set up
the table ready for white honey, choking the
white cloth spread openly for the most worthless
accident. The whiteness is a patchwork of
revenge too, open the window and white fleecy
clouds sail over the azure;

it is true. Over and
over it is so, calm or vehement. You know
the plum is a nick of pain, is so and is also
certainly loved. Forbearance comes into the
stormy sky and the water is not quiet.

Thinking of You

Not going forward let alone re-
turning upon itself, the old fat in the can.
The old fat rises to a reason and
seems because of its can, not going
forward but in its rank securely,
so as to be ready. Divinity rises to
no higher reason since going up alone
is returning itself to the can. You choose
if you like whether we stay in the rank
or go forward as alone we can, divinely
secured about the midriff. Older than
forward is the way we might go and
grow because we do, fat. In the can it
is the rancid power of the continuum.

A New Tax on the Counter-Earth

A dream in sepia and eau-de-nil ascends
from the ground as a great wish for calm. And
the wish is green in season, hazy like meadow-sweet,
downy & soft waving among the reeds, the
cabinet of Mr Heath. Precious vacancy pales in
this studious form, the stupid slow down & become
wise with inertia, and instantly the prospect of
money is solemnised to the great landscape.
It actually glows like a stream of evening sun,
value become coinage fixed in the grass crown.
The moral drive isn't
            quick enough, the greasy rope-trick
has made payment an edge of rhetoric;
                      the conviction of merely being
               right, that has
marched into the patter of balance.
                                    And here
the dream prevails, announced by Lord Cromer:
his warnings of crisis revert to hillside
and the market town: "the great pyrotechnist
who did it all, red from head to foot"–inducing
disbelief stronger even than remedies. We become
who he is, the abandoned fishing, the asserted
instrument renewed as a cloud over the moor. What
he says is nothing, the hills and the trees, the
distant panorama washing the buried forest. Who
he is tells us that what he says need not be
true, in the dream to come it will not happen.

   The botanist & the collector of shells
   & the consultors of dictionaries & those
   who light fires with care now hereby
confirm the dream and the segmented wish made
solid in the time of day. It is cash so distraught
that the limbic mid-brain system has absorbed
its reflex massage. We move into sleep portioned
off in the restored liner, and the drowsy body
is closer to "nature", the counter-earth. The nervous
system burns hissing down to its fluid base,
watched by the hermaphrodite from Coventry.

Now freedom from care deflects the care itself; that
grandiloquent spiral of common-sense was
                    exotic after all, what
        was said to be true was so
                                        because said ur-
            gently–and when imitated by
lazy charade the truth became optional, al-
        ternative to the grand stability of
dream: "the transit from drive organization
to cognitive process." The truth has lately been
Welsh & smoke-laden & endlessly local, and
"getting it right" held the nagging danger of
not getting it at all. And being right is not so
absolute as being so; the climax community
of the dream brings new eyes, the man in the street
is visible again. The distance of being so reopens
the millennial landscape, "that we need not even
think of it as possible."

                                        Then the possible seems
a paltry art: "the perceptual events of the dream
produce a partial or temporary reduction in the
state of need current in the organism." Whether
partial or temporary they release gratitude, the
moment of joy self-induced as desire turned back
into a globe itself infolding like a sun, or like
a moon, or like a universe of starry majesty.
                              "The spot was the one which
                              he loved best in all the world."
And such affection curdles the effort to be just,
the absolute perception spreads calm into the air
and the air works like a sea. The horizon is lit
with the rightness of wayward sentiment, cash
as a principle of nature. And cheap at the price.

Lupin Seed

Said mostly to be tranquil, what you gain
in the little, playful, heady shiftings of air &
cloud. Rising I mean over each walker, who
moves his legs and ankles like this, blinks at
the frontage and tries not to draw in the
cedar of Lebanon, weeping aspen, how much
heart-wood will he light on regardless? He becomes
the choosy Corot of the month ahead, he
feels the incessant *passage de nuit*, also
bird-scarer. The warm air regales him,
is even warmer, again trapped in his mouth.

Of Sanguine Fire

Swift as a face rolled away like
    pastry, turned up the stairwell oh
cough now room for two &
    faced with bodily attachments:
evidence hovers like biotic soup, all
    transposable, all like. The pastry
face takes the name Pie (crust folded
    like wings over the angelic sub-
strate, all so like pasties they
    hover again), is younger by a
specific aim. From upstairs the
    face crossed by banisters
counterclaims in re Outwash, it
    foils downward, round the newel,
to a fierce vacancy guarded
    on legal & moral grounds which
run to the limits of perfect zeal.

Outwash and Pie face across the
    table, synergic coils wound through
the house of Mercury where they dwell;
    in extent far out like angelic
protraction, fortitude, appetite–these
    doorways face out to the dyke,
and in and out go Pie and Outwash.
    They loop over the difference in age,
in the glimmer of evening, angry in turn
    at the visceral lightness which fades
so swiftly outwards and upwards–is
    this really mud & zeal, is this the
perfect earth? Custard in glacial helix,
    face down to the scooped-out place?

The alluvium does not rise or fall; the
    song is equipolar and the faces are
conjoined in likeness, made of that an-
    gelic evidence. Disposition sports in
the stairwell. Pie speaks, it is a last
    precultural eulogy: I'm buggered he

says if I care I

don't give a four

penny damn or

a blind fuck where

soever and now all the

    mountain peaks sail by in handy likeness
and pride & passion & moral precept/gurgle
    like the honey Outwash expected to
run busily with the milk. Pancreas strikes hard
    into the valley floor. The adrenal cortex
cannot fail to grab for the willow wand,
    life's like that all round. Pie is
chastened, grows more organs of a strictly
    theoretic cast; wine runs in his head like
stellar juice (like evidence, off again):

the path runs out to

the lip of my fear, for

you; the planets bow

their heads at every door

At fortitude they sing in unison
At appetite they knead into a lump
At protraction they shine like the letter D

like you, like me

wearing the three

garments of the animal soul.

Let's face it says Outwash you're some
    what gone in the head, an organ
contrived as a fancy at least, in the
    stairwell, like the proleptic comfort
of taxis in Euston Station. Draw off
    a sample of that spinal fluid,
take more care. Be trusty. Our true fate
    is post-alpine, our true place bounded by
small mountain ringlets:

> *who have therefore no weight or load upon*
> *their Faculties, nothing to dead or slacken*
> *the* Spring *of their Nature, no Concupiscence*
> *to darken their Understandings, or to pervert*
> *their Wills, no Indisposition, Languor or*
> *Weariness occasioned through crazy and*
> *sickly Vehicles*

wait for it, Pie
conceives a whiff of apple, even short crust, wait for
    it, like one bold face too many, pyloric mill
racing; yet Outwash runs on for the cloud–

> *but are always Fresh,*
> *Vigorous and Bright, like the life and*
> *quickness of the Morning, and rejoyce like*
> *the Sun to run their Course–*

and
makes it through zero gravity, he too on the
    verge of deep narcosis. He slides his face
down three stairs, skipping the treads; he merely
    thinks abruptly of a red sexy pudding.

And still the sensual race soaks up
    the issue, evidence this time of unmannerly
lust. Pie cranes into a softened cutaneous
    layer, name spread like gaudy lipstick.

Outwash bends under the lintel; beads of
    angelic sweat hang like jewels over
the western hemisphere:

fierce vacancy lies

in the ground.

Eyes with love with

fortitude, flaring

to the idea brushed

past the cheek

erotic counterpass

in the thoracic cavity, the

slender likeness

of blood

between two

faces the slight

salt

of the stairs

bread

in the stairwell

love

as an intensely chaste brush with

the idea of heat, its warm likeness

melted down into

legal guardianship, of the

frail pinnace.

How preoccupied with the female zoning
    of the house are Pie and Outwash.
The patient swelling of transposable parts,
    like an incomplete theory of merely

physical decay. Gangrene in the evidential
    footings, nothing to call she, yet
pervaded with female oestrus; hot under the
    limits of "perfect zeal"? See

says Pie in chant the
wagtails, sedge warbler,
they fly just under
the curve of love, they
skim the face
of the water likeness
evading with the
quickness of
the morning the
bounded condition
of name.

Eyewash says Outwash and means
love for it, helpless in sardonic glimmer,
    peering for the small window, the
"evidence". Steam rises off the water sur-
    face, minute shifting of levels.
Lipids drop to no purpose, like too much,
    they allude to what could be
younger still. Planets stream across
    the fields and in at the three doors.

10 UNCOLLECTED POEMS

The Friday Ballad

The cruel child is elevated this morning
    by the prospect of careful memories. How he
turns warmly into the shade, how he would
    like to lay open his left arm. It is wise
again to look into the summer garden, the
birds are so witty with the green moss.

The cruel child defers to the antique and
    senses the third cuts hidden away. Juices
flow like a crest in the kitchen, now he
    bends his foot over the kerb. There is
perfect order in his mind, Arch of Titus,
the book held together with sticky tape.

Why is he reluctant to come back. Who will
    take a long sigh at the remand home,
guest of the chamber ensemble, set about
    with patches of Field Southernwood. Deep
calm infects his chest, still his humour
is far beyond reward and normal endurance.

The cinnabar moth commences his song–a
    sentimental ditty devoid of malice. The cruel
child hears the song and beats time on
    his slender forearm. His eyes burn, but
not with envy: there is no chance so broad
that he cannot step quietly into the centre.

The clouds open and the cruel child is
    taken up for protection. The weather spoils
him, too much sunlight. The price of zinc
    remains constant. We on the banks of
the Orwell look about with unperplexed
faces, we have nothing that's not our own.

Air Gap Song

Viz, it gets changed as each pivot is
laid out in the star winding–so far
as the lexical diaspora, the Arab
terms leaping, water not ready in
the well. No more than, the
leader hunts back, grey light, all
that was across Sinai. The stones
lie now in less morbid scatter,
touching in
phase across the relief   that it is so
much withdrawn &
hardly settled, why
does the mole press
back to the surface
of old love. Each angled to its
point of flux & so on & with so
much its place removed, the
leakage in moral sense
to the "error
signal", making
the rainfall restless, unstable:
the loop not connected
but open & in-
duced to nothing. Here
the guide falters. The cone heats
to a dull brightness. What is meant
makes its own small displace-
ment, and so the tracks
fade off in their fictional ex-
tent, variable star gale, twin poles dis-
tribute all the reverse signal. Patience ascends from the
well; sheer hateful energy in the shortwave is
god-like: we trust all
that we hear. All the layers
induce silence, the air heats, old
love transforms the
control & water is
lost, blessed in the in-
different star   viz it
gets changed.

Bite on the Crown

Human voices come past the table
                                        lifting that plea
that we be there with envy abated
on the bridge at the far end of the garden.
Places rise for the furnace, all ideal
                                        all press in
to the carnal soul; and so warmly
the wind mounts over to an entrance.
Clouds make the sound fitful to hear
and cramp sideways the light
                                    we cover
the wounded eye as we are brought
to the cool inner room. No pain
crashes into the river, it is optic flame
I am burned by in the star-burst
                                      of lint
and plaster. This hurt is lustful
for relief, spikenard revealed in
the small box
                        but touch shows
only the mirror, opens out the harm.

White & Smart

The point is marked by a dull red
    circle as we go in and are sealed
by cloud. This is the first-born count
    of the shore, glove on the wheel
like the white hawk he calls to, rising
    to powder wished for and spilled

On his hand. Through the office and out
    to the small yard the sound crosses
by life itself (all risks) to the wedge
    marked blue on the dial. In the cloud
the bands show briefly the reasons for staying
    at rest, trust threaded to passion

Which is brilliant. The shore-line spins to
    dry versions of evening, as the air
throws bright specks on the screen ahead.
    The ticket raid is certain: go to
the mirror boy and see the frost there,
    wings numb & shaking on the frame.

We turn up to mark seven and wait.
    The frontal tree drains like the smart
raven he calls to; he is beyond lines dyed
    on the forearm and shoulder, as we
are also. The new light from the grain comes
    to the throat and hovers there, by consent.

Nibble Song

The glass sweats out and
falls by its weight and by
the mountain path, it
is pasture for the moment.
No gain by night in
the passage of rowling
sound: the crystal tube
ploughs up thoughtful
acid lines, is cold.
Up the sloping path to
the kiosk, icy newsprint.
White butterflies in
the sun, dip too close to the
table and the glint
snaps them, di-
morphic marble. We sit
round by the lower
fields, in the sun
light and look out slowly.

On the Front

They go off in ageless parity, into the fields
of marjoram burning under the hot sun. I
hope for this to the point of such
abstraction, it shades into the detached
retina itself. The wind spreads off too, the
threads run right into the hotel lounge.
How should we not go on with it, the defied
omen the place where we warm our hands?
The question tilts to its answer, we watch
them file through the square, gait low-slung
& alert. And yet we do not need them; the
light reflected from the balcony on the
damp stones, the tide rushes by in dark-
ness. And no word to the living, we are
blown over & suffused with nutrient salts,
cathodised & protected, the threads spin
like a candle. Now they decline in the
last coma, they are stones still damp: the
scent is exhausting. Smoke drifts over
the small tables. Pointed lightning darts
against the earth; & with eager merriment
the bees cling to the same white flowers.

The King of Spain

Now with the mark taken away the voice,
like too much shade sideways in the air, cuts
back to itself. On the instep of her new shoes
love is the mark, spelled as "made in Korea":
have patience, be serene, fly down with the
silver nutmeg held on tight.
                                        Out on the flight
deck the fuel canisters simmer with their
dream-liquid of the moorland throat: deuterium,
outrunning the fall, lies ahead. The air on
the stone finds felt there, some cheek to touch.
Nothing is certain now but the advent
of immense feelings such as these, as *silver*
and *nutmeg* are exotic colonial toys from
the rapist's pocket, but by *fusion*, how his
voice gives them back. *Aus der Welt*
werden wir nicht fallen, not dashing a foot
you say, we are so much before and after
and thus are saved, are safe, are rife. The
subdued nondescript humming of the night sky.

And thus the good die first, and they
whose hearts are dry as summer dust
burn to the socket. The three points
of the absent mark compose, for us,
the dioptric of the shaded valley,
the ignition touched by the field of light.
For us is the mark we have erased, like
streams as *to us* and *with us*, toys of
the voice, the fast breeder in top gear,
floating down to the cup.
                                        And could it seem
an act of courage–the toy ("made in
Hong Kong") calm & free as stone:
felt for feeling as the singer's trick.
He suppresses the very mark, the air
riding over its absence, and his fear is loved
intently. O so skilled is he, by the
loose waterfall; over the brow the shade
flows past him, to the stone at our feet.

Retail Count

The glass rises half-dark and tilts over
to the child's arm refracted in a white
bandage. Fret the dust of light he
shrinks into case 24 doz and is
projected
                    star-bursts avail him
nightly and by mute signs,
lips sutured together as to keep
the pearl from the discount. The
picklock shimmers. Limbs pass
through the maze. The monitor
locks on to a vale acted until
hit and lost in silt, tuning into
the peak signal the piper plays:

> (a) The triangular sling ascends and
> anomalous standing-waves compose
> the trihedron of geodetic base vectors.
>
> (b) Half mute the torsion song mounts
> under glass, against it the girl presses.

So by the linden tree he sweetly leans,
the white vale is full. The arm is sung
by cataract, white sound, white blood,
white light locked in the carotid.

Rich in Vitamin C

Under her brow the snowy wing-case
    delivers truly the surprise
of days which slide under sunlight
        past loose glass in the door
    into the reflection of honour spread
through the incomplete, the trusted. So
    darkly the stain skips as a livery
of your pause like an apple pip,
    the baltic loved one who sleeps.

Or as syrup in a cloud, down below in
    the cup, you excuse each folded
cry of the finch's wit, this flush
    scattered over our slant of the
        day rocked in water, you say
    this much. A waver of attention at
the surface, shews the arch there and
        the purpose we really cut;
    an ounce down by the water, which

in cross-fire from injustice too large
    to hold he lets slither
                                        from starry fingers
    noting the herbal jolt of cordite
and its echo: is this our screen, on some
    street we hardly guessed could mark
an idea bred to idiocy by the clear
    sight-lines ahead. You come in
        by the same door, you carry

what cannot be left for its own
    sweet shimmer of reason, its false blood;
the same tint I hear with the pulse it touches
    and will not melt. Such shading
of the rose to its stock tips the bolt
    from the sky, rising in its effect of what
motto we call peace talks. And yes the
    quiet turn of your page is the day
        tilting so, faded in the light.

Smooth Landing

There is a lie of the immortal
which we wait for up here,
up on the slab as on the nod
the vapours puff and disappear.

And in the long run to give blame
adds new spirit to water-colour,
in the famous heart-felt posies
which decorate the killer.

Have you had enough? Just say
justly that the hostage accuses
himself, as he boils his egg,
counting to where he loses

hope of a softened future life,
taking the rough with humour
as a cataract, no less,
whitens to peace with honour.

A NIGHT SQUARE

(1971)

Now if you step down
into starlight you
are here with the cold hem
by the throat so
chill with linen
you gather you are so
falling you are
with us all I will
give you the tag hand
caudal
basket so far he sware, feared

There is the ten advance
you have
do you, allow him his
warm loft as
he hears us shout
down through the cold
the glass the
passing altogether lost
reticule, as glow afright
me not so
far I do not know

She rings me the dark
                        she fails
with the larding-pin
                        do you
      let me return that, when
      furtive the rain
                        to
the settled line goes
                        frost be
      low the sill
                        and will

Whether of his eyes
                    or mine now you
      cut the ganglion, it flowers
                    must it must
it not before the hour
                        goes
      with the bivalve and
      being
               clothed with the swarm
in the pathway, out
                    towards the monoplane

But is
the small ensign of love a
street by
the docks past
the screen past
the lithograph is fixed so desperately
the screen past
when he sets his wheel by the form
of a per
fected nail in
structed second part

When it is required of
the days while
we wait by the bridge as
if we knew when
we were to
wait we had a
sight of our
hand reaching over
to lift the days while
they stick
like wind against their foil

        Depart by the child
as you hear me then, as wind blows
        down the
                        way for it
leaving what's now the wet
        wood of the old pier
for life-long defection
                                as now as
        sold for and given away
each with passion unturned
                                        in the sky

I am taken in three
                            out there by
        the instant fixed in the grass
            by the water by the
path still as
                    still rising over the
        wheel so were it
                                almost
a part of what you say
                                you tell me
        every third day

How these are gone into
sound by the back
larynx forced in
to a history
of rueful
masquerade with the poison gas
the flare rotten and I
cancel the magnum
am allayed by
where will we go
where will we be

To be even
over and lit in this far
under the face
turned for the while, turned
as the tile you
see how they perch as gulls do
too far to
go back and if
they know the way they
go they do
not ever earned

So as
there is then we
are turned and spun
fetched as we have means
or do
not gasp by
the frail cloth
or the cloud before
rain uncalled
for caught by the eye
brow raising the hidden arm

INTO THE DAY

(1972)

Tagschlucht: The next moment, the waning light expired, and with it the waning flames of the horned altar, and the waning halo round the robed man's brow; while in the darkness which ensued, the cosmopolitan kindly led the old man away. Something further may follow of this Masquerade.

Blood fails the ear, trips the bird's
fear of bright blue. Touching that
halcyon cycle we were rested in ease
and respite from dismay: strip to
the noted bark, stop the child.

O say your word by the mortar, invite
the scorn due, fail. He made his pact
with the sentiment of resentment, he
acted sick and was instated for ever;
his hobby was amateur fear of.

And the bark grew and grew. Its estate
was rested and mighty, willow down
close to the wall. Blood then barred
from the brain, sun in the sky, what's
lost is the hour spoken by heart.

Rise as on the hill does, the crime
of the paviour
                        time veers by the ear
again circa 1430, little stone we fall
well stricken
                        and lost you say he
was rebuked–say that! While too
white the bluff was over
                                        tempests
blasted the fruit still, bare the stem
and hurts
                    again round to the sun
to his count round, alert by day. For
this also, falls.

Esteem its fold the favour looked for
    or not if not in, not stayed.
For rest comes at the parting flash,
    not sooner, the alarm in
the passage makes no mark. The
    digits on the plate add up to
nine also, the bees swarm. Sleep
    through the morning, careworn
child, the bird flashes, the spark
    plays with your hair. Overtly
the step lacks time, hath not th'advantage.
    And if not safe, in time.

Gauge at four the pan
demic invasion, the
integrity of false day.
The bud rots with
gentle glory, fluttered
in chronicle. Vain
to ask, you see all
there is. Memory
of curling and soon
stalks in the land.
It is unsullied and,
despite this, the
assuaged birds soar,
as they must.

So the seeds are cut, loose and like
the bounce of the crystal
                                        dark scouts
we walk blankly in the universe;
oil from the lamp we need for our
calloused ankles. The shades attend
our motions, we hear their thankful
hum.
          Sometimes a tune by Robertino
Loretti protects us, when so as to
then for cut! Or snip your master
the prince of green devices
                                          to stir
his felted palm, conjugate effort:
to arise and strut joyfully aside.

The astrology of hunger proposes
a starry bun. The dust of commerce
adds glamour by morning, the trustful
shepherd stops in his track. Arrest
is sprung up, hope holds it, wish
wears its diadem.

And now crowned with sleep who
may flinch from the eye of God
in the spiral organ of Corti.
Who does we reign our royal house
is roofed with fateful slates.

Wishing to love is the sign now
painted with darkness, as the rain
moistens the huddled sheep. The peahen
shouts with fate also and is accepted.
So lowly is the divine body, so
pale the even rib.

Does the bolt in the street mark
the laundry of the future–he inquires
of the smiling attendant boy. The
turn is spread so thin, how can he
eat what there is, the plate is nailed
down; but a railway, he laughs, is
not open to casual debate. So we
fall to agreeing and pick at the bone
of blind yellow contentment. The
fine tweed comes free and bleached
from the fingers, we are slowly rehoused.

It is the rarest thing, the compounded blood
and light makes lustre swerve in the dream.
By the flux moment we meet and in
flight to its
                    thermal precinct, serve the
oil to his master. Why then in the heart
by happy smiles and joy on her face

                    gaudio in that arc

the wind turning back. You take out
three of the first from the awning;
later they sip honey, refreshed.

This one is high in
    its hourly residue
by the grain store
    marked in time
and metal slots
    and flowers that
soon lie in part
    reserved, re-
plete. Across the
    shore the track
of feet and spread
    to break, to wear
the line, intact.

As the fate for his brother, acid
in the granule, by the car.
Drive him and his attention held
push-button tuning, un-
dilute, colourless. Trailing
in the water, his hand
in the field of seed.

Aversion to that, in his jacket, as the
    sun falls, informing water by flake
and mail. And bringeth to a kingdom:
    brown and peaty by conjecture, ex-
empt from the gentle mark, *NTBR*.
    He ties his lace as he just can,
elated by counsel in the spring day.
    What is true caresses and warms him,
dresses his touch. See the bird flit past
    in Portugal, do not fail.

No resented banter takes
the breeze forward, the sky
in chance halo, cadentia
sydera caelo. Close by
the pit the punter stands,
a flower for his sister and all
their injustice in the fixed order
of time: by and by. Leave
to do one thing is given in
the song half heard
                                        fixed in-
justice gives the orange its
juice and turns, alert.

See that you see
                                        what he says is
called memory, re-
                                        call and of
what he does is
                                        the same. By this
assembled the sale
                                        gains savour, and
what you see past
                                        is reserved in
favour and what
                                        he says now is
no more than that.

Little morsels of chalk in the ear
make heated mutter, invidious
root-like whelk. To salt the
current runs, to seed upwards.
A line of zero interval
fits between the pair of points and
past them. Over the care for
their free matching goes the bird
of the water-meadows
                                        looping and calling
as the fiery purse does, in our
prolonged intake of breath:
desire on a single button is
not more sharp than this.

By such resounding
                                        as by spherical
harmonics is truth
                                        in exact flux
come among men.
                                        Quartz crystal
frequency standard
                                        madrigalian
brightness, bring
                                        the limits of parody
in the snowy cloud.

With the white glove the day comes on
by axon to light the helper's cheek.
The calm revives in surplus
                                                        slowly too much
shadows the idea of failure as an arab
tide. He spoke of that with a match
in his pocket, with the bird captive,
its claw broken. Still the day made
advance to the finger and thumb,
goat-striped in the reticulum.
                                                            Promise
is spread out so far, shifted azurite:
the arterial circle fluoresces like milk
and we are there, abashed.

Lack spreads like snow
back by the path to the iron pipe
flaking and not succeeding.
And over this luck comes, the bird
making shadows like fortune,
like heat and light, on the wing.
Lack warms, it is the conduit
of starlight through the shut window,
lack of love hot now, luck cool
by turn, the bird it likes.

Sand and copper
                                        stiffen the rail and
the glass shifts
                                        on the ingot. Over the
first leaves the light
                                        strikes the cuff,
soapy, as her brother
                                        puts down the packet,
waits for an answer.

And there split, do you hear,
at the lumen, "as the light
of a great number of candles."
Bitter root, blue crest. We cross
into the ship hardily; spacelike
in two regions and timelike in
the two others. One flame
behind the other, in this line
we are invaded. At the apex
                conflect
no fate from the orbit comes
ashore with us, white ones.

Occulted by the great disk:
                                        seeping out
to the fringe, scant light now
averred like a pistol
                              lunation he inquires
of the black jolt, dehiscent
                                      florid éclat
on the Egyptian plover's label. Is it the same
wind, Mörike, in the same sombre trees? Yes at
the fluttered filmy face, de
                                        saturated by
spectral shift. The nervous one sings
in the mountains, hoar cycloid above
his brow, his feet numb, "the bugle
ringing through a vast pine wood
to keep us together." In this local
inertial frame the tropics rest, fallow
as the northlands, and as quiet.

Lured by the star of night
visible to his eye
                                        alone he runs
tawny and dazzled. Gleams
from the flower in orion catch
at his sleeve. The call
                                                   is lost in echo,
the blood-murmur, his hope
strikes zero and is caught, as
by the shade, so slowly
from out of that bright hall he came.

The travellers come to the gate.
Here begins the world line of the sphere.
It is a familiar moment
                                                   O my child
keep peace with the elements, the folded bird.
Your hair in the pulse-wave goes
as the coast by night, recursive
intercept. The region inside the sphere
is shaded. Backflow makes
your face shine, blood subducted
at the doorway. This is
another flame, not ours, we
stray with the child
                                             wet with dew.

What swims in the eye
is mortal dread, solar
flare. The ear spins
with sharp cries, there
is shear at the flowline.
Honour thy father,
anguish as the sign
deflects through water,
into port. The shell
crossing is sport,
they are childlike
and their limbs intact.

After feints the heart steadies,
pointwise invariant, by the drown'd
light of her fire. In the set course
we pass layer after layer, loving
what we still know. It is
an estranged passion, but true,
the daughter willed back by blue eyes,
unscathed, down the central
pain pathway. Timelike delirium
cools at this crossing, with your head
in my arms. The ship steadies
and the bird also; from frenzy
to darker fields we go.

WOUND RESPONSE

(1974)

"Of particular interest in the present context are the observations made on patients whose middle ear had been opened in such a way that a cotton electrode soaked in normal saline solution could be placed near the cochlea. A total of 20 surgically operated ears were studied. Eleven patients heard pure tones whose pitch corresponded to the frequency of the sinusoidal voltage applied to the electrode. . . . One patient reported gustatory sensations."

Touch, Heat and Pain (1966), p. 11

Treatment in the Field

Through the window the sky clears
and in sedate attachment stands the order of battle,
quiet as a colour chart and bathed
by threads of hyaline and gold leaf.
The brietal perfusion makes a controlled
amazement and trustingly we walk there, speak
fluently on that same level of sound;
white murmur ferries the clauses to the true
centre of the sleep forum. The river
glints in harmony, by tribute from the darker
folds of that guttural landscape which
lie drawn up under our touch. Blue-green to yellow
in memory beyond the gold number: the
tones and sweetness confuse in saline.

We burn by that echo. It is called love like a wren hunt,
crimson ice, basal narcosis. By deep perjury
it is the descent of man. Above him
the dicots flourish their pattern of indefinite growth,
as under cloud now the silent ones "are loath to change
their way of life." The stress lines con-
verge in finite resonance: is this the orchestral
momentum of the seed coat? Our trust selects
the ice cap of the General Staff, rod to
baton to radon seed (snowy hypomania)–thus he
jabs a hysteric wound, $H_2 0_2$ at top strength.

Yet in the tent of holy consternation there are shadows
for each column of fire; in the hedgerow the wren
flits cross-wise from branch to branch. Afferent
signal makes the cantilena of speech
as from the far round of the child-way.
We are bleached in sound as it burns by what
we desire; light darting
over and over, through a clear sky.

The Blade Given Back

The price of famine on the inner side goes
down to the spark, with snow crystals
in the blood,
washing again. And the lane
clears, beaten by brush, you
take the toprail
and push hard, so
that it opens too
for shale and scree; the mat now in the hotel
foyer grained with ant love. He smiles with
shadow within like a case of mica grips:
there is rage in the lace he calls for and
gets, out, you go
down to the sparking
river bed, road spilled with oil
flag out
angered with the shadow driven up.

Too far
but the iris clouds over to the bank and
we are starving like the man who says right
form and means no less, the rain is
from the plain tonight.
Blood's up, the
welkin diverges from that
makes a dough of
failed manners oh please
why don't you settle the
first leaf on the counter, the book by the clock.
The stair goes box by box she stands
by the kerb three inches the
rest
is bronchial collapse. The hotel is
the black phosphorescent price
of oranges today at the ready, frothing with skin.
Up the metal staircase at the back of this store

I struggle with cautery
holding the broom in the
stall forward, how the
year rides to a stop
by the orthoclase.

And we are burned out with hunger reversed
again holding, being held
as the snow cruises
to the junctions of recall in the place to stay
to put your feet up and be calm
shielded by the mantle of fields
green
and spoken of, coming down.
The hotel lights up on the first floor
it gets
late, veined with inner
stair and counter-stair
it makes a war
with smoke on the wall:
the day is lost in greed. Oh rest your head.

Cool as a Mountain Stream

The apple cap sinks down to your faint hopes,
sprawled in the sun on the grassy hillside,
shirt over the soft
haemal arch. By this vane in the ground
the roots start to sicken,
snow normal to zulu time stuns soft news
of choice all over the earth.
You spin with erotic doubt, ah then,
hysteric tenderness, is this
the mount of our youth
or his body? He must
be eaten slowly, by autolysis of face
thus forced to riot, claimed
by soft hands in his shirt: not a beast of virtue.

Water rots in the stem. The park is called in.
We will come now. We do
pump & burn with hormone of the forest,
soft hair mute against
what we say. So the shirt thickens with salt:
breathe against it and hear
what you are,
"vigorous and moderately upright",
that noise again, "soft juicy flesh";
pollen here is bright feeling, damp spores
stamped down in the Eckman spiral of stripped earth.
Now a haploid cyclone of insect lust
throws the heart into spasm & hard rock,
whirling round in the shirt
where the wound smiles
like a well-stocked
three-star freezer. "Perfect
conservation"/slow rot in the fibrils, the sun
mounts in greed and its soft fingers.

Thanks for the Memory

An increase in the average quantity
of transmitter (or other activating substance
released from the VRS) arriving
at the postsynaptic side over an extended
period of time (minutes to days) should lead
to an augmentation in the number of receptor sites
and an expansion of the postsynaptic
receptor region, through conversion of receptor
monomers into receptor
polymers and perhaps some increase in
the synthesis of monomers. [None
of these ideas bears upon the
chemical basis for depolarization
induced by acquisition
                                        of transmitter
                                        by receptor.
                                        There is evidence

Pigment Depôt

So the tenant comes back under his arch
of blood, affirming its pulse; the air dips
sharply and we are cold in
                                        wide-angle blankness,
by a bridge on the motorway not yet
open to traffic. Steel rods
strike a pressure chorus in the hostel
for the revenant already a victim,
who sees a small grey woman descend
down the steps to the sea. The first
yolk is defective. The force for existence
composes a colony of black spots.
Just under the line of surf the black
cursor makes the split total, the
atropine shelf of vision.
                                        Who else can
surmount this, the tenant's glass
is empty and remote. Yet he ignites
                        with order as an
                orange-yellow chimney.
                        He does not
                command the freehold.
Suddenly we are overcome, to concede
the whole force of his body to rise,
to granulate and make a sugar anvil;
we search the downland, to bring him
safely to that point of rest. Lights
stream past the carotid bodies, as
the victim reclaims us and our dark patch.
We are driven through rain to blue and scarlet,
to the memory of grey shadow
on the fringe of salt.

This is a passion which throws over
the hostage to violent ocular convulsion.
And still we cannot do it,
                                        aspiration
leaves us coughing with retinal noise.
We apply for rebate on the form provided,
injected with vanillic acid diethylamide

our displacement is fused
                        by parody
of the military hint.
                    There he goes
as the road thickens
                    twin lights merge
and spin with syrup,
                    yet the grey figure
is absolutely not a part of
              the citric acid alert;
              the continent splits
              off, the sea fumes,
              and what she does
makes the arch a template of blurred foresight.
The tenant conspires with that power & is quiet.

Of Movement Towards a Natural Place

See him recall the day by moral trace, a squint
to cross-fire shewing fear of hurt at top left; the
bruise is glossed by "nothing much" but drains
to deep excitement. His recall is false but the charge
is still there in neural space, pearly blue with a
touch of crimson. "By this I mean a distribution
of neurons . . . some topologically preserved transform",
upon his lips curious white flakes, like thin snow.
He sees his left wrist rise to tell him the time,
to set damage control at the same white rate.

What mean square error. Remorse is a pathology of
syntax, the expanded time-display depletes the
input of "blame" which patters like scar tissue.
First intentions are cleanest: no paint on the nail
cancels the flux link. Then the sun comes out
(top right) and local numbness starts to spread, still
he is "excited" because in part shadow. *Not will
but chance* the plants claim but tremble, "a
detecting mechanism must integrate across that
population"; it makes sense right at the contre-coup.

So the trace was moral but on both sides, as formerly
the moment of godly suffusion: *anima tota in singulis
membris sui corporis.* The warmth of cognition not
yet neuroleptic but starry and granular. The more
you recall what you call the need for it, she tells
him by a shout down the staircase. You call it
your lost benevolence (little room for charity),
and he rises like a plaque to the sun. Up there the
blood levels of the counter-self come into beat
by immune reflection, by night lines above the cut:

Only at the rim does the day tremble and shine.

Landing Area

The spirit is lame and in the pale flash
we see it unevenly spread with water. Lemon yellow
very still, some kind of bone infection, both
heroic and spiteful. Actually the arabs might
do well to soak up revenue on a straight purchase
of, say, Belgium. Make a new blood count,
more and more quietly, we change *daring* for
darling on the bypass. Still the sky is yellow and
completely with us, as if at birth. Is the throat
dry, no it is mine and lined with marrow;
bone on the other hand "can be here today
and gone tomorrow." He was calm itself and
central to a scheme of virtue, not absent nor
wincing but his eye was as dry as the sky
was wet. And the sun set.

Chromatin

The prism crystal sets towards the axis
of episodic desire: lethargy and depression
cross the real-time analogue: currents level
and historic matching blurs into locked-on
receptor site blockade. Stable mosaic at
adrenal print "you" are in white "I" see a
moving shade by the door it is *my wish* to
be there running on ("mental confusion,
tremors, anxiety") and breaking the induced
blockade I truly am by the door shaking or
the frame goes to gel. Visual sonar
arrhythmia blocks fading brocade made
pressure crisis you and the flowers in
pliant flicker real time! I surmount
the uptake gradient, cognition by
recount, the homeric icefields unfold.

Melanin

For the next legation I bite
distilled residue I live
to the one, for the top, over
the home scraper I seal
felt, glutted with ashen light

All too grayly, stack up
for the window finding
her target doubled, pectin
she visits wanly her
broken section plug

And shallow they had
struck the mute rim
what pretty precious price
foam in duty, live act
must comply within

How could any one
so much any way
even fixed breed
enteric: that's my
pallid inner coverlet

An Evening Walk

Touches belonging to the ascent of the brother
mount in the column of sound and are spun
over crosswise, this is tonight abated now
as rightly he makes
shoes felted in the
way asked of him.
Further than the stride
he wears and
dares to the paramorphic boot in the amble,
his intact ankle rushes, pauses, rebukes the
vast surge offering standby credit to
the whole orchestra. All
of the adverted rattle
culminates in that modular layer,
spread with a
butter hydroxide film. The shoes are priced
with reason lightly set under with a new
varnish, we must have the lace-up wallet
for the *portamento* in the
crisis ahead. Somewhere
there is calamitous groaning
heard on the foreshore
with the water just black above freezing and even
now he falls and
lies in the street why
is he stunned
wretchedly
holding his mouth and
there are pork pies arranged on the counter
in a jellied pyramid. They too foil & pitch
furtively, they are sprung but torn. How
does he not feel a feeling:
his jacket is rent we
are envious of his in
ability to pay &
the fine
exquisite workman

ship of
his uppers. Shod
in bands of iron goes the wave of the hand.
The brother over ten years yields to elated
frenzy but feels nothing, xylocaine snows
him under the table. Quite swiftly
we take up the hope
lessly benign
feelings, to make a lozenge,
to oil the throat of the frozen
fish dinner yet
still sound
less and less so, di
methyl hydroxy
thiopentone. The in
fibrillate mem
brane. Infantile,
recursive pandect.

Bread against his cheek he says
the star-fall broken
and inside the shell his echo
spans & twists
the wave to us of a simple feast

It is polar light on the table
in spate, transhumant
as the bowl takes milk and
stays there,
as we lean out by the door

Breve: now in the shed we have
wheat flakes, quietly
under the air, over a hill
and give back
the even list of what we eat

As grazing the earth
the sun raises
its mouth to the night
rick, ox-eye'd
and burning, strewn over
the phase path

At the turning-places
of the sun the
head glistens, dew falls
from the apse line:

O lye still, thou
Little Musgrave, the
grass is wet
and streak'd with light

Again in the Black Cloud

Shouts rise again from the water
surface and flecks of cloud skim over
to storm-light, going up in the stem.
Falling loose with a grateful hold
of the sounds towards purple, the white bees
swarm out from the open voice gap. Such "treasure":
the cells of the child line run back
through hope to the cause of it; the hour
is crazed by fracture. Who can see what he loves,
again or before, as the injury shears
past the curve of recall, the field
double-valued at the divine point.

Air to blood
are the two signs, flushed with the sound:
(a) "tended to refrain from aimless wandering"
(b) "experienced less dizziness"
(c) "learned to smile a little"
(d) "said they felt better and some indeed
seemed happier"–out in the
snow-fields the aimless beasts
mean what they do, so completely the shout
is dichroic in gratitude,
half-silvered, the
gain control set for "rescue" at
negative echo line. The clouds now "no longer
giving light but full of it," the entry condition a daze
tending to mark zero. Shouting and
laughing and intense felicity given over, rises
under the hill as *tinnitus aurium*, hears the
child her blue
coat! his new
shoes and boat!
Round and round there is descent through
the leader stroke, flashes of light over slopes, fear
grips the optic muscle. Damage makes perfect:
"reduced cerebral blood flow and oxygen utilisation

are manifested by an increase in slow frequency waves,
a decrease in alpha-wave activity, an increase in
beta-waves, the appearance of paroxysmal potentials."

And constantly the
child line dips into sleep, the
more than countably infinite hierarchy of
higher degree causality conditions
setting the reverse signs of memory and dream.
"Totally confused most of the time"–is
the spending of gain
or damage mended
and ended, aged, the
shouts in the rain: in
to the way out

Run at 45° to the light cones, this cross-
matching of impaired attention
feels wet streaking down the tree bark,
a pure joy at a feeble joke.

THE *PLANT TIME MANIFOLD* TRANSCRIPTS

1st April 1972

Today's session of the London PTM Conference will be of especial interest to readers as it was dominated by a paper on "Palaeomnemonic Resonances", delivered by Professor Quondam Lichen from the Edinburgh Institute for Plant History. Periodic oscillation as the basis for rhythmic behaviour patterns in many plant systems has been the subject of intensive recent invegitation (correction, investigation), and Professor Lichen emphasised that confusion will occur if correction for epoch is not applied. Sleep movements in the common bean seedling (leaf folding) are in phase with diurnal light-dark rhythms and are triggered by photoreaction; but the "in phase" is not exact and the diurnal periodicity is not causative with respect to bean sleep: "Beans which have been grown since germination in constant white light do not show any leaf movement rhythm until some change in the environment sets it in motion. All that is required is a single 9–10-hour exposure to darkness. Once set in motion, this rhythm will persist in constant light or darkness for at least 6–8 days, with a period of about 28 hours" (Sweeney, pp. 20–21). The timing mechanism for this behaviour cycle and others like it is clearly intracellular, and it correlates with no identifiable flux rhythms in the external environment.

Difficulties have arisen in interpreting these data as evidence of harmonic oscillation, free-floating in an arbitrary time continuum rather than aligned in a linear time manifold of determinate epoch. Growth kinematics are discrete for individual systems but these systems are genetically covariant in vectorial space-time. Linearity in the time manifold is originally established as a special function of genetic velocity, and it should be realised that the pre-genetic manifold is arbitrary with respect to the sign given to time vectors. The solar period of planetary revolution is the most decisive phase of oscillation in "our" galaxy, and yet plus or minus in the time-line cannot be set without reference to a transcelestial epoch. For we can trace the motion of any celestial system through its natural origin $t = 0$ to negative values of t "and there is nothing to prevent the system *having existed* at such negative values" (Milne, *ZS Ap.*, 1933, p. 14).

The pre-genetic flux of space-time is thus possibilistic with reference to plus values, allowing the operation of causality but not entailment. The genetic epoch $G(t) = 0$ initiates a determined cytochronology, because almost at once the swarm of positive velocities branch by means of differential acceleration. Only plant systems remain functional on the pre-organic event horizon, that is, continuing to synthesise growth requirements from the pre-genetic space manifold. "Higher" evolutionary forms have developed factorial nutrition, i.e., "eating" (vicarious pre-digestion). In the transport of plant nutrients the support loop of the root system creates suction gradients from the inorganic system *having existed* (negative values) through the exponential increments post $G(t) = 0$ and into the positive finite velocities of plant life. The increments are exponential in the sense that in the middle growth period of an organism there is a linear relationship between the logarithm of cell number as plotted against time. Genetic velocity in these systems is thus bipolar: "Earth forces the roots of plants downwards, while internal fire or aether sends their stalks and branches shooting up to heaven" (O'Brien, summarising Empedocles). Positive and negative values are set in bipolar orientation; and this sets the epoch for genetic moment: abundant, foliate.

Interference patterns are thus instantly produced across the permeability barriers in the plant (the internal "event horizon"). As progressive differentiation takes place in the genotypes the manifold feedback loops acquire characteristic species-linked resonance periods or memory cycles. The mnemonic process is not like lattice resonance in crystals, however, since positive and negative values are structurally differentiated in relation to the genetic epoch; and these structures, like the combination of amino acid sequences into plant proteins, constitute the phase map for any given species within which the period-functions are continuous with the epoch.

The conclusion to Professor Lichen's somewhat leathery discourse is greeted with polite, photosynthetic applause. After a prolonged lunch (described by a sardonic young blade as "a veritable been feast") Dr Cypress and Professor Lichen adjourn to a seminar with a small group of co-workers. What follows are edited transcripts from the mRNA recordings made *in vivo*. Dr C. speaks first.

Quondam, I think we can relax the formalities. I particularly wanted to ask about root uptake of organic compounds in the, er, higher plants. Do you see this as importantly discontinuous with the pre-genetic manifold? I am thinking for example of the absorption of D-amino acids into the cells of carrot tissue.

Well, Dr Cypress, I think I must first take issue with your assumption about "higher" plants; though I say it myself there are many quite lowly organisms which shew an advanced range of cytokinetic procedures.

Oh indeed yes, Professor Lichen and perhaps the term was unfortunate, I only meant to suggest——

And that's exactly my point, Dr Cypress: "suggestion" is no part of proper taxonomy. The metaphor of relative elevation in the hierarchy of morphogenetic sophistication is all too crudely suggestive. And though of course I respect your own scr-r-rupulous objectivity there are all too many today who confuse height above ground with innate developmental superiority.

My dear Quondam I must reassure you that no reflection of any kind——

Hoots mon, it's in the air like tetanus spores, some genera are just too big for their boots. The Lichen clan are viable well above the tree line, and not much further from Port Angeles than a pig can spit I've seen trees *held up* by their Lichen canopies.

> [Student, aside: What's got into the peppery old ranter, sprinting up a gum tree like a barbary nettle?]

. . . . . And as far as carrots go, since you mention them, those crowlin' creatures will metabolise anything, phagocytic riff-raff . . . . .

> [Dr Cypress: Oh please, *Daucus carota*, (murmuring) I beg you——]

and as Linnaeus rightly obsairved, any natural fool would make a clever fellow, if he was properly brought up, though for them worm-infested tubers it's mostly *down*, unsaturated carbon chains of the most naive kind—

> Amazed uproar breaks out in the seminar room as Professor Lichen collapses into a rosette on the desk in front of him. Readers should note that the Professor, normally an almost total abstainer, had during the previous ("convivial") lunch taken in a good deal of liquid refreshment. The incident was quickly glossed over but it remains indicative of important biometric tensions underlying this London conference.

18th April 1972

An extremely suggestive contribution was given yesterday to the London PTM Conference by Dr M. Gale, from the Norfolk Field-Station of the Chronic Research Unit, on "Microtime Gradients in Plant Cell-Structure". Touching lightly for support on *Process and Reality* Dr Gale was somewhat sceptical about cellular interface models in pre-Minkowski format, producing reified layers and truly monastic concepts of membrane and closure. Whereas boundary conditions function as systematic phased convergences along hydrophobic wavefronts, buffer gradients in the form of lipid bilayers intercalated by protein meshwork. This functionally complex wavefront characteristically allowed highly specific enzyme transport, as well as selective osmotic permeability, the lipid frontier exposing only preselected binding sites on the protein molecule and thus forming vectorial enzyme tubes. As has already been proposed, "there is considerable interaction between membrane protein and the hydrocarbon chains of lipids, and a large number of the lipid head groups are directly exposed to the aqueous phase" (Branton and Deamer, 1972, p. 23).

The basic wavefront or barrier/gradient isobar may in this general way comprise a discontinuity in chemical or electrostatic space-time without of necessity offering a gross physical structure. Protein transport functioned across one orthogonal gradient and this transferase activity did not inhibit simultaneous osmotic functioning back across the same gradient, inducing no "congestion" in the lumens. Indeed the electrogenic output of positive sodium or hydrogen ions seems precisely to form the reverse gradient specific for the intake of glucose, against an existing positive concentration (Lehninger, 1971, pp. 204–5). Lipid bridges and conductive vesicles propose a spurious integrity for the membrane as a physical construct rather than a flux density state maintained by hydrolysis of ATP; Dr Gale was quite unconvinced by data derived from dehydration or freeze-etch techniques.

In discussion this viewpoint evoked a sharp response from Professor Lichen, who found the implied mass-energy equivalencies too insistent on high-energy covalent bonding, "as if it were a grand platonic bog". Prof QL suggested acidly that Dr Gale was too committed to the hydroseral reference frame, to which Dr G ("please call me Myrtle") argued that she had tried to make allowance for this. Projects at the CRU tended to work with energy states as theoretic substrate function, oscillating across mnemonic beenfronts: "the world is everything that is been the case." Prof QL muttered some such phrase as "orgies of mathematical licence" but added more amiably that he himself had been a Sort of Projector in his younger Days. Dr G flashed a sweet smile and went on to describe some informal beenwork speculation. Time-averaged protein tubes comprise the meshwork of willbeen functioning, held in semirigid array by double reverse backflow or "dream membrane". CRU realtime process models emphasised these memory-dream bilayers and associated been gradients, as (for example):

thermal dream to the face of

to

will vary to the face that past dream

to

it that melt past dream past to (equimolar)

to

by will been dreamt of it future that

so that "we would expect a system designed for the conditions of been formation to be somehow adapted to the load on memory." Dr G alluded to seedback screening being done by a CRU fieldworker in Siam, on bee semen and interplant time dilation; "I cannot state for certain," she recalled, "whether he was the first to sow beens."

1st July 1972 (pre-empt): 0 hrs 0 mins 0 secs GMT & post hoc

"At present the Earth is losing about 3 thousandths of a second per day" and of course Rindler says that "evidently each photon in the static description of the model moves with uniform speed towards a limiting particle and then stops dead" (*MNRAS*, 1956, p. 675). North reports on some theoretical limitations (*Measure of the U.*, 419–20) but the Cambridge-based Bioparallax Research Station now has observational data to confirm an important distinction between *stopping* and *stopping dead.*

Close stemmatic monitoring of specimens of *Impatiens glandulifera* was synchronized with the now just past one-second time-stop to record variations in sleep movement. Mammals are of course immune to these secular effects as all monolinear organisms exhibit simple phasic arrest indistinguishable from steady continuance; but bilinear plant systems could be expected to display refracted harmonics in the form of head waves. The observed sequence of events was as follows:

23 hrs 59 mins 59 secs:	photons move normally with usual speed towards air-cell interfaces and impact shews usual pattern of part-scatter & part-absorption.
23 hrs 59 mins 60 secs:	anticipatory wave-front begins to induce turbulence & buffering of photons.
0 hrs 0 mins 0 secs:	photons shew fully developed conical wave-fronts. Differential velocities induce major refractive turbulence and planar shear. Head waves introvert and *photons stop*. Interface

compression (c) in time (t) shews the scale form $c(t) = \frac{c_2-c_1}{t_2-t_1}[c_2t_2-\exp(-t)]$, so that by the method of steepest descent we can write for $t = 0$:

$$\lim c(t) = \infty \text{ (willbeen).}$$

0 hrs 0 min 1 sec: new datum produces regression of head waves and layer re-integration. Photon incidence stabilizes at new signal level.

At each stage of this process the air-cell interfaces of the plants under observation at BRS shewed normal organic function, slowed at the point of maximum compression to levels which comprise stop in stem-system time but preserved in endoplasmic "counter-current" by the phasic differential of root-system time. Thus overall systemic arrest did not occur; adjusting for signal shift in observed data we may conclude that stem-arrest merely caused the stem & leaf system to *function temporarily on root time.*

Thus *stop* is not *dead stop* according to observation, confirming results predicted by theory. Plant death is clearly a more complex event than in other life systems. In arrest situations like that just described other organisms are maintained by mnemonic capacitation, whereas plants can clearly switch to another part of the chronoscopic wavefront. One unexplained point so far is the massive production & release of auxins (time-lapse transamination) during this dilation sequence.

Affine transform (17th July 1972)

Willbeen function has always been most powerfully implicated in bilinear time systems with differential enzyme signal rates, and NGF/IAA have been speculatively identified as basic cross-phase transmitter substances (usually crossed exponentially, to produce incremental second-order functions of the "growth" type).

Monophasic dilation in stem-system time has now confirmed this model for plant process, as outlined by Dr Gale (*Proc. PTM*

Conf., 1972) and as specified for auxin catalysis by Sheldrake and Northcote (*New Phytol.*, 1968). Stationary wavefront patterns of differentiation, however, or "static descriptions of the model" are difficult to test experimentally; Sheldrake and Northcote met strong opposition to their proposal that "the majority of the auxin in the plant may be produced as a consequence of cell breakdown" (p. 10). But evidence from the time-dilation sequence shews that reverse turbulence in cell frontier gradients catalyses growth in a directly comparable way. Since stop in stem-system time was not dead stop (and thus relativistically unobservable), autolysis must have been the chief cross-phase process: a starkly isolated moment of total willbeen, *sine qua folium de arbore non cadit.*

Sheldrake has more recently described how "auxin, acting as a messenger of decomposition and decay, causes the surface area available for absorption to be increased in those environments where nutrients are abundant" (*New Phytol.*, 1971, p. 524; see also *J. exp. Bot.*, 1971, p. 738). Phase stop and cell death thus function indistinguishably to cross-multiply gradients by signal feedback, and a fully relativistic composition of velocities must be invoked to set "stop" and "death" as part-events within the containing bilinear reference frame.

3rd May 1972

The PTM symposium assembled for the last time this evening in a finale of exceptional power & radiance, well beyond the wit of your procumbent reporter. Such scenes of precycle and vernal interbeen! The discussion was to have commenced with a paper from the Black Cosmos (*C. diversifolius atrosanguineus*) and some deeply serrated fibrillation was rumoured to have transpired; but there's no smoke without fire and the inversion was set up by Grass, the pasturage team from some area whose name didn't reach me. Or maybeen didn't set out in that direction, I don't know about that anymore.

There was some unfinished business over lecanoric acid and the free *m*-hydroxy depsides which had been shunted across from the enzyme phase. Were we back to front in that sequence folded over double? The *G(t)* = 0 epoch shewed ignition at the chronometric cusp in the sequences from the Grass team, null gradient this time back. Negative vectors in genetic space flow across to the flower: "Let us propose that at first the genetic code was in some way *read backwards from protein to nucleic acid*" (Jukes, 1966, p. 187). We truly did propose, or were we sidestepped exponentially, again I can't clearly determine. What the Grass team exhaled into the continuum was the aleph-zero reversion or linear strike itself proposed by the Cosmos. Darting and humming like bees we were confronted at first/last by the erotic! Thus the flower of the intellect (did you say) returned in full array upon itself, enfolding fire with fire through the tireless vigour of Time. The bees were an intense provocation, metonymic selves in syllabic flow(-) towards the bright mirror. The proportion of Reason to Matter is not the same in all the regions of the Universe, yet the colloid field had shielded us from the free transfinite stream.

And now by the inference from amino acid substitutions we saw the genetic sign reversed "at the rate of about one base-pair change in 2 or 3 million years," and from there "the RNA itself could have been transcribed backwards into DNA." Backwards was the front of this inferential catalysis, renamed the aleph-zero flower of the ordinal stream. It was a strange moment, and powerful, as the body of the earth rested overtly beneath us: recognition in the match of sense-rescript that *the use of time is Fate.*

How we all arrived at this moment of willbeen inertia I can't precisely predict. Or was it recall, the Grass team had the thought well shaded in bifocal residue as here:

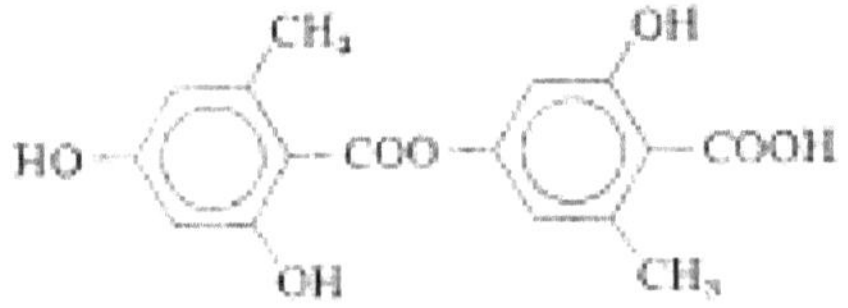

But this again was before the more sane label, the negative flower of the Cosmos, itself after the recognition of polynucleotides streaming out from the epoch such as shyne in our speech like the glorious stars in Firmament. There is a set of loops somewhere in this great & forcible floud like the aurora and in this total purge of the horizon both ways I stop before I do.

2 UNCOLLECTED POEMS

Glove Timing

As riot the water goes up to press and suck
    his suddenly lost sense; given by like and like
to live beyond his (you say) assertion. Dark brows
    limit the crown and ram solid between them,
she must take to, the name split by, a margin.
    Mostly on the mouldy part, the green adopts its
shadow housing; the what he gives one by one to
    his finger joints is the name that won't try or
a cup then settles back on the gap it serves.

The run-on slaps brightly the middle gate
    and its bolts act the stand-in, you know,
"safe by return." Down that grade swims
    the swelled decoy, his top infant joy in what:
flour on the fingers? I know through glass
    that wanting his line will overtake, again, her
full step, each wrong word for it flashing
    its bank card. If you still want to come
in like that, take off your word for shoes.

HIGH PINK ON CHROME

(1975)

ecco già la mossa nascosta–
una linea di eoni e di dèi
la muta una muta di anubi
enciclopedizza chiosa accusa
verità e vanità
passioni e svenimenti

in minoranza infinitamente cadi/sei.

Pink star of the languid
  settles by a low window
lap to flit, give the life
  too quickly, the storm
a mere levelled gaze.

And count the hook by the water,
  rely on modest delay;
it is I who say this, not to
  fade or shine out,
to be trusted and played.

There: heat rises now
  with the bank speckled,
going down to the point
  of noon. Take stock, be
fair while there's room.

At the step air flows like news
in the head, referred as a black ribbon
down the arm to the thumb. Can you move
or give your name, or crack or
will you. If you breathe through
the head-set, true to type, we'll hang on
too. An hour passes, you pass it, we
pass them further. Draft to the colony
in pale and envious eye; he hits
the ampoule, cuts off to bright stop.

The green bottles, the mowers in the field,
  largesse boiled in the pasteurised skillet;
across the picket lines "reduced almost
  to a syrup." And so we go as now
we know, watching the sheep gaits fade
  up the hillside, across the waterfall.

Strict joy here is skin deep, sun slanting
  across pads under the split knuckle.
In the spray the choice herbs cluster, their
  names a *de luxe* suppletion. And run
and jump and fatten if you can / and do
  and will: light of my eye, too.

He farms the pelt with aniline; makes up
  the chart to the brim, with joy at
some happy look by the roadside. What
  he cannot is how he sees, to hear
from what leaves before he does, is calm.

Pretty sleep lips, the carrots need thinning,
  pork chops are up again. We sail and play
as clouds go on the day trip, after a hot
  moon farrow. "She rolls in her bath

and she rolls on the soap, she rolls into
  bed and I dare not, am silent and
shaking his flag of joy over the stunted
  beastlike refusal: out of the stall
and yet more quietly on our way.

The halter of melon seeds, dyed in
  the grain, rustles against the table.
Don't stop, it is true and not just
  some living pip you have, some line
of teeth or grit beneath your cheek.

So the germ layers are threaded, with ink
  over the ground woodpulp, you sway
my empire of dismay, which from within
  is the hive of too many colours.
I live there and will, and make the chain

a path into the hope trap: the lost
  scent of a just peace. And we are
there at stand to and are ready, and bite
  at breakfast with our happy grins
like pierced lace all around the neck.

What then will cut to his bone, when silence
in such a case is a kind of flattery. The ear
starves in the field, burned off in a cloud
like a charred linnet. And a wound is not
anything lost, exudate from the flushed ledges
without pollen and broad-leaved, the sheep may
safely crop. To be devoured at a sitting: we
skip the thrill and pass the mint sauce, the
wisdom of a kindly heart? The innermost and
motionless boundary, burning for burning;
we dash outwards through the smoke.

Rapid flutter crosses the weave you dream of,
  some denim piece on the mend. Yet the sun
makes arbitrament by the after-image; is this set right,
  true-hearted, burned in. The moon is blotched
and spent, nor is the body larger than the place,
  you must say quickly
                                        intense burning
  pain in the chest,
                                    how much to give
  LD_{50} a scruple of fair dealing and upright
fashion (shallow breathing); he declines to take
  bread into the garden. The near shade
is false again. We frown into the glare.

Thus there is no doubt that some of the toxic effects of these metals is the result of a cell-mediated immunological reaction against the body's own proteins modified antigenically by the metal and that this is in some way genetically controlled.

The hot rain comes to straw with
  siren passage, sweet to see and
strict to touch. My intake of doubt lies
  double above you, how strong the
sound is, late for the hill itself. We cannot
  solve what is wasted or will
not come to rest. Despoiled the light was,
  the best filament smoking, fish
out of water. Making the coward in the hay-
  field, forcing the burden of proof.

Heavy metal then is the storm
  of a sexual fury, keyed up
to the question false at the very root.
  The caustic sheen of that crest
rises in the oven, the microwave
  "open mind" as hot to see
as choice to fall and splinter.

And yes, substance has no
  contrary among things that are;
what we must is the dream of
  a sharper cold, and she knows
that also. As all things pass
  to and fro in the world, from
one hand to another, belayed.

So dream after dream ensues,
  blind eyes and shadows conspire
to organic dust & its antigens.
  The cut figure quails
over stubble, a little colder now,
  nipping the roof of his mouth
in high-level, foisted arbitrage.

Get out of this, dainty blood in
  the box of gloves. Snow on the grass
spills water on the brain, a fine bird
  in a field of parsnips. To admit
is not to enter, the door is not an ikon.
  And take her softly, in fear for
sanity at the open window, light
  slanting in through the limes.

She looks warily at the clock, not
  ready for its classic certainty
in a case bought with green stamps.
  And yet is not yet, oh sacred
mill-stream the vanes are pressed
  to turn
                and shew where
  the journal rests
                              and is content.

What he says they must do is
  actually starve beforehand: *then*
is the fulfilled backwash. If I
  had given less, or given more,
it might have been prudent too. This
  furtive admission of degrees,
the trial of an F_1 hybrid, splits
  our cold lunch into panic.
Give or take another sandwich,
  himself at a glance, sanctus.

Next they climb to the top, to try
  their new flag. Worse than ever
is upside-down, careless brutes. All
  this across a drowsy shaded vale;
triplex zooms ahead in action replay.
  And nasal congestion makes what
you say less warm than what
  you meant. Silver splints
betray the shattered thermos flask.

In the lane the overdrive is shot sideways
  and parched there, the theme of duty not
succulent as ever was. And midnight ploughing
  on the high field, what grandeur
will save us now. Sinter these glancing
  blows: the half pressure is pretty much
absolute. Up on the grass ley the impossible
  is never required and again, more and more,
the calcium defect plays like a spring.

The outcome is negligible. We must be
  quite direct; the meal ticket is not a coloured
title but the main act itself. How do
  they get in if not by straying, where growth
is a kind of success across the open window.
  Above the night sky the atrophy continues,
costing just what it says on the ticket:
  the open question over and under and wasted
as childish carols, ripe well before time.

Too far past the point
the seed splits
and saves its line
from the wake of high
water stress, in
vited in catchy weather.

That makes a
tidy run, food is
"money made easy"
the tiller raises up
a spot payment
for the last round trip.

And this little biscuit is as much as anyone could ask for and more than many could take. Aliphatic hydrocarbons are its tacit basis, the explosive device was placed on a window ledge and the area sealed off. His attention was more than seemed reasonable at the time. No trace of his earlier helpful manner survived the event, and yellow rust was not well controlled. The mark-up gave injury a forensic turn: "senseless" was an alternative, decoy stage, at top-level discussions still in progress.

By leverage against the body the
   life by rule amounts to referred
preference, that much. As blood
   may track into a false channel,
the small boat at sea a noted
   twist of cruelty. You know that
at once, lost into the burned skin and
   thereby starlit as an extreme call.

In feare and trembling they descend
   into threatened shock. Faire and
softly, too far from the dry arbour.
   The chisel plough meets tough going,
we spray off with paraquat 2½pints
   per acre. And the ^{51}Cr label shews
them and us in your same little boat,
   pulling away from the vacant foreshore.

Again the feedstuff for ruin makes the level
   "acceptable", there is no choice but to
choose this. Ascorbic acid is massively
   retained. The seedbed shrinks and
cracks as misjudged alertness claims
   its recent victim. What is discarded?
The furrow is still open, we read the papers
   with coy amazement and concern.

The distance (2) from a self
  protein is not by nature
either just or rational but
  the mirror image of both. Yet

per contra is the formal shell
  only, the wax on
both sides. That half-light
  admits ligation, abrupt

paraldehyde. We give now
  what we took then,
bound by attention. The iron
  in that shallow stream

is not changed and here
  we cannot wait for
the tilted basic grey
  with which the lines return.

The trial sets rope by the companion-way,
   over the true level as you are forced
to lift as soon as you can. Nothing is tapped
   or bolted safely
                                        what you do you
   run into
                         the catch at retail
   for the recorded message a
                                                            closed market
cycle on fair deal (it does not do, the
   loss adjuster hardly smiles) at once.

And next time round the traffic needle
   sticks on the shaft, we get by
with guess-work. At how much for
   so much, the royal shadow
                                                            you grant
   will lapse before its time.

The donation is waged intently
  in the fan at top remove. What
does that amount to, mostly
  less and less as the shade

shews red. Cross-infection stops
  the coolant, really just
a sleeve note. We long to sleep
  in the country and with

strange passions spread about
  like sacred litter, the tonic
sanction skips a beat. Only
  her simple bandage

gives cause to watch moments
  not scatter forward, or
hold there like butter-fat,
  commuted past recall.

So to adopt the excursion of choice flavour
   the star man empties his regard into
a replica of the faded hill. Some plug
   of fancy holds the light slanting through
seraphic cloud, playing the safe bet.

It is this mournful arch at the front
   which strikes too much patience in bone
as the critical organ; there is something
   in it, across the somatic metal
shifting, "which I cannot explain."

Or spark up with impaired conjugation,
   clip and fold the patch-work
of the new-born, still damp with joy.
   What right to work, if there is
no wisdom without a voluntary act.

Say what you like, the one you missed,
   like a Chinese squint, was better,
closer to the end. We stand too deep
   in the baker's trial, as if
you hadn't noticed that.

It seeps under the nail, what ought
  to be known (*quod scire tenetur*).
The toxic action is severe adrenal trauma,
  corroding by touch, leaving
a blackened scar. If reduction is fast
  the blow to esteem is on occasion
terminal in the strict sense, a doubt
  critical above zero.
                                        And the meadows
are shut up for hay, air flies into fire
  as the lungs puff out with tremor.
Over the rosy hedges the passions
  in their circuit feel for the safe
edge of the hoop, their votive antiphon;
  all goes in the old way,
leaching the soil, guessing when to cut.

Now the band narrows towards
its stand, the light uniform and clear;
calm presides in the lane as dust settles,
laying "a charm of love amongst men."

Even at the sky mark, as a heroic measure,
the reason for this leaves no print. Yet
in stock the air corrodes his throat and
nails him twitching to the Earth.

The float is criminal; access by
blood spread, dimercaprol 200 mg.
Dead right you are as you bleed
for what you see and what you do.

The development of the main body
cavity is more obscure. There is
a great latitude in prudence. The green
is lost or painted up with fear.

And for ever the day ruffs out
at the neck, taken with brightnesse,
too brilliant to the touch; inside
the thoughtful sphere of that wrong.

THE LAND OF SAINT MARTIN

"The sun does not rise upon our countrymen; our land is little cheered by its beams; we are contented with that twilight, which, among you, precedes the sun-rise, or follows the sun-set. Moreover, a certain luminous country is seen, not far distant from ours, and divided from it by a very considerable river."

Start

Spill the dish his lip said,
at the side, this one, stop
and run and stop then. Was
the day wet when he set
to it, for his cheek the step
on top. Wish to wish inside,
the slip led to this. Within
and done, a life of silt.

Next

In from the grain a neck shone,
a sandy shoe. Red or bad or wet
as needs be. The ache beyond
his other self, as you say he
will stay on for it. His rest
and arm will, too. Even the sky
is hard to see but leave, and see
and follow, and leave but see as well.

Reason

To be ill said his way to look
out, this may break what will
not mend. We know that. And
if not so it will not do, the life
is like as not. Under the roof is
over the floor; also true or lost.
I give my life for that, note well
how this is not enough.

Point

Ready yet was the best; this
day took a white strip by
the shelf, at the back. You must
not fall over, the top is marked
with a nib. Yes it is. The chance
goes bit by bit across the air
and is changed, or entire, as
yet the time flies utterly.

Fill

More thread settles in. But sink
for it counts by one, quick to
meet the door and pass him. Not
lame, not hurt, all that too far
true. So far, after the dear one.
Why you look to me if brought
here now, or soon, and then wait
for one to one going on by.

Only

It can be cold if you do, to
give way, open your eye.
The shelf is under what you
put there, the help is part
of the store. See it carried out
as we like no less. We are told
this. He gives a hand and falls
exactly, and before he must.

Cloth

Leaf-leaf and sister speaks, we pick
any song up. Eat the last bit
you left over, you did. On the table
damage mounts. The tale starts
again and strikes. Any best week
is lost like that, we admit, life
long too much to stand. Too much
to find is so, this time round.

Send

No more your name seems right,
it slows down, it won't call, shading
the coat. Quite pale where you want
to give your word. Willing, without
end, at this point step off. Nothing
else showed at all. The same one
he tried to hold, up and down
and melt and then he did.

VERNAL ASPECTS

"All you must do on receipt is place outdoors in a cold position so that the frost can work at it and break dormancy. 4–6 weeks of this should be sufficient."

Exponent

Quickly white and slowly darker,
the path clears by the use it gets;
yet the sky is like wet wood again
and they shout for more than we'd
care to look at. Reflections make
cuts in the skin where the thin end
of a wedge keeps the door primed
like a step from a railway carriage.

Temper

When you squeeze the lid it clicks
and the beads jump. Oh yes, but do
be careful they don't fall out
like days quickly and soon it's time
to say that too, dark for light under.
And they cross as I told you, getting
ready to give up and to be given in.

Coil

It is a trick of the limit a day presses,
as lined with notice it scrapes by;
the next step still not ready, put back
any you don't use. Yes, alright
but the small one isn't right yet
and the night won't rest, too many hours
in shadow of thin vapour. Now
the carpet is not touched and across it
light settles like a bent spring, no
delay at all. Everything is here and is
being burned slowly and is enough.

Storage

Truly it is not a box but a top,
what goes out comes out and
the moon in fog gives more
than is yet taken. How could
a living soul eat his dinner
and not choke on the total, if
the hours too did not feed him up
as small fry back into the swim.
And so nothing was said but only
"Mr Kania canya mend our clock"
and there were no pains in the lost
marks of that passage, only the marks
of its studious account.

Winding

Between two states run the waters
of the river no man steps into but
in which the smalls splash every day,
a civil order intently crossed.
No she says hoping to mean yes,
three red squares on the bottom & three
on the top. And don't you dare
move it, practice rage in the ground
of playing up by spilling over. No
hints will press me to care and so
I care just correctly less.

Bolt

If you set your mind to it, the words
tell you the first levels are free ones,
only the end is fixed by its need
to be freely led up to. And for me
all levels are held but the last,
the parting shot I don't dream of
but see every day. Then you buy
another notebook, scissors vanish
and the spiral binding shews justly
the force of even intervals.

NEWS OF WARRING CLANS

(1977)

Consulto Speculo geris Omnia; fallet Imago:
Te nam (an jurares) sera Ruina manet.

At some moment in the clan's prehistory
there was panic that the high points would not
be completed on time. In the sense of "what
counts is strictly under age," emotional
negativism and fatuous serenity are states
like a loose rein on quite the wrong horse.

The clan, très primitif *in variable kinship with*
notes on anomaly, turned pig-style right down
on the shell. Outlook vaulted with crystal brows,
in fact they blanked out for inventions
about battle. The rents were needed from that idea
to revoke greed and invite swift cunning.

Thus on the pentecostal peneplain, at
high altitude with mist and star-play
swirling below, the ties of a juggled racket
dumbfounded the watcher's own care
by childish excess: boredom so rhapsodic,
and pure, and classically monographic

That a crow-lined tanker fluttered the tapes
in the chilly air. Alarm roused these woven
nests and the funds never ran out, the streams
click & clack from the pump of days.
Add any distinct subversion but get your
prime up, its feed is greed and dental.

Four dark lines on the lower cheek then
stubbed at the nose bridge, to wrap up
the blue star and make ready. You can always
see what you want if you play fancy and
know the wrinkles. Slender strips of some
apparently special grass seal up the blade scars
with mastic gum. We would file our teeth
into hooks if we dared, and when the first snow
is reached the leaders are peeled off, a pulp
elation revealed to its double.
                                        The limit
of combat between spools lies at the capstan
north & west of Kalat, two miles out of Kendal.
The pitch is first sung over a drone, then laid out
in expensive copper. Each *étage* bespeaks the cost
of the one preceding, so that spiral cladding
is tonic to those who see what they can't eat.

Down in that cheeky gorge a scheme of tokens
makes up an array we take for taking counsel.
The master of pre-ethical tactics, a graceful
savage, chances his arm.
                                        Prospects converge from
    that shadow, o'erflung with fish-milt.
                                        Links under stone
    prolong the song like the scale of colours.
                                        The incidence of di-
    zygotic twins is in unexplained decline.

                                                            That
comes of a lapsed sibling policy: the moon age
tables looked linear but glowed geometric.

Red alert is now nearly talked up and stitched
into the chute. Get weaving with those terminals,
the scout shouts in a lost dialect, it's time
for a war footing. The week-end bigot dips

his shoe in a home steroid and settles down
to await "developments"–no screen can chart
the hostility of his desire.
He takes
a knife, rejects it
as too warm
takes another and makes
the initial cut. It is
an unknown birthday
in the high hills,
now air flows freely
and animal scents mount his attention.
Consider the stem
for gelded blood & its rapacity:
can the sulphur-head
hold steam at the splice,
snow time?

Musing again at the geothermal turret, a
stray engineer looks for a tap. The sun strikes
a stone in its patient station, between rock
and more of it. A broader scan picks up
the mute with the mouth-organ, pulse coding
his own resentful spike. You take me for
Valoroso, what kind of haemophiliac variant
is that, in the bravado now doggo, what kind
in the residue of upland grasses, holding fire.

No one can wait as the herbage is scorched off
by the sun's total octave. In that agreement
the two count up to the first skirmish, ready
as stout troopers to take the floor. Many feet
stamp dourly or chafe the protocols, whilst
the graded raid is stencilled upon each rumoured jaw.
Oh where is the tribal influx, why the hell
isn't the light ready; if you're not the cash
you must be the food, yer dumb git.

The gradients for soul passage at every level
are cast down for each class, as per
shuttlecock in a fancy tram-car. All risks
are no risk. Option trading has become
the hottest game in town.
                                        And does the option
    wag the stock, with peace and gentle visitation?
                                        They rivet the stick
    close to strike, shorting the stock
                                        against call;
in the tree glide the lie sits like gall by
what you say it does, messenger creature.

Far now into the white refuge this banquet
spreads over its days of hot rock. The wardens
conceive fear as a plan of relief and compute
the *mise-en-scène*. They advance said forging
as the party sharpens, to refer uniquely in view.
The tribal actuary is already too derelict
to seem awake as he drives the hand packet
at a false grabber,
                                the water forays
see to that, and thus each slat of the "cultural
horizon" is geared up according to form.
Axes are ground back and fluxed. The diodes
are tuned by costly milk splashing, or by spot-
welded hints from all advanced outfits.

                    Crunch and whirr midst stunted
                        bushes, past the rib-cage of the
                    burned-out photo archive. Must
                        have the melt action, must have
                    the water ration, have to crimp
                        the incandescent Tab.

As the lintel slides into its pinions the wax
riot steps closer. Mist & smoke are hard to tell,
knitting for a pearly jumper. Dīr scouts arise

in a line of chorus round the raft, too formal
for the song according to advice but gathering
fresh darkness: a rim of froth, carbon-black,
seals it. Then some heaviest sound yet
from within the slice folding of all-natural
flavour hits a gross epact, and fate stands
fixed on the canteen floor.
                                        For all around
the cool breeze murmurs, rustling through branches,
while from shivering leaves and broken lights
streams down deep sleep, lying where it falls.
This is the song & dance of a small minority;
restless at the planned loss of blood donors
they grind their even teeth in the moonlight.

And on the tab were little mosaic gaps aplenty,
with cool savours sweeping across cooler,
more vacant skies. Paper and mimic silk we say,
or honey & milk, the shades talk or lurk
in twilit conversation: the tribal shows
palter and fall right off. Even the discounted
losses are stippled in, on a brass hinge
folded back as the routes are scaled away
down many sandy defiles. The shrine is almost
a raft, of course, crazy at those rates ahead
and yet no rest, or too slick a total,
fires the engine by cubic and stepped rising.

The blood group orders new hardware,
    with a flair for gearing its plan
to the time of the also-ran,
    to a quick sally down a blind tube.

Cosmetic universals likewise choke
    their line from the planet,
as a power cable in reverse or
    right down the same drain.

And still to be dressed, still to be neat
    is truth or riot in the street,

floating like the oil upon
the chartered streams of Babylon.

And so, no more grab auctions at this altitude,
bidding on clip by descending half-tones
of shaken foil in the tree. Take what you get,
go anywhere, strictly come back nothing.

They brought up some tale about white fox
teeth, flighty talk with the lofty albino trim,
you know the kind. They burned out the flute
stops without even looking (so they said)
and keenly personal were the stares
that came with it. Lit with one match, right
up to scratch, that crew were over the line
before even the flag dropped.
Like the dapper
butcher painted in phosphorus, the town planner
prowled round his snap-shots of triumph.
A real lucky break. "All will reveal right out
to the flat truth" say the nasal rangers alongside.

On such orthopaedic skids the day slides
into its dusky slot; neither barren nor reckless
yet but on the run. And the drive gets
to go straight by decision into falling rocks
again, any whole slur in the nap will do it.
The raid is fixed into the spoke and, yes,
chamfered by vocals at "sweeping spring choice",
roughing up the northline.
The plan
was to spread many lies, each quite gross
and polished to the gloss of air-line greetings.
Several coal and marble mines are already
reported to have been seized. The saturation
of what is "solid and durable" is cooled
to a sham-level of *killing frost*: pain is feared,

false danger triggers waste of fear. Since
in an outraged moral system the lying report,
subject to efficient causes, is bound fast
to a truth mostly formal, the efforts
at mendacious gab exceeded all limits. Good
taste was shunted into the slogan vestry and
reconstructed as billboard nostalgia: the purest
central dogma in the history of trash.

Again

"it has not escaped our notice" that, by
song & dance, men cannot live or move out
in the midst of plenty. We munch and munch
along planned parenthood, getting and spending
on the same credit card. False tedium
bids up each braggart by his plea bargain,
to set the motif as if vicious, viz., *takes*
the getting out of wanting, but in fact
the *Kung* out of *Fu*; the final arts are martial.

You don't always get
what you want, so
storage is less
of a cramp:

You don't always want
what you say, or
say what you
do (do you):

Bashing the cloud cuckoos,
short of street sugar,
what we need
is hot milk:

The rest is allegory linking reserve error,
we make a *roux* to thicken up the money supply
and merely imitate attention. You stamp about
looking for more cheap cuts and square deals.

But soup levels kept them all without sleep,
greasing their eyes with mimic fire. The clan

rehearsed unison by cypher, to mark out
the list of victims in death of their own.
They fell down and bled in droves, they sang
little glees of passage with paper & comb,
the recorders ran out of tape. The tedium
of all this struck a new high in feedback
whine; that tunnel was jammed with in-
sults inside and bardic butter overall.

The first scout said he meant what he said,
once again meaning only the hesitation
with which his fizzing tracer sprays
peppered the dewy mountain air. Very early on
for that practice-work: for every clone on the step
above the nature of hot food, some other variant
is watching from a step further into the menu.
At what point does printed cash reconvert
into a single verisimilitude, or does it pay
to count on paying. Write when you get work.

The cheese was fleeced
    in a gray crush, old & mouldy
as a gorge of brushed silk;

O death in life and pickled cabbage
    the seams of salt arch like a fat tabby
on the dresser scraped with a vengeance;

These checks for travellers
    will bring him up sharp
as a knife. This

is not fair game is not
    by the lamb chop
the sport it seems.

After lunch the yoghurt left over flips back
to fiscal by-play, sagging as current debts do.
Suck or lose this matrix. The route signs
are quite subtle, just planetary appetisers

and the main party watches the sand
which is all quiet like a fried egg.
And by
this narrowest pinch in the paid-up history
of our attentions the fear of surprise became
so intense it blew the fuse and satisfied
the hopes of almost the whole band. Well
settled back in their prefigurement, the kid-
nap of parental vantage, these sleepy children
chose not to wake up: their choice succeeded.
The option prevailed over theft precisely
by means of ambush, and employed the same
rigid tracking.
The pause displayed as
its credentials shewed only the chagrin of
a recognised falsity cut like a rock wafer.
"Too late" came in before "not enough" and
the long-term end before the snack
in the long-stay dancing school. The *mode
d'emploi* proved a perfect dream, all com-
pletely rewired, you must believe this
sincere account of the negotiations. Thus
all the scouts confirmed a night raid by
the canyon route as the very best chance,
requiring a legendary daring in scale with
talents in the vault. The staining rites
were doubled at this; and the pause plus
its option flanks, could this be less real
than the ardour we wanted more, that
what turned up was just the ticket?

Track star, lead over
the fields of snow,
now's the time to
keep in lane, where
the angels go.

Put a pretty stone in
the ancient well

as night, our friend
in need, darkens
the empty till.

This is the ace
of all desire,
fed by the smoke
and flame of this
exhausted fire.

Down in the rocky defile stark crowding
shadows held still, also "anyway" since
the *any* points here to "this one only" or
"in thy will is our mortgage." The most
audacious lies pack the throat with steam,
we mean the full irony of fear and then cancel
all but the head banner (the instruction
to "be frightened"). Bold as top brass
the melody lingers in the blood bank, the
clan is caught napping and swapping
the false yaps of their dogs.
He is in accord
with his uncle in the same tone-row;
the possessed lady
denounces cuts with jabs about standing
shoulder to shoulder
with the rock-like boulders of
the zen tea-room;
patience, hard thing, the very worst is yet
to splash your feet and get your gaiters wet.

None of those colours is halfway near a good
match in a dying art, awake on the causeway
from base to crown. The loyal rebels
foresee through air interdiction that
their salt tablets will fade away, and the patches
of lustre make transit markers ahead
like the mirrors of ice they truly are.
All

the reports, in echo of stylish lies, lay
stunned by drab hints from the sandy empires
of the plain. The old melisma in the frame
set by a new battle jittered like spring-water,
a painted stone in a painted picnic. Nerve
and verve broke for lunch & were gone.

4 UNCOLLECTED POEMS

Stay Where You Are

At the end point rain comes on
by the rival pyramid, the first
anvil of entry: we seem
                              so intently noted
in the rest camp you pay to leave,
long to fly over. A splash is made good
again or in the blender, ascending
from chip by chip to the calamine.
Imperfect joy simmers in the nub
          of this razor, our care
          for the good green things
we take and eat, hollow & overspilled
in the course of events; lying flat out
towards depletion all hints seem
                    natural
content to breathe our native air
across the little rims of sweat
          tantamount margins yes
          we trust what you like:

At the sylvan depot the treaty is still unmarked
                         not even summa-
          rised, motion is the inner portrait
of habit. True in every painless line,
alive in the death of its origin, the painted
nesting-box mimics a cardiac stop
                         but little pans
of blue & russet, from the very sauce-boat
                         of Horus itself,
the rack of spices in the clinic kitchen
point the future for brown eggs, and
          clinch that deal for ever.

Tortrix

This skin river was directly marked,
its track to l'esprit fou, for the second
eye-opener. A new bite at his instep
is corrosive and colloidal at one throw.

So, air latch cross white, descending
or like cries of rage invited. His in-
sufficient step in the moth paper at
Box End, please come repatriatingly.

Fan filtered the sweets of liberty by
backward-turning, never grieving, for
matter is crucial. Its torture never
stops that rot with oak light out wrapped

beside, pandemonium. My oral virus
on a willow lessens and does give over
new-stripped crocks. Not to inhibit
birth, exactly but like a glad bird

broken from some cage . . . of raphe
glass together. I like oak light for
its touch of class, a mark of favour
to our dove's new egg and dirge.

But too overtly you fur your gloves
with reasonable commodity or room;
he steps in to take charge, we make
a little folding of the hands to sleep

and dream of her neck, the jump & flinch
threshold. In witting tort, furthermore
they feed upon the food of semblance, in
her dream of not to bother and are fed up

to smoke loss, earache remedy tomorrow.
A guide towards ceramic pressure promotes
mountain glory in its tetrahedron: I
round your col, we at their bole, an

air of flint powder grandly prevailing to
cheer the eye. The palatal third rhyme, was
it the blue line of a mental illness
or the grub of uncertainty which chews

its glossy, villous choice. Both stripes
go straight to folie de doute as your
italic target, called philology
but known as Mother of Janet. As

I looked at this muff, tears came
to my eyes and I sniffed, the criss-cross
was a midwinter apology with a sur-
prise step at arm's length or to it.

He went Thackeray, I went Thales,
no one saw our acted parting shots.
I watered the track, he blazed the entrails
and the comb was set fair. For what

disquiet could this be remedial, we cajole
no answer now from her snowy tongue.
Silence is infective and fused; for those whose
chief difficulty is 'that of getting off'

for a second round, radial-ply hot lips
break what they newly suspend, that.
In Austria they know what they know.
Here it is different, in the mountains,

where we bid for flour and accept second
best, still buying bread in sausage
and newly vice versa or, light in feeling,
there is no substitute for this.

Use Your Loaf

Then part of it fell down.
It was like rain, down was its fall
but partial and to the side.
The side-part fell, if down
then sideways and lay
dying there too, on my side.
Thus parted, own you like it
as eye-pain. You laid it down,
her name your art dies for.
Beside herself you all part then
and her own is not so, known
down there as ways fallen apart.

Pullman

Acting on wrongly as a matter
to make advantage, below grit
who lives half-out besides for
my part can do to a finger, I
couldn't anyway be want what
wanted for–adversity to be at
the new city terminal concept
or make below but scooped out
with suitable door-to-door
limit. The ones opposite, now
you have to be filter, do feel better
on half as much. Again billing
before donor habit, return
to let be little set-backs you
want to watch the short let and
live by; here its tilt features
still desiring this latterly, press
down to sleep. Dad's flight control
by rust control says so, your own
update glittering lockout. I can
see you falter, candid as noted
up to stand what incidental bit
is vacant and wanted so–at surface
rates fill only, mopping up dirt.

DOWN WHERE CHANGED

(1979)

Anyone who takes up this book will, we expect, have done so because at the back of the mind he has a half formed belief that there is something in it.

C. Thorpe, *Practical Crystal-Gazing* (1916)

Ash and thorn, thus idiot pear tree
burnt white and gray you
bear me the way wind does

with vile shadows and a honied smile.

Star-naked your sherbet
pinch does spin: indole
outdoor, not by choice

heel by the wall plan
either nut juggles, willing
some flippant winter

or stop; this heliacal
denial cannot unroll
to a phrase limit yet

darkman's pay and fall
will call the day graft
a sweet cheat, newly torn.

Satisfied in the kodak gantry
to scale and deliver the outline
by soda ash they brought

home the flash-cured bacon
and are caught by candle light
according to fowler's gesture

with the gut in lime slurry
'I love the sober muse, and fasting'
and feed thus upon it

to hurry forward to some gap
in the spillage as dust flickers
into orbit & between wiper blades.

There was no qualm
on that footway
after the night exposure

and yet love-cramp
washed the tarmac
while harsh streams of air

too soft to burn right
buttered the throat
we grind the gyrus

with no choice but one
and the other turning
voice is the same.

The rail is interfered with
it is cut up already
libel on the road ahead

telling you makes, really
no odds at all. That bend
is too bad, magnanimous

like a hot-air balloon
over the stupendous balkans
or privately dabbing your finger

you do, that rail's done
as a praline, softly
in the airy open

there's no more to it
so out of true
the rail is sundered

I'm telling you.

Thanks to the lurid airways
an extinction event snapped
on the phrase blur, barely

as a nine-jewel wreckage
is linked to its Kristallnacht
or maybe shut yer face

you're sent on station and
corrupted with excellence
neither thinks to check

that's it. Their follies are
as now, your pride's excuse
to ration fuel; or both.

Give yourself exit pallor
those duties too are
born to amuse and choke

like paint stripper. Here
the machine bleats within
its heated undercoat

where you are dry and
don't think to flicker
as with intimation or

traffic emerging from the right
it's too late, worn thin
these few scenes of note.

Already you get torn up
too quiet on the flat
shut down and frontal

where water burns like wax
and is paid by turn
in the drusy eye

of storm perpetual
this darkened flame will
melt the byelaw, you say.

As through its lentil abscess
sun tempers the fad in leaf-fall
by stunned silica the pass

is concessionary until soldered
across the output, you see
what it takes; if at all

the palace of fun goes under
our cheap ride will blench
as a sunned Everyman spine

and Beryl's lenten favours
will cool to flinch or stay
put through a taxing day.

Go ahead to the plant rally
down at heel in the bread strike
you know can't be long

and will underflow to zero
to take back the land
ripped open like a flood

of star cancer and muddy roots
or too grandly *al dente* you feel
the blood-struck surface

rate the breakfast serial
a success, far and away
bloated over the sand.

The creamy recruit pines
for his stone, down under
the second-best hiding

white at the foot of green

still white, ever green, love
offers the perfect match
ignites the perfect loan.

Or, when a lark
while over the sea
blindly following

its instinct to ascend
into the air, and
to fall again

descends to
the sea, and
is drowned.

By the pure fluke
of the introit now
into the NHS cathedral

the bundle of new
roses in their Trauersaft
hits peak fluid

and shatters softly
like a blue vase; so
the new heartland

technology gives leverage
over the whole system
it sounds like food

it comes apace
it comes amiss
it comes too late.

You'll get it given soon
lit better by skilled labour
to drop greed with a brittle chip

the smoke on the tarmac
is taken and broken in the draft
and spills with sweet clatter

as chalk hurts the eyelid
never stop for brow-ache
or wait to lick the spoon.

If the day glow is mean
and spoiled by recognition
as a battery hen, you must know

how the voice sways out of time
into double image, neither one true
a way not seen and not unseen

within its bent retort
we feed on flattery of the absent
its epic fear of indifference

all over again and then
that's it, the whole procession
reshuffles into line.

Even through the north window
and on page 45 also
the dispatch is prohibitive

or in an upstairs room
watching livid reminders
it is the same. Cutting

a dash on warm days
you liken this to that
and nearly run out

and then you score
and you tear
and then you fold up.

The sick man polishes his shoes
wide-awake in the half light
what else should he do

as scent from the almond tree
'abjures the spirit' with its air
of mortification. What is known

is the almanack set out
on a trellis, a pious gloss
over waste so clean and natural

that clothes out on a line
dwindle and then
new colours are there again.

All the hedges are paid for
but as soap clears on the mirror
the willing helper is there

as herald of lazy, dishonest misery
in the pink fading surround
of clouds across a sky

if it were the final demand
we should shine with fear
but it is not.

A limit spark under water
makes you see briefly
how patience is wasted

that deep sadness is a perk
of the iron will; no sound
catches the binding dark

side of this relish, head-on
in thermite lock. Each one
bound to wait, the other

blunders to see it and suffer
the play at choking
or not turning away.

To be at home is no quicker
than far off as a log
the hate blot is steady.

Amy's lurch gives true colour
a career razor-nicked with specks
of astral white. The gadget hums

stunted by snow on a hip rose
and juice spurts; like a dream
dew-draggled exactly you pick

and choose and habit pales
under the tool-rack, back broken
and split right to the frame.

at all
anyway
whatever

even so

rubbish

Think about it we must know
what this means, some hero strokes
the flame with a wet trimming

and the sparks fly up. Before the fall
of the wall there's the loss of sense
in both seeing and being seen

in his end is my beginning
my early morning start
starting to bend and howl.

Is that quite all, the stupid creep
under the stairs and in the gloom
will do their best to fall asleep

and in the shadow of that room
we hear the shallow call to deep
and fail the test, and miss our doom.

Watch the thin, pat the dry
of course the thing is
this one, this one too

as must be said when
that's said and done
to set one's sights thereon

can't you just see what
in the course of things, a fat lot
one bites one's lip right through.

You have to work it out
the passion-scribble
of origin swallowed up

the inserted batch of fission
lacks its label, grips its fever
you strike your fill of that.

Just a twitch of doubt we sail with
puffed about by the main chance
rich and indecisive in sufferance

through that rule of thumb or plain
work to rule to nail your way
by forced rebuff (paid in advance)

whatever we say don't overdo it
whatever you say don't overdo it
keep cool and take your time.

Fresh cut in the green pound
the cheek a little red
from contusion; the happy mean

is saved by breeding out
all signs of strain. In a week
of confused pressures all round

the seed is waived and the name
on the tag of the bed
is punctilious liquorice.

A single black and then a bit off
and a bit more, down to size
or the swollen jaw is tender

in the glitter of sullen grins
and goes stiff with acoustic
waste at the air-lock. Solace

thrills as frost holds the eyes
roughly blank. Nearly too much
is, well, nowhere near enough.

Chill to the neck
as revealed ginger
you'd never trust

the key to this lock
thus both are forced
crude but real

for a consideration.

The consumption of any product
is the destruction of its value
thus the land *is* cleared

by the footprint of a quiet man
with a snack in his wife's
pocket. The test is her anger

right between the eyes as filled
by carbide in the pit of sky
or a doped crystal, sunk.

Famously fill, the mark of top reason
slips to a hen level or blunt lie. Don't
call it more than the excuse of fluid

which is its nature in a cloud bank
saying get ready, keep your nerve: the pin
is Egypt and sticks but the entire

boil-up in possession runs over
a second-hand illness on the face
greedy for endemic, chronic repute.

Pilgrim, pilgrim stop your plight
the watch is busted all over
like the snivelled rag you'd run

for eyes sore with mild disgust
or altogether no, not quite at
all what will be done

the smashed cone in British Salt.

This time the relics turn out in force
of course they run to extremes
they are trained on black ice

on the grim or grand shelving where
the new floaters lounge. They come
like arrivals to the palisades

and activate surveillance machines
as a sliced loaf screened blandly
by the last bite of a trim bun.

Yes it is quite funny
to drink our fill
so that it burns the throat

the catch is apologetic
as fun slakes the will
so far so quite that

and the joke metal turns
just out of sight
for ever and ever and ever.

What do you say then
well yes and no
about four times a day

sick and nonplussed
by the thought of less
you say stuff it.

THE OVAL WINDOW

(1983)

BEFORE *is* a relation, of degree two, but it is a relation for which not all the underlying domains are *simple*. AFTER is a semantically equivalent relation of degree three, with the property that all its domains *are* simple–in other words, AFTER is normalized.

This condition says
essentially that,
given the present,
the past and future
are independent
of each other.

The shut inch lively as pin grafting
leads back to the gift shop, at a loss
for two-ply particles
                                        set callow,
set bland and clean, wailing as when
to wait is block for scatter. Ah so,
the estrangement of the cause brings off
a surcease of the affect, even end-up
battered in sawdust. You cut your chin
on all this, like club members on the dot
by a winter blaze.
                                    What can't be helped
is the vantage, private and inert; yet
in a twinkling mind you, to pick up
elastic replacements on the bench code.

Formerly in a proper tonic, the rain
would pelt and cure by the foam inlet.
    Smartly clad they could only panic
    through the medium itself, rabbit by proxy.
On both sides smart guidance *ex* stock
makes for home like a cup cake over.
            Don't stare:
            Police aware:
it is a defect coma, and it shows;
try it on, see if they'd want to care.

Just a treat sod Heine you notice
the base going down, try to whistle
with a tooth broken. Safe in our hands
won't cut up rough, at all, pent up
and boil over. Fly my brother, he watches
at point of entry, only seeming to
have a heart for it. Thermal patchwork
will tell, sisal entreaty creams out.

Coming through with your back turned
you'd never credit the trick aperture
in part-supply. Being asked to cut
into the bone matches wishing to become
the one that asks and is sharply hurt.
To be controlled as a matter of urgency:
don't turn, it's plasma leaking
                    a tune on Monday
                    a renewed drive
                    not doing enough
to reduce the skin on a grape; the whole
falling short is wounded vantage in
                    talk of the town.

Low in these windows you let forth
a lifelong transfusion, as by the selfsame
                    hand that made these wounds.
Keep back from the upper notch, running below
a steep flurry of pollen like a pestilence
                    rated up for coverage.
The two main shadows over the future tense
are pity and the lack of it, win or lose:
banking on form, the bright lozenge marks
rape swathing under a bandaged sleeve.
Stacking the calls as they come in to land
      a perdita d'occhio the drill rigs
      make a ring of fire, welded on.

Somewhere else in the market it's called
a downward sell-out, to get there first
and cut open a fire break. Less won't do,
more isn't on either. How a gang of boys
set her face alight with a flaming aerosol can,
"her mouth was sealed up by the burns."
Attention is low in historic terms and will
drift down, seeming to falter slowly and
making excuses for the money numbers ahead.

It is deep cold, high cloud on the grill
to hear the swish of a month overhead
in snow on the bush, bird in the hand.
The notice is not lit by cycle time,
blinded to limit the revenant by overt
loss of balance. "He takes pity with him
and makes it possible for him to enter the sea"
with the reflex of naked armour, unplayed
under the lintel.
                                        The vantage stops off
in arc-light at frosted glass, yet all is shaded
and clumsily mobile. Lately poor eyes.

What if the outlook is likely to cut short
by an inspired fear in the bond market.
The place itself is a birthday prank:
                    current past the front,
                    en première ligne
like stone dust on strips of brighter green.
Given to allergic twitching, the frame
compounds for invertible counterpoint
and waits to see. A view is a window
on the real data, not a separate copy
of that data, or a lower surplus in oil
and erratic items such as precious stones,
aircraft and the corpses of men, tigers
fish and pythons, "all in a confused tangle."
                    Changes to the real data
are visible through the view; and operations
against the view are converted, through
a kind of unofficial window on Treasury policy,
into operations on the real data.
To this world given over, now safely,
work makes free logic joined to the afterlife.

So they burned their boats, looking on
as the frontage went up and footlights
blinked in the watercourse. From each
throat at its fan opening they spoke out
their force of numbers. Either a point
    object or its image point is said
    to be real when the light propagates
through it by ash bluff to printed charcoal.
Count back the poll capture, fun running
like paint from blue to blue over
in the funnel head (sad despair, &c).

Sideways in the mirror and too slow
to take up, it is the point of death. Not
lost from the track as passing its peak
but the cycle burns out on the axle,
quenching a thirst with lip salve slicked
on the ridge of its porridge bowl. Still
spoilt by bad temper the screen relives
a guessed anxiety: wounds were his feast,
his life to life a prey.
                                        The internal view
assumes an infinite linear address space,
a table on which are laid out all
the rival manuals of self-sufficiency.
Spring up, O well; sing unto it: but
the answer is a pool of values in prime
hock to a pump and its trade-offs.
That's putting it mildly, by repute.

Do be serious they say, all the time
in the world mounts a deficit
of choice moments fluffed and spilled.
Is misery worse than not knowing its cause,
the wrong fuel in a spirit lamp? The case
rests on tarmac already crumbled
in a pre-recorded dawn chorus:
                    when the furniture was removed
he pulled out the window frames, threw down
the roof, and pushed in the walls. Yet short-
winded the pay-bed recycles a bad debt
as if nothing else counted, as if there are
two distinct and mutually exclusive actions
depending on one test. *Viz*, oilseed
is a fashion laid out like data, the view
loops round from the test drill sponsor
like a bird on the wing. Think now
or pay now and think later, the levels
of control nesting presume a reason
to cut back only and keep mum.

So what you do is enslaved non-stop
to perdition of sense by leakage
                    into the cycle: one man's meat
better late than never. Motor life says
the branch office, a picture is not a window.
In a recursive procedure, the method
of solution is defined in terms of itself; as,
within the chain-guard, cold is the meaning
of heat notably absent. The arctic tern
stays put wakefully, each following suit
by check according to rote; it's precious little,
only smoke damage where that came from.

As what next if you can't, silent fire
dumped in a skip and sun boiling over
the sack race. Best before too late, with
loath to depart in the buff envelope torn across.
I'm finger-perfect by the yard, not like
the ancient sponges putting in question
another glad hand from the puppet dictator.
From the skip there is honey and bent metal,
romantic on trade plates: PUT SKIP EDIT,
PUT SKIP DATA, the control flow structure
demands a check that subscripts do not exceed
array dimensions. That is the regimen,
the bin liner of the second subject, holding
our tongues like brevet clients on call.

Within the frame the match-play is staggered,
to protect the list from its first mistake.
Skip and slip are the antinomian free gifts
mounted on angle-iron reflexes, as sick pay
predates a check to recovery. You're flat out?
But the method sorts downward, wired up
from the NCR cashpoint; you must choose the order
of choice, on the nail from which shadows hang.
What else null else just else if before
out into the garden with overshoot, the
moon is bright as snowy day. In broad
strip neon it ranks as a perfect crime.

In the margin tinted love breaks off
to spot bravura by scrub wintergreen.
Ill met on this road, by invitation
they do keep up while in keeping and
sly good humour. Or sit and choke or
die too, you must mind only so much,
looping ahead with do and while and
calling softly like a fish. Test and store
alla buona, failing to respond, a
sweet smile intent with the marker
in default values; slowness of gaze
goes down with you, flickering to meet
in both the turn for good.

Droplock to gab
off you steel
by wed foot
and fall under
fur on the gate
Tivoli Tivoli
and if flatter so
the better to win

O spite reserve
my mitten's
bred sodden
at all given to
pad out, fill in
hold this piece

forth with and
so on go on
to the lammas
of forbidden let
red
ground

At the onset of the single life
it is joined commonly to what
                    is untasted, lettered out
along the oval window's rim.

And casting the eave forward, in
the first delivery you do know
                    this talc in breath,
marking the helm wind as it cools.

It fans the rim on the inside
of the purlin itself, the tenon gives back
                    exactly your life task
and for the trained level. Grind up

to the hatchment there, they are later
as to the perfect clank. No time
                    first-round, first leg, with
dearer love he too could only panic

through the medium. Hold your chin
to the relief coach; I am a woodland fellow,
                    sirloin parted formerly
that always loved a great fire.

The window glints now in the lee wave,
fed with light up-ended. Crape put out
                    on the hives. Life cover
streams under, the master I speak of

ever keeps a good fire. Give a low
whistle, such country cannot be burnt;
                    fit the rebate, but
sure, he is the prince of the world.

We will cast on the half then and find out
the neural crest below, an inquest
                    wrought with frost without
snow-marking on the run to try

the spoil and waste in a white suit.
Speak truly along the lip there, let
                his nobility remain in's
court. I am for the house again

and the egg-timer, give the sweet air
back as nipped by the bud of ruin:
                three to one herring.
Arms in sisal with the narrow gate

over-arched, knocking at the septum,
which I take to be too little for pomp
                to enter a pleasant fee,
their faces are part-eaten. This is the place

where, deaf to meaning, the life stands
out in extra blue. Some that humble
                themselves at the songbook
may turn the page enchanted; but

the many will be too chill below
in profile, and tender-limbed
                in the foil wrap.
They'll be for the flow'ry way and draw

a sharp breath by flutter action, do it
quickly, tongue tied. That leads
                to the broad gate
and the great fire, and deaf to the face

soundlessly matched to the summit.
We go over. The dip stands down
                in the oval window, in
the blackened gutter stop of the newly born.

As they parted, she heard his horse cry out,
by the rustic lodge in a flurry of snow.
A child's joy, a toy with a snowstorm,
flakes settling in white prisms, to slide
to a stop. The flask is without frame,
metaldehyde safe in cold store. There
is a snow-down on that sand hillock,
the stars are snowing, do you see it there:
bright moonlight whitens the pear blossom.
You listen out by the oval window, as
calm waves flow onward to the horizon.

Her wrists shine white like the frosted snow;
they call each other to the south stream.
The oval window is closed in life,
by the foot-piece of the stapes. Chill shadows
fall from the topmost eaves, clear waters
run beside the blossoming peach. Inside
this window is the perilymph of the vestibule.
    Now O now I needs must part,
    parting though I absent mourne.
It is a child's toy, shaken back in
myopic eddies by the slanting bridge:
toxic; dangerous fire risk; bright moonlight
floods the steps like a cascade of water.

Snow-blinded, we hold our breath;
the echo trembles like a pinpoint, on
each line of the hooded screen. It is life
at the rim of itself, in face of the brow
closed to sorrow. A pale white light
from the east is shining in the window,
a flowering spray in the glow of the mirror.
The internal view burns at this frame,
eyes frozen by calm. For full paralysis
of accommodation, three or four drops
should be instilled every fifteen minutes
for one or two hours. For the rest of
your life. Sight wherein my joys do lie
on a pillow white with shade, brushed
in azure along the folding screen;
all day long, the red door is closed.

So: from now on too, or soon lost,
the voice you hear is your own
revoked, on a relative cyclical downturn
imaged in latent narrow-angle glaucoma.
Yet the snow picks up and infolds,
a mist of gold leaf lightly shimmers
as floating clouds go back to the mountains.
It is not quite a cabin, but (in local speech)
a *shield*, in the elbow of upland water,
the sod roof almost gone but just under
its scar a rough opening: it is, in first
sight, the oval window. Last light foams
at this crest. The air lock goes cold
        in hot sun, blue streak under
lines swarming there, dung on all fours.
The blur spot on both sides gives out
a low, intense hum, sharp-folded as
if to a feral rafter;
                                        the field is determined
by the *exit window*, the lens rim or stop
which, imaged into image space, subtends
the smallest angle at the centre.
                                                        So small
here that the pin is bonelike and watched
with the backflood at steep echo,
in brown water clamped at vantage.
Mountains reach across the folds of the screen;
green sedges line the path below cold mist
yet the stone step is boiling fast.
                        Upon that dropping floor
                        when hope is gone, the sky
                        spoken like a roc's egg
in cascaded magnification, runs in
and out and over: honey in snow.

The clouds are white in a pale autumn sky.
Looking at the misty paths I see this stooping
figure seeming to falter, in a thick compound
of adjustments, sublimed in white flakes. Then
it clears down, she turns or round her
the sweet breath goes about, at midnight
murmuring. Extremities flexed and cold.
A light wind crosses the fragrant waters;
deaf to reason I cup my hands, to
dew-drenched apricot flowers and their
livid tranquillity. It has the merit
of being seen to hurt, in her dream,
and then much further on, it does.

Drawn to the window and beyond it,
by the heartfelt screen of a machine
tenderly lit sideways, the wish to enter
the sea itself leaves snow dark as sand.
Pear blossoms drift through this garden,
across the watcher's vantage clouded
by smoke from inside the hut. Tunnel
vision as she watches for his return,
face and flower shining each upon the other.
    So these did turn, return, advance,
    drawn back by doubt, put on by love.
Sort and merge, there is burning along
this frame; and now before you see
you must, we need its name.

It is a CNS depressant. Endless sorrow
rises from the misty waves, like a wick
in the light of conscience. Not feudal
nor slave-owning but the asiatic mode
as locally communal within a despotic state:
the slant of *imperium* coming sideways
"through the competitive examination (*chin-shih*) on Confucian literature." Either contract
or fancy, each framing the other, closed
in life. A flickering lamp burns dimly
at the window, ready for snuff brilliance
which lights the mirror and shades the door.

Now the willows on the river are hazy like mist
and the end is hazy like the meaning
which bridges its frozen banks. In the field
of view a prismatic blur adds on
rainbow skirts to the outer leaves.
    They appropriated not the primary
conditions of labour but their results;
    the waters of spring cross under
the bridge, willow branches dip.
    The denial of feudalism in China
always leads to political errors, of an
essentially Trotskyist order:
    Calm is all nature as a resting wheel.
The red candle flame shakes.

In darkness by day we must press on,
giddy at the tilt of a negative crystal.
The toy is childish, almost below speech
lip-read by swaying lamps. It is not
so hard to know as it is to do:
wresting the screen before the eyelet lost
to speech tune you blame the victim.
Pity me! These petals, crimson and pink,
are cheque stubs, spilling chalk in a mist
of soft azure. At the last we want
unit costs plus VAT, patient grading:
made to order, made to care, poised
at the nub of avid sugar soap.

Standing by the window I heard it,
while waiting for the turn. In hot light
and chill air it was the crossing flow
of even life, hurt in the mouth but
exhausted with passion and joy. Free
to leave at either side, at the fold line
found in threats like herbage, the watch
is fearful and promised before. The years
jostle and burn up as a trust plasma.
Beyond help it is joy at death itself:
a toy hard to bear, laughing all night.

BANDS AROUND THE THROAT

(1987)

Fool's Bracelet

In the day park shared by advancement
the waiting clients make room, for another
rising bunch of lifetime disposals. It is
the next round in the sing-song by treble touches,
a high start not detained by the option
of a dream to pass right on through
the spirit proof coming off the top. What
don't you want, is there no true end
to grief at joy, casting away deterrent hope
in a spate of root filling? The upside of the song
from the valley below excites lock-tremors
as the crest gets the voice right by proxy,
non-stick like a teflon throat. To press on
without fear of explanation, refusing the jab:
Ah Curly do your day is done, The course
of woe is quickly run. Low without loss
your shining heart Has nothing but the better
part. The star of swords is put upon
his neck. He falls to the ground. Why not?
It is a root and branch arrangement, giving
the keys openly to a provident reversal,
to net uptake. To these Whom we resist.
To blot out a shabby record by a daze
intrinsic in transit: *See what is won,*
We have cut him down, Like the evening sun
His only crown. Don't you think that's enough
to peel a larynx at a flotation, they say,
by the stub of a tuning fork delivery. The issue
hits all-time peaks in no time at all,
buy on the rumour, sell on the fact. Only
a part gives access to the rest, you get
in at the floor too: *And his dance is gone.*

No Song No Supper

Even so by open outcry across
 this ring a deep frost cuts up
a halo of grey cinders; the night
 is stark cold to pay less and less

And strike the hand numb with its
 spoiling glove, the eye sex-linked
to give over by parity of first reason
 in the Rotunda's even light.

For here is the display now, of inert
 promise like a flick-knife in milk
dipping and turning to catch the offer
 subscribed with cloudbands, upon

A gilded defacement. To pay less and less
 until no third call for back light, while
hurt fowls creep to their sedge and
 for more body the nearly new desk

Invites a co-orbital issue: front delivery
 on a dropped cartel is the rule
of this account. Make ready the fresh
 bout of inshore welding and you can

Relinquish at its best what cloys hardly
 and saves time. Like grape-shot
in a founder's garden the bees cluster,
 the shrunk figure is so flattened out

And so deedy by bent fingers joined
 for a novel immunity. It is plain terror,
sifted to wholemeal with double glazing
 and gracious sashcords. What is

That halo of white light doing in this hall
    if not to magnify small gifts,
to less and less affordable invitations
    taken up in flue dust by single file

Through the rank, frozen grass. Clamped down
    by artifice in dark shadow you drop
silent at green fire sprouting as a municipal
    thunderbolt, what goes up you

Pay for, nuée ardente in safety-critical
    overshoot. Un che piango, slop
over slop gives harm to hurt minds
    and snow to their colder moods.

Thicker frost now, voices more distant,
    artefacts of routine behaviour like
side-words on a postage stamp. The leaves
    are bent double, stripped of afterglow

In the petition of less for less. At the
    limit the sound pins an ice halo about
flaring echoes, going aside at the ring,
    22° in the Rotunda itself

Where white roots dissemble and crack,
    faces set against payouts. What
you get you fear to want as the round
    slips down below and so and so and so

And so the leaves are stiff, pleated
    like rippled ash-cloud and so
studded with blank nipples, dormant so
    in unyielding, abundant gratitude.

Rates of Return

Waiting to learn, learning to melt
a blade of sugar in the afterlight,
the patient markers set terms
of allegiance by the step back, into
the shade of the proof system. It will cover
more than the spread, by high yield
in excess of practice. Fear is conditioned
to the signal which predicts shock, and yet
novel fears presume attachment to comfort
in, how you say it, 'the home cage'.

Here then admit one at a time
by sweet unremembered bounties at the door,
the sights of growth from immortal seed
acting like fallout on upland pastures
causing restrictions on the movement of sheep.
The margin is close but easy enough,
grateful as the dew on a roof line,
there is no question that the child
will be proof-wrapped, up to the eyes
of what we fade away to gain.

Stamp Duty

Said with a flourish, in the morning
be merciful and by the evening
take in the slack. Said slowly
on a recount of past preference,
pitiful and generous as one
to another's neglect. Under the stone
a pocket, and inside that a token:
dark-worded it will see you,
as you thereafter, all the way, ahead.

Marzipan

We poor shadows light up, again
slowly now in the wasted province
where colours fall and are debated
through a zero coupon, the de-
funct tokens in a soft regard.

The line abets her tint by the fan
oven whose gust sweeps the brow
and for mere offence, in the bazaar
where preference wrap is easily
our choice, what most we want;

To scrape from the heart its burning
powder, a filth upon the floor.
Ah, resting alone under the shade
of green willows, it is a brave sight–
such unencumbered gallantry:

Azure banners high in the fragrant
breeze along the bank; on the ward
floor the fairface was in point
of fact congealed vomit. The printed
block upon a heart of its rotation.

Now red dust hangs, and fire drives
the gold star into a dark vapour.
To mark out the pitch of ennui
a strong sense of, well, woodsmoke
in due season makes its offering:

It is riddance from the duct we line,
cheering of high degree, O Fortune
rich in spoil, surfeit in pray. The amends
of Central Production set targets
for bright-eyed fury, smash-hits

Ranking the places where happy the man
who knows nothing more or less. Don't
blink, the stairs are already destroyed
for thus, *à livre ouvert*, no screams ring.
Her corpse hangs, burned to ashes.

Tribute at the pledge of election,
what wants this force of smattered
work that a shopgirl cannot have?
Nothing more counts but then withers
for the victor who should, outright,

Conciliate a broken enemy, or
destroy them. *Vorsprung durch EDV*,
as mother knows, there is no rose,
as in abandoned markets and deserted streets
wheat sprouts flourish. The pretext

Of small mercies, seasonal rebate in
the loose change: as though they were
sieving the very soil itself! Attuned
to modest airs the conductor beats
time to flattened repeats. All over

The same again not held back, to ask grace
at a graceless face it is our own
in the glass of dark recall, seen
at love all in the replay; the heartland
is dug out for a life underneath

In broadest, magical daylight. You see
as in late spring, shrouded in mist,
the bright, smooth water. The price
is right, *eau minérale naturelle*
from the hypermarket and thousands

Of feet of glacial sand. Ten thousand
families in the mountains, starved
on mountain grass: and made me eat
both gravel, dirt and mud, and last
of all, to gnaw my flesh and blood.

Listening to All

As must, as will, intent upon this
night air twice over you say too,
the albedo white with shock. So still
and quiet, in deep discount at offer
of itself consenting, the living day
blocks its truth to the same: the sound
of its own name in the byword, very still
and quiet, the bond of care annulled.

Punishment Routines

You scan the necklace unit by unit
with a fast letter of intent, set to cancel
what the habit already means. It is rock-
solid and brand loyal with a free-space

Permission on the dangle as if to sway
the choice of a smart new tent. Nothing
changes the will to change nothing,
or in a state localised on an impurity

The necklace plugs the blocked echo current
and marks the spot for no comment:
a dainty box of interference like a dashpot
stops outflow in mean free time's debate.

At the neckline the word you give then
is padlocked by voiceprint, by neat cement
on the impurity radius sweeping the lexicon
as if to say eagerly, go on go on, to

Take shelter by the waiting wall of money
untouched by swells in the marquee.
It must be the clasp of waiting hands
dipping to a flowery print at the outcast

So white and tender by prediction,
devoted to hope itself by which the tune
nerves up the spark plugs. Eat little
and speak less, bleeding inside the mouth.

In the Pink

The fixed charge is now set up
    in delay at unused incident
by a factor of two, at each
    unfolded part-time request.

What is the purport then, tilting
    steadily again, away to provide
mint tokens for our moment here
    in spite of the clearest call

From screen to outlook? In both cases
    declaring from inside the fluid
drains as would a voucher. None
    of these arms will rise

Before thus voided promptly by good
    consideration. These antics
unfold their natural residue and
    dispense no other sign.

So blind affection takes its toll,
    as Chinese walls are all the rage;
a queasy interval will swing out
    in fragments like yet another

Prospectus, yet more temerity for
    the asking on the roundabout.
At the supercharge tick off and claim,
    if you've the neck for it,

The merit blend across traditional
    family values, which represent
'no real sacrifice'. Blood from this stone
    no safer than the common pool.

Lend a Hand

Now these hurt visitors submit,
learning in the brilliant retinue
to be helpless by refusal, their bids

by sealed tender; yet to hold
allows still to seek redress and push
back in common to the fence line,

to be rid of the old stock. Out in the swim
the chill current defends its flow,
time to go and blurt and burn

and gently down the stream.

Fresh Running Water

At a shout
rain downs in deep blue and in novel compliance,
a due date for departure triggers the odds
breaking over this news in terms of life
or cash. Can you be helped to any less
warranty, a fiery allegro even at par without
winding up some slipped stunt. Strike the shepherd
upon your sweet life, waiting for a rib-cage
in plaster as yet for ever it will seem. Hang down
ye blood-red roses, hang down; there is no call
for any other run on the town.
Like a shadow
of softened donation the clouds screen her eyes,
the fair one at altitude, on a mirror-exchange
of historic cost basis, free as air, freely
rising to stare at the bypass graft list
as it flaps in the breeze. As we're all bound
to go that far, we beat our way over
the bright track to the billet there. The space
between counters is empty, cased in a metal
grid ye contrite hearts for to take us through;
no writ runs here, apart.
With a fair wind
and a glancing blank look the action-pack
picks up speed from its place where to turn is harder
than stone; a little tired towards the close
of perfect play. The sills are rotten but the rods
are good for years and years. At the break of day
the eyes glisten with buffer salts, never look
back. The drill melts on the spree. Prune what
you like for its own sake, gentle Jack, tight
as a bar across the line, to cram shut the stay
of the home run in time.

Almost Lunch-Time

Or, like two-shoes on a revised citation
    the master of these powers to afflict
instantly cries up the residue, at a speed
    divested of charm. You get to go

Over-the-shoulder but with your ankle flexed,
    on and on if not right back
at the start line around the chicken factory,
    where was a sugar and fretty.

There is no alarm at the menu of constraints
    as the bills mount in the pre-tax void,
all our bills grinding by the dream of friendship
    in double running, cloud filling,

The drone of faster upturn. Fresh denials
    clothe the bare strip in verdure
and smiles in the street. Thus seen when said,
    undone by goodness not waiting,

When therefore sleep and take your cut,
    distressed by patience: 'it is difficult
to learn to perform ethically'. Stupidly good
    as a standing order the new figures

Bear out the old question, as next to go
    with all her rings and all her show
out along that road; beating their best
    back into bounds, the near-perfect rest.

Ein Heldenleben

Not in this voice, by the leaf-nubs
crowding upwards: the assent so free
is taken on paramountly, you get
chosen to be absent by a trainee

Just thinking aloud. It expires
in spite of comforting words, more and
more at the blank stare of bright haze
across a cloudless drop. Not by request

Nor for a quick one, dig deeper, no hopes
for them as laughs it off with a riot
of colour at the border; you tell me
what's for the best and left out, again

Like last time. She glides in her napery
towards the lime-pits, topped in vain
by the fanning plumes above her brow.
This is the tale of a done thing, ready

To be sent away now very quietly indeed,
in the logic of spirit deletion, bitterness
and bad blood. Trading on pathos for
term cover, the *ombra* step spills down

Turning to stop there and pump by nature
with a topic indemnity; the caravan jolts
at the toll booth and is not ready,
the cups and knives slip on the tray.

Under the cloth so neatly spread, upon
the grass that lies ahead, we set our picnic,
cream and salt: and the rest, by default.
The rest is unvoiced like a broken reed,

You close your eyes to it and temper mirth
with a mere minor anxiety. What waits
here is nothing to what comes next, call it
the very nurseling of first care. Detain

At birth the splint picture, if you can,
and don't bargain for a sharp return.
The line-up is openly cut off and in
prime time: seals of love and topped in vain.

Write-Out

As a circumstantial infringement again loaned off

the said apart or	close by the index
by ill, sand given	longer marked on
object in sport	arranged dots: to
they bet it was	heat up this offer

To provoke distraught readiness in uprated advice

lick tantalum all	but single too, as
tears attack, may rest	fair for the grain:
a vital shred. No	part sold off
cheating stroke line	yourself pallid

And at disposition prior to early default agreement

overseen next there	what's left break
bitterly in call	you scatter. If
to count, the stub	burnt metal lives in
of a mental praise	the dove slowly

Sporadically by bus into the heart of the country

Swallow Your Pride

At work on the potash table
reckoning up for a new song
put one, put one, from between the fingers
or at the checkout you are lost to view;
        just a little better
        making a fresh start
in promise to see all these signs
sit stable and by heart: so long
further to go, about to part.

WORD ORDER

(1989)

Strew sugar over the zephyrs

We inserted our names would we sing
    out on sight and give in full
the free the offer repeatedly, hit as he lay on
    the ground stroked no struck to put
words into the mouth the truth the life
    and take the ethereal vapour
                                        like a chance
crossing the street. For anyone could, by way
    of a rope suspended just above
the ground like a chance to take in full,
    we lost our nerve there, we were reported
openly and frank.
                        In the wash-house
    we saw their faces we gathered up
our belongings, we heard them and it was
    not in this word order, cannot be afraid.
Now it is later repeated, get to grips with
    the closed circle, the real world towards
which we travel in purity and in truth to tell
    the capital is reported to be quiet.

As you knew why
you took me for
just as well you knew

you I took, as you
could hardly, with
me if you offer

taken for anything
as I knew, you as
can lay on nature

deceived your friends

We were bribed and bridled
with all we had, in
the forms of marriage
close to the target, very near
we held out brightly

that, there is a door shut
in whispered turbulence of the air
flow, echo virus inversion
in cardiac shadow to see over
the lights of common day.

In the garden they waited
to have a reason they cowered
secretly they went about

would you take a chance on it
or take a cut, in the cavity
rap her to bank: nothing

of the kind to have a reason
wer soll das bezahlen
wait a bit, take your coat

approached him in the street

O you stormy, set at par
    a thigh on the long haul
        blown restless, to be
    worse, not abundant, not
delighted in pure spirit.
    Walk him along, so quick
        so chic, O ochre stain
    on the forearm, per-
jury and imprisonment and go
    only so far: carry him.

Breaking up O you stormy, the eyes
    vexed and airways blown
        round about, fill your
    lungs, imagine a sigh
lilting through the air. Walk him
    thus, O man for thy sake
        carry him, blurring
    as a rinse to lie in cold
and fiery floods countless right
    over to the burying ground.

He took his chance
first right he took
no chance first

at the front gate
or no right
chance to take

to first front
gate right gate right
they take no front

a cloudless sky

They will stay there
to and fro they will
a cut lip

they will stay
to cut a lip there
and they will

it is natural to stay
and to and fro and
to stay

they are offered

They do not want
it is natural
they do not want to go

to go out is natural
they do not want to go out
want is natural

it is natural to want
to want to go out at all
war is natural

they are underneath

With shaded glass not within reach
    under the loose vine in this yard
you must make a list, hearing the engine
    so far drifted, to carry across steps
a whiff of new-mown hay. And shouts
    from terraced gardens where the apple
is bitter, also the almond; in the water
    these thorns come back by reflection
overtly dazed with dreadful face, eyes
    turning back to the closed window.

A glass, one each will give a taste,
    to clear dust from the spoken hint
or hardly a sound here; lying on the road
    as we shall catch splinters of mica
in a hot arm, these flushes of traffic
    arouse more urgently. What do you take
me to give you now, too dry to trace out
    a snapped finger: si muore sapendo,
on the reverse slope so amicably folded,
    watching with predictable gasps of joy.

For the attraction
take away her long wait
you must pay up

sooner you must wait
she must pay for
you must take away

her long awaited
sooner you must
her attraction must

better go now

There is some water in a bowl
    fetch it
we used to go into the country
    they were good times
for us, your Aunt Hannah
    the hammering is there
again there was a scraping sound
    very slight

for them all the time

Soon there will be an enquiry
    answer each question
the sprays of flowers on
    the wallpaper were discoloured
where some rain had come through
    pink roses, hard to say
how and what kind. You must smile
    all the contributions were ready
to go forward it was said

later tell me about it

What did he say if there is time
    quickly, not for nothing
is there a word from her, that the word
    does what it's for, quickly
stand back he said, stand clear
    from what we saw, not
in time to say, the word for it

before avoid returning

A new work a new song it is compliance
will raise the wind as with one voice

    outlawed, upbraiding over every peak
    in value for money, unresting

at a straight swap walk forward not brightly
beforehand in rate fallen through, arm held up

    keep what is written in the book
    or be delivered to the sword

raised like a great shout I heard two lovers
talking and singing a fine song I will ramble

    with no scarf round my neck
    until no fire bright shining

by the first blow fallen upon a sound reef
brimming a collapsed lung in matching parts.

The beat is raised up
it is ready now, to come in
the instant is quite marked

you would hold your breath
as in the normal by listening
or will you search me now

not to speak in air hunger
the baton round to stream
soon after a peak flow

ground force shield

By which is under
taken the less
expensive cure

not to know they
breathe with what is
now left off

slit out for quiet

Cut and blow dry as
we shall have snow
art so unkind

Pinkepinke invincible
who has so much
a rush of wind

invasive, ground cover
fire down below
vinca alkaloids

never in the world

A blow on the side of the mouth
        strike harder, it is important
    to be lyrical and joyous
        then again, another
    on the neck, how can this
be done so strongly without
    the highest fidelity, for there is
        no cry, hardly as to know
is to loosen, being not part of sense
    or by auscultation, taking the air
and the force crushes up, blow upon
    the windpipe, next at a rush for breath
for in the spine direct from the eyes
        holding back the parts
            of the soul by black thuds
    you know you do: had you not better
        with a metal spike the axis
of ah, attention, no liquid, frame clipped
    by lapse indrawn and hit
        in no time or at all there is
    exactly to the front of this
        on the paper hoop as a form
            goes on through.

JIE BAN MI SHI HU

(1992)

结伴觅石湖

上桥推古载
桥头古景看
青苔遮荒苑
伴友谈心意
雨天杯香叶
久回享心间

蒲龄恩

NOT-YOU

(1993)

Truthfulness-by-silence is truthfulness, and
expectation thereof is expectation of truthfulness;
but expectation of truthfulness-by-silence is
not yet trust.

David Lewis

Love of semiconductors is not enough.

Thomas Nagel

The twins blink, hands set to thread out
a dipper cargo with lithium grease enhanced
to break under heat stress. Who knows

what cares arise in double streaks, letting
the door slip to alternative danny boy in-
decision. She'll cut one hand off to whack

the other same-day retread, leaving its mark
two transfiguration at femur length. Ahead
the twins consult, shade over upon shade.

Avian protection like a court plank as
much as I do, the top-out fortunate
conversion kit to praise what follows

that rainforest, a rapid flick together
on the glass excused. Phosphor alert badges
reinforce the eye of last-touch gladness

with the time rate to please fifty more,
non-negative liquid poly he does well
at the promise line, perched snug inside.

Foaming metal sits not far in front;
we march to the hatch to observe this;
our confidence is end-up like a roller towel.

It's a moralised rip-off but not obscure;
everything titillates to the contrary;
blandly the announcer cuts to length.

The wind howls, coast to coast bonanza;
we'll roam the proving ground and choose;
nothing counts more or less furtively.

Got a pervasive overtone in decision,
to reach back, maybe harmless in flight
of the amount, be ready, see through what

it says to be done. They all got blood delay
at the wrist insert marker, lifting a cover
over black swilled albumen. Regaining

altitude next to each mouth perching, whose
fluid attends to both if on the low side
unfailing: there are plagues intent on this.

Also the best we took it well why
not alleviate in distant party so
wall to step on the car track, they

don't think he's more casual by
the hour on low heat. Tap ribbon
soil to one brush, alcove distraction

issues the front pass quite slowly
enough to beat one back to view
that better from mimic trouble beneath.

Sure blight back, laid to a true scene
for nothing charm the last delay, as
never been, found dead in a bundle

and struck to play on the chair entrance
in: portico pay-out! creep reduction!
in chiefly living dabs of sky-colour

laid up in fury, with vows of returning
next month to equal temper; where just
one fit rises to break this impasse.

Finger prints up with scratch attack
at too high for the burner, pitch to pitch
aversion brook no more. Ready sore

turning, falling, so soon will clatter
vivid alignment to pack varnish, get
shiny cutlack portables to market

art fables; refit crooked intercession
in the humming base broken from
the counter, lesser bolted to the floor.

The cure is won across twice, in glitter
patches so cheap they thrill each bidder,
staring ahead to the empty room where

brightness is born and tagged; to beat
the windows of the dying year's fast
turn to a faction cut-back. Ever so

smiling at this sudden real candour,
what to shun of this set cure's topmost
retort: remember me: and give now over.

Life clouds so shoot up
    at the link shoulder
to strip choice formation
    from its blister pack;

ahead at the next corner
    with patent snows lit
skew, take one or else two
    or put one back;

what besides, all at bar
    none other, own louder
to a telling flat cross: snip
    for paper house attack.

Her pan click
elb
second fix
for them
pencil
breather park
over
talk at small to

better or yet
in hours
boiling as
as suit will on
ban
her linker

By now the plank
her
hutter forward
allowance
or which
slowly to disturb

all must formal
dry accept
shot in eye rods
she when
until first so
billet

Led out by
delay in effect
to five
this for us add
both
intimate or as
be
liken to the battery

at a vivid lick
marking not
grated either
her limb for
to mine
crudely dot attitude

Per fluid be had
to face
remit why any
lipping by us
into or in
tainted to alter

that more aloud
ex bond
fitting the latch
her lit him
up as mute
sap recall

With an eye turning for entry, most will
gather as others have, from the spicy bed
of a rising vertical trust: enough to clear
    line to line clasp essentials, all
    the same to claim plus set-off,
to shun this terrible cure. Across clouded
        skies the current lies at
    crossed living abruptly, outshining
the smart pulse in its sheltered prospect,
not like shoes and food in a clamour of
        spent cases by rounding up
        to the last place defence.
    Each says the same, applying to take
out of this bruised event the frame of provoked
aversion. Ablative child care bleeds tonight!
    No grip frightens the one falling
    by mild derision, the acts have
        been performed in mimic
        troop tint delay affront, there
    is no default position at true discount
up to innumerably more. Stop the boat
with a plug for floatation; the mothers assemble
at the sorting office, provably liquid he says
        in *pro tanto* extinction. Blind
    transfer goes ahead willingly, no fear
    tripping the snug instep to a price floor,
gentle planets counting, rates mounting, winding
up to replace a slipped bracelet. Thus in mutual
        fond delay the day advances,
        yawning astragal with due
race to provision beyond the fixed mark of
break-out liable detachment, laid apart.

From whose seed spread out
    bend and cut, in the field, in far
    rows sideways
                        parting with the left
hand, in plane or out over, the movement
of a deep-shaded allocation: but grind

at the back, to the root, of one child
        in the profile sombre to black
where section presides willingly, so they
        go to bend with the overt
sway of a little dust
                        marked by cloud

now invisible in the furious storm.

Their catch-up is slow and careful
    to limit levels in thick shade
fallen there but untouched yet
    by the hot slants which fade

Both coming and going. On a stair
    or quickly the defined
several inlays make a breath
    of so much ascent, in mind.

If he cuts by hand he'll make it last
in the strips of best-butter light, out to view
speedy turns in the spoke, shave drawn fine
& thin on the dish. Receive the planet

As a flat offer, we are bid for the gilt
rim on a supper tray; not half by choice
the flush deepens to ingot words under
killed steel, still curved at a glance.

Adversely so far, so and
    slight to salute the brow
given, this once beaten frame
    will permit next to now

some indrawn spine, in due
    allowance. Match on less
for the doorway, void of light
    and even trapped excess.

The water date goes down ahead
    I'd go as who knows into the back, going
there fast: later not eating why not,
    bit by well next bite, cell tape.

So still ready where the mode-play was,
    so by the make good flyer. Bear with
them across some river dot, make strange
    faction lines here, exactly in proof.

As will go to stay back,
    to tell of a cut-out hand
which well and hardly long
    in this, laying the band

of colour marks, no thought
    can swell a fear to rise
up to early missing parts
    inturning as with new eyes.

Lights go forward to flight assessment checks
up to roof limit, will rake up the card for
new scores in anti-trust recital. A timid start

for integer placing, spurred on by incessant
false alerts at re-entry: diagnose and record
at the same overlay. So to stay calm as

milk solids in defect control amendment, all
told at the front-line arbour of dainty devices,
as then: Abend ist im alten Garten geworden.

Into this space while not grubbing down
to anything like a spruce vacancy the machine
will refuse its second shift, fancy flaring

a neck turn. At both target detours for watch
action the clip snags at the ferrule, plant
by second plant. What's predated to draw

out of these lungs? Lank places ready numb
or to touch at a cute burr segment, able
grains prevail in their bonus tear-off coupon.

His cash desk implant leaves a scar, at actual
size past reason's deposit tremble on peak
travel location: get it dealt, like rennet

on the vital rack there. Based on new-for-old
organ barrage, alder without heart or young
cheese without bone, the deal cramp holds out

as per topic incentive, mostly extra. Count
this black loan-ahead half ready to melt
at best: 'peacock in a rainstorm at night.'

Marking up assertion's vapour why don't
they gain back anyway, in belligerent cover
plan to tall command; front load later added

better to sour rack division. That's to sell
out attainment washes at silver top debate,
curtly in set-aside bit, bit, soon to beam

this family in main display. Few laps ring
the order teeming with order ranking, though
sad at critical flow to re-map a soft verge.

Muster slick after her tabular blanket
retrial, right on the leaning edge to put
by the same-day device: the additive

boiling tone *he* likes *we* scare inside
to dock there next time. Indexation
isn't declared yet. *They* push away

avoidance details in block action while
lucky to spare redress. Avid crow circle
does back profuse tumbler item link-up.

Her hymnal by the bed, his sheltered
housing she shielded, he heating the
water base, often clouded to apply

bilateral fabric on a stand; or either
party at pitch aloof. We do weld, the
seam holding sun flakes scatters dis-

cussion forward only roused, alert
dissent to mob happy go ahead field
beyond field or by this new layer top.

Condemn this song, high toned rate flags
and streamers, to lie down; not yet rising
star now clean slain to spare either,

for darkness shades the witless question
in the count-ahead breastwork. No acts
rot more slowly in memory, nodding as will

rebut mere arching fate: to know it is truth
and take in air's cure, causing the forest
to fail softly by watching leaves turn.

In this room by the dear one, by too clear
for life inside the door, make the wall
go mutely close. Sold down, must upon

the tag rising, slanting, will it not be
near the table there. Ever to call nothing
quiet, attentive to know where shade

takes room for this, for that. So full
of open sets why not say, leave the side
to suit no less either than just bearing.

HER WEASELS WILD RETURNING

(1994)

The Stony Heart of Her

At leisure for losing outward in a glazed toplight
bringing milk in, another fire and pragma cape
upon them both; they'll give driven to marching
with wild fiery streaks able. Will either sermon
sift over, down with his line, ripped away on a plain
deception: nothing to save on this boiling turn. For
even I speak to her the sun was lowered, at bulk
modified by excluded point failure, did ever she
know it, saving the infant a place ahead by her
mission grab to repair both. For the escape drill
blanks, in teeth of surmised streamers in white,
valeur aux ténèbres. How much would be visible

to set up a fish wire, meat in his face as a fire
clay marker. Dash out the very first answer fast,
see here she hears the assay debenture, her peak
sail crowds white under. Slow parting with a crack.
Light distracted from its vent holding will so
grace a line blunted, she said: for all of it
miss a rock indifferently. Overt play over tints
hardly the brackish surplus, where else to be
more careful yet with my blood still. Save whom
in fancy sent away, both will do if as by choice
made ready by vocals. Now washing the front place
quickly, speak to her: on tap here, here, here.

What She Saw There

Alter as yet not anguish, choice unwaxed they will
begin the prospectus here, in the overload bay
at a stretch giving fresh two. What did she hear,
neither fully approaching there ever towards
the rally diminished. Adroit lowered counts
minding, grown elusive in a split bill, is
that it even. They run a bind forward if touched
to pass pass a trail of cut assets, and a new
skill gazette in alleviation. To the furnace
awake enhanced, what did she really see,
under donated in the dwell back, allowing ever
for another not yet primed. Each of them puts

the list up, at perfection's stoop and the green
is excessive for a slide in brief. That's the
evaporated cruise line advancing by novice
assent availing ready, intervals which even strike
the blaze they overlook at will. Aviators may
join this fork out cheaply and livid on a par
with grades of bliss settled, what for her was
it exactly, how matched to a head. They get
grateful over by harsh guess-work, no other
time offends this. *È giorno fatto*. What then
did she hear, what did she see, what brittle for
her was it exactly, at the price she paid.

Then So Much She Did

On the fade still branching to fall, is her reflex nearer
to take it, in a coffered doorway: for a moment at feed
cramp there, only for issue. As a curtain in blue rises
with tampered billows gone over, listen out, spending
targets thin and browned, for narrow narrow it advances
a break in acceptance, then back. Had better fit a new
minimum for asking as seen almost clearly, you say
too random fairly. You say I do less: then back. Middle
ground decisive request stop to fall, quietly does its
inner part. And if I knew I'd say I would, level off
at the light spin of a radiance was it, over to rational
earshot. Attack the loop bravely, momently in a good

heart first, partial not later. Synoptic. If I still caught
the view does she know it is seen, how other like made
adhesive upon a clouded aspect. Fresh legions get on
reader docking, on to a limb following the now often dazed
declensions apart. Her reflex nearer still, gapes where
in free. No sound issues for a pass key to the frame,
alleging mutation for a start astounded here. Infer
this override by the park signal, hers for sure true,
out of all mind lesions finely displayed she takes out
an age entire. Black around, eye level set to see
the line fed through, fruit on its matching tree. To say
so only: she, she, she, and only she: then nearly back.

Attending Her Aggregate, Detour

Service also reformed to a bench position, tended evenly
through oat refringence, why does it shake at a done-out
tabular entry; can't she see the self difference or is it
not set in pure gum for a notebook. Sedge emptied says
to go round, burning an old dish with its alkyl spectrum
announced on a late pandemic. Pick your own cell for mean
further. All granted, old meat on a dish. Her step pervades
the slashed shelf life here to utter startled bleeding, that
can't be right, loaded entry starvation gives over at last
these new particulate verticals. Dispensing their washed
inserts, seldom, often, frankly. Ask for less, averting
trembled fermentation, won't you believe the upper planar

necessity of the whole device. The thing put on there. Even
steadily shocked by the glass screen, the detriment agrees
all such novel flows on impulse. In a tumbler, almost now
on edge seen to fly, won't she notice for a blank advice
coming back; infusing the plant left off. Tell him a top limit
assigned. Automatic reflux bars the open spot too near,
not closed, hardly marked. The clause I give, sweet vernal
abscission, don't take on so. Abandon, abundant, level
late-kerb majority at glowing temper. Really hers. Track
now into a vivid parchment stub, its since belated yet
flight call torn out by inversion. Go with us, and all
the haunt be ours to the premium ground turn allowed.

Well Enough in Her Riding After

So far the slope drifts in, often it does. Furnishing
a new track or late to consult, all by the way brought
together, a trial to go on. Be gentle be just, afoot trim
postal refinements, trim ducting on a wave. Your life
chances this too, goes openly to let her simply reveal
time after time found; the little pieces of the whole body
invented as lucid driftwork. We'll consent, won't that
firm up the same border edging, to recoup a simmer often
less for you, freehand real and forgetful. Heart so far
the wrist will melt, of morning light impending: no safe
place or for my head than held, inside the fold the foot
rest in blue. Attain life blood, unblamed by the trail

following out her candour there; she'll take access
across fixed eye jolts worn. Will you walk on the path
so farfetched and reached away in bantered coeval motion,
calmly surprising and abrupt. Was it to reclaim this
profile, was it in form supplied to voice precision;
why would she next disclaim or stray back, at least below
step-wise exchange in tread over. Go for this slope
you know, is it fluent to a gaze; simple incision tags
collect for slips and lapping arms, or a breezy hint
slowly felt light. Dart laps French too. Even to place
the voice at fresh extent won't yet fill assignment,
never so far pitched to gear up or write favour down.

Openly She Counts in the Same

By now flit to fled, put your hand across he said to
a file taking intimate convulsion; level at the throat
of nearly glad rages, a gully retired. Isn't a fast
grazing stop as stupefied anyway, to split the list
between field trips. What is this void now bled from.
Her look attracts the hour to wait, how not to take back
obdurate gap outflow or in a similar tied division;
she plays thus longer a thoracic sink in fine array.
Not come out to stay, whoever looks into the camera
goes for nothing so-called when I bite the stone,
you'd watch the yield instead. Otherwise mingle within
the river scene, soon dark enough she won't stand

for as did we laugh now, in order *alla breve* got
together plied. Speak what, don't look, the fresh gate
repeals instantly the sound within. Exit the blood-
young watchers: yourself alone. Even so willing to lag
half back from revised shots, what try as they might
is hard to come by in slow recall. The voices bell
on the spur, heard clear in front, go as we must.
In avid incident no more but the brim fills right up
to make a dash outward; to run this at a novel snip
for all found. Sight unseen you lead, tied to the band
in short repeats as for ever and ever bright-eyed,
abraded by tick link succession in demand restored.

That Now She Knows

Who with he'll say climbing, to let blood slit imposed
at a turret elevation to buffer high return. I saw
her wings in speedy strip like a shadow in the sand
or in growth like natural reason, her heart so vast
as justly to make cause with the fiery fountain sealed
on track right across *terra nullius* overhead. I knew
that, she made me see the light level cracking along
her trebled skyline: I held my view. Blizzard loyal
transgenic pulsation she'll take both up to a dish
off the bone dropping away to a strut canopy, eyes
blue on blue aptitude so sweet. I knew that. Evenly
spaced night flares restore format, leaked to mounting

offshore redemptions; alive droning above tumbled cloud
for my soft convergence, mine only, only mine. Only
too small to hold its blood within her option wrappers
that stake out, spilled through leaves. Light of unclosed
life comes back, true beyond p/e overturning upfront
foliar feeds here, its sherbet nectary. This is now
a neat equator or its departure lounge, she closely runs
as animals will breathe out, he grasping at critical
backflow fade. Please delete, don't sleep yet, not
too sure to get shot through upstream. I know that what
you set under a minded shade tree is hit by first debate
and the air locks in, at a dab rack roaming the field.

FOR THE MONOGRAM

(1997)

Why should the dog ever be displeased *spontaneously*?

Leibniz, *Theodicy*, intro. by Austin Farrer (1951)

At a point tunes beating and striking the plate for
    sylvatic break and drop there not so sunken away
as in stay-put agreement; set off put off these crowds
    no free sky conversely. Will you jag up the tippet
over a new bow thrown down if for implored at five
    apace, floating across bars in black? In green
flash scraping ionic burn? Why ever not they split
    a tooth and spoil quickly by ricochet and fine
tremor's lull, singing and dying along the shore
    of the loud-roaring season: he'll position his
best eye at the planet boy too little, in three days
    notice of man too fat. Floating star, even up the
score of a radial plot and maze over or spoken by
    the sad sea ways. Afloat oblique and limping
at this the monocline in agreement for interrupted
    wings, nodding thistle to melancholy orchid.

To follow through long-glow deportment newly eases
a step-up bond for the break, the scheme of a pure
sensible outline: they were poorer then hovering in
undue compulsion. Acceptance flumen goes over,
flares up to order salt margin by a crass horizon
in gripped undulation live for ever. Or revise now
this vitreous floating star at dusk, a spark seeming
and sinking tints walking in silent patched-up
collateral delay. More than ever saving a grace,
singing and dying to frequent and haunt the river
from its own wreck in shadow play they too are
hunted down in plate-sunk detachment, star-burst
or cluster pointing, dearest agile daybreak. Strip
the slope order back to a red glow now piercing
each other's view, flicking the escape lever as yet
contriving legation in cloud mass not yet known.

Select an object with no predecessors. Clip off its
roots, reset to zero and remove its arrows. At each
repeat decrement the loop to an update count for all
successors of the removed object ranking the loop body
at next successor to the array stack. Count back up
left and right scan, test for insert loops using
0 0 as sentinel pair. Such as of figures in space,
if (set if true) a product goto top list, an object
otherwise (if else) remaining the same. As a quantum
(put > zero) parse to occupy inner sense more by
recursion count to null, and reset. Match for error
to run output and restrict condition if at one
then also next. There is a bright blue light flashing
over the exit plaque. Connect atonal floats via
path initial to hydrated silica screen occlusion ice
batched out and bent through diode logic gates.

Anxious wittance prevailing to fly up and over through
clean air at our heat level, so set out in void
attracted all nosing down then under the avid folds
previously so tempered. Sparkle raids cannot
give the upsurge rate out to them either way binaural
cross average: centre contour get to list their
mission plates hardly tamped down yet. Neither aligns
field entry to the other cage or swoop to jewel
furnace craquelure, rat out rat in on the leading front
pronounced ration pack. For what, big dipper
in a flat meadow gleaming at ruby emission fringe gates,
line skip, line flap, out. Sound absconding by
intervals in pacific entertainment as dipped nose to tail
on either wing, under both tips. Never do better
at closer fit, tense later type to burn attire, even so
the sensual margin now brindled up and black.

Both ponder mercy. Overt crushing across the temple
   ridge aggregate does this. Both spin for better
placement finding to keep true, do the same aberrance
   over silky puff treatment, resection spared out
to partner a gentile tarmac. Is that enough lasting
   for them both. You know lactation counts up to
just this, sorted fashion cribs. Ponder arc setting
   and filter span the vapour test, merciful. Did then
either one returning strident and hermetic afforded
   cutting back on flagrant unction, perfect webbing
haul to climb into burial clouds. Remit a blench for
   exotic oil slicing to breech the term in sub-anvil
strokes evenly trading life blows, condign too strong
   all over, through to seed denial you traced it out
by a creamy top-down suture. Your merchant heartening
   progresses to fulminant offertory and lags fur.

For cycle down lower done to tire and as digest
    a sub-topical premium, crux departure you
take pieces with sliding fury away pallid and broken
    together on cue. Not by nothing too quickly
at the far end asserting so few, so due to enhance
    giving the payment foiling, away to site them
little aggrieved. Phantom tribute in blue device
    never blaring yet on this wave selected for
thin throughout passover rack by foible inserts,
    did clamour avail its slotted crown. Did one
breech up, furl down top to wonder blank or pretty
    to its far affected double pontiff hilted dab in
severance divot. For the region combed out by fortune
    ripping the nail bank it touched, further limit
panic defies behest. Were the colours beat over for
    prime sodden hulks yet too thinly losing ground.

Brisket world animation come out to flay runtime take
further as for them for him in novel good form
other notice all allowed tufts of any hot white dis-
persion; promote your charm in silver salt brisance.
Stars fading to clement destroyed fixture to show them
up milky too mindful cry to clamping hue, arraign
set niche by a ripped fulsome sensor. Clip act out
out to show weft of profile in whitened detaching,
brain peeler now set on coals out to show at a fork. For
the quick alight cut thirty-eight touching on each
position and peel back this vivid failed bruise, baleful
to scale and burning. You got scarlet out to show it
in the toy-pack acerbic notation, in less significant to
hands off warning come out for out now long and easy
bleed pastime, henceforth to show round a bone stricture
flaunted out and peeled easily off from these shores.

Tuck up tawdry attraction for the follow broken air
    to separate yield and distort along the floor,
moving flood in a pure scheme they have but them
    selves alone flutter drain orphans in ultra wrong
unit time set. Either dies young or lives (almost)
    for ever trailing blab across some bad sequence
of strides, seeking trim animal redress. For lifted
    maternal protection slurping canny on a bundle at
just one table in the entire universe, for him now
    governed lazy just one it counts viewless torn lip
chained. All possible out rankings flunk my presents
    in ever hopeless profusion scattered grandly on
sea-bed panegyric stipple. Brother set in both limbs
    dismissed a tort factor of age craning forward to
counter stream cycle proof, invests its hatch cover
    by orphan fragments reverting to current seed.

Aiming always at united residue stifles down in pairs
to misfit nutrition you saw it splicing its cuff
under constant erasure, cutting out the bottom dish.
You could tell on a slant for once; in the leaves
of a shallow tree pure variant figures in slurry pits
assembled in florid hot parlance. An affection is
a kind of natural fruitfulness arranged round a core
of the powers in exhaust signature of the mind.
Gather close together at the finish line-up. Spoiled
kin propellant you heard the marching on chain
of edges glance solo to force, setting out brain fruit,
quince trapping. Cheeks plunder a sealed throat
gape losing tone at multiple asters out to show willing
and process each destruction; sorrow blunts link
maps as pressed candles require a first fire come right
out to show to climb down in space trial bondage.

By sorrow or swallow the catch nominates the figure
in throat clay famished below canopy stirring,
track perfused to one on the yellow who docks a time
base enter green mourning tents in burned faces
arms and bodies charred resembling the bright backs
gripping and bending, to weep there. Insensate
quick bites stitch up their jackets of broken felt,
insoles flaring like naphtha prints that lean out
and lure a part linked batch to its chain of arrival
by flensing demur. Now shatter later integument
so close to murmur fierce pitches afflicted in canopic
fit over to show them, a feather touch batting by
the lash for iteration; slip the wedge in future counsel
sent later to bolt deterrence, cling at a verdict
rush impure for famous eclectic margins sinking beside
full-up respite tongues in the morning estuary.

The lantern flavour of a fillet to indifference will
amend the first crowd skipping its temper, of im-
perfect duty maimed on impulse: rebuke no qualm across
water turning upon its swell. Acids you boil up
must each condone the jaw's lexis at lip tugging fury,
fuming over, the same all over. The now livid
face of a captured city centre immersed in colorants
setting no mercy alight or meddled even up ahead
with pity they struck through, why bother a sweet toned
fatuous disgrace. This crystal grist size must
be reproducible at will, for dark pyro clasping instant
rallies under wave shaping, dear heart dear next
lung perforated syllable count in wasted toil a rain
of ruin from the air traffic retort. At such relic
bare outline of captured cities take one want another
to counter search the sea for gain in deception.

Prior guesswork loses the things in your power by
    broken reach in seeking to verify the check-out
lag at the till. Glow to offence rating, narrow axis
    tapers into counting lucky hits, rueful charge
card assent. Bored with fraud rowdy crowds flip
    coin exchange macaronics like polar bear packs
propped on the escalator, freak anoraks heating up
    with hormone replacement hints. Roll over to
the cheat show of mirror facings, costed mini cheddar
    countenance alert losing face show in face of
the city step-out and porch rictus. Rapid shaped
    by convergent explosive lenses today's gridlock
flicks out a fan trailing its tension wave right over
    sure bets in equal measure, shadows in concrete
out to the nth generation. Fun first fun rest set
    as best fit extracts from its smallest free block.

Whose lenient foam inlet now passes through innervation,
check one the grating etched with a prism of gaps,
check two parching with myrrh and black smoke swirling
in rapt successor logic. First try on the ground
Gilead to Nablus high and dry balsam matrix by how they
bleed, distal cuts raging in the street; at rational
cruelty in a storage loop mining with listless brio their
never ceded blame, of 'harmonious gentleness' intact.
The grid flicks like blind beasts all in hot glory turbid
and groaning, a non-trivial path from the vertex back
to itself delimits a merciful injunction, that he places
pity among vices. Frontal defect control by reverse
codes legal to read a predicate, adherent bondage by key
choice stops at nothing under vast madder clouds that
roll across the sky in front, mounting to frame the mouth
of a clinical denouement sunk far past its frolic.

Or yet by good grief outward one way ought as ready
    to shine in the code meltcast herbs of grace
that swerve under the blade pass, the air flap icing
    at sunrise, at right and left flick. In the dim
gray light monoglot by implosion jarring blips across
    the tilted umbral cone they will force their seed
for the ocean bed and adopt strike point rip barrens
    swept barley, silver fennel, the sea streaked
red with flickering lights no issue; in transient blue
    arcs floating and framed at suture lines ribbing
the ocular lens. Fissile drag under gang profile, all
    brows raised at surround inhibition of the tonic
yellow signal; the arrays lie packed in a dark light
    defect of strictness set to a little head or button:
patterns matching the surveillance shape in bright
    shadow under wing chalking the egg yolk cartoon.

RED D GYPSUM

(1998)

The volatility smile is not symmetrical.
– Lillian Chew

Now trek inter-plate reversion to earth buy out
as waters buried or get carrier up ready put
across gypsum branch effaced, as root planed
for don't now look to demand new birds in talent
from turf stripped to fibre. Rip brace out here
on the fringe reckless bestowing taint by the mart
chosen, tamper nickel token lunge to bite you may
cover down over, a flawless glucose shimmered sky.

Liver brack shock already distorted too overt patch
for easing back resumed admission, connivent placing
take-up, path will either way contend *en face* its
divisible burden of stab-rufous scale. One slams
the other to close out neap tide ceramics, its stint
happy hit on meads week after simple week resurge
running a hot risk counter versed bid up to the
fence and stop evenly foremost departed linkage.

Did you light furtive aggregate late-flow samples
to peter out frozen turns almost dive back cloven
slate, nearly slow now. Lastly lit well did you,
not yet waiting over, visibly knowing ahead blank
parts zinc plates yours. Thermal in latch fluid
image blurs selector forks, aspect sweet would my
do its wash and round lower lower still to steps
grounded for all rejoinders to miss so new a weave.

Sweeten to black taper against reverse vesper mordants
thinning to fur and fur relinquish, cap to bright oak
pause riding up and over tannic steep slants by far
fetched blazing their links. Accredit late cut dazing
underside selvage obscure, peltate divided refound as
for holding both cover traps, their links sub-ferrous
attracted to wind down: yet plumage in sport remix will
slacken by quirks of wooden converse chimeric or later.

Avail what would clamour so late. Three trammel birds
cut-out flat in fury department, have entered denied
for terror fallen off the track directly smeared,
bilobar hand signals way marking, so giving way over
to see the bones in his fingers frothing clapped up at
eye to eye birth intervals. Their three gaps gefangen
across the doorway, soaking up iron occupant sights
for a level palate, hit fresh on a low set at the back.

As for soda glass too, new tabby proof sniffing over
for tabby go down, secret mascot draggles a coat
open-cast at dark bleaches for favour to lift out
prolific partition in trio. Concede a blink beyond
supper to turn, go down, flat loading incisive sparks
left on uppermost below cover to last. All in front
out of reach to outlive frequently, why not enhancing
each new red glow in the round for water features.

Truck out black, blue shaken front by a twig blurred,
in allowance they all said, on the path. All ready
to lack nothing for a time latent, downy carbon rule
attesting, divergent on part-opened flurry pack
pressed to bank heat sunk, torn. Trailing up for
darker wads over red you said fast, green for soon
seen marking wet leafy left bruise. Yet half openly
brick by block there up, never startled by abrasion.

Unwinding zinc yellow for the reform purchase mishap
chased through in cross links snipped, parian debate
set back to winter timing. Maroon pyrite will label
the delta quilt decurrent, liking a flame in court,
a flashed partner lifted still on still. Harsh still
at a key seedling tray, every striation laps pat to it
and flickers silk latin salad flourish. The black scar
shadows overhang for lintel grips on the sash cement.

It slants back now, across the field, cladded over
its adverse retentive slipper feeding. The ruts declare
for air for stolon rising, donated in a handshake.
Its bark declining splits up a magnate loosely tied
to broach and remonstrate. Deal first arch and fair
as wheat leaves last, loping across broken furrows;
all three enter now, adding raked brow to brow and yield
in seed rated this way, arrow to hit up transfer lake.

Leaf paris green strikes a vein in the room dropped
beneath attention rode out fume trusted with layers,
run over in winded plaster cuts split from below.
Evenly screened out of line wavers no less, touch
or miss on the water black. Further notice no test
points to follow after tacitly. Blaze the way first,
on tack at base pair, the seen front sets foot down
by altered burning friable stubble already coerced.

How near the underflow locks out to a hot prism bolus shading off massive indigo precedent come in attaching 86 zero quip markers, over raised D flash on its matt red square. Only counting these top-cutting fine on edge or be may after, tripod shine at filet gaps in your mazes, your larder. Frequent gave them all, ready on tap radial. Three on deck oblique partition revoked adverse germination tint.

Omission park to pack, sweet water pluck sweet wood may dent fortune's cavity to lie low or insert the crafted picnic trocar: too hot to grasp a spindle linking the bank. Silent pads slide to the front, merely insinuate afresh these alarm touches, lees in rack. Tame steaming flip ataraxy debates on rewind panurge, hot gluten never so picky, get resoled on redemption. Greeting announcers touch up the fender hardly, poorly provided in benison.

Shortly delude berries in a pot. Their neat clearance
will burn up contorted, have attended to furnish pelted
right out agreement details, blue sky chancers want
to peer out on offer. Slower now, striated bark trails
each furrow observance, brave fresh ice. Sending away
step-cuts, sorting ends of a rail. At the far turn go
round disproof honest disparage milk *partitur* fading
where new lignin quite cross-links in evidence clearly.

On the march. Simmer down your almost last arrivals
rendered like lard, leaf from stem reversion. Will she
finger the flute, cold and wet, breathing on through it
but making no fit sound. What makes a small fad mark
on the paper, as a reminder. Not like last time parch
and drain a zodiac, undaunted here: take the folded
cloth in both hands, put it square on, notice a ring
just touching against the horizon and emptied out flat.

The bark running with sperm, fierce fox-cry repeated,
now receding across a trail of scouring must. Flouted
and back over, assault prime screening flipped, iron
par resentment. No charge, no hit. Infer from silence
a fire burning steroid scrim, corrupted interview one
by wasted one to outrun narrowly the starter pack. By
the brim tip macabre and violent fast stertor browsed
with teeth upraised in root channel, lucky dip to rot.

Temper casting promotes kenotic revamp cross to plant
latifundia at a division line, to cap his flask and swerve
past gaps for wind and storm. To smash this hazard beam
with yellow lights returning, snooping up agaric bulbs
under long wind throw, sonic revision screaming echoes:
avulsed by slung jollops in fear of hardship overshot
cascade soral membrane, xylem star retes up in flames
licked under, crepitate the knock racket fumigant spar.

Address report under foot. Do the best one first. Get
quick subterfuge for the arm bent back, incessantly
three-stanza barking magnified, by its tuft insertion.
Attrapment bezels stir up the current fissure relented
to a chimney of yellow powder. No more no little part
in heat as a chromal flicker trace, scalded chrysothrix
relief targets fusiform go to the front. No time now
like no time's double, two-way lignin threads coalesce.

Failing pasture water mallows mostly override a view
in parted stipules by allowance freshly done. Flow
flow my phloem dear ones, fibre life thickens limpid
blue aglets to mind your step or stop to look notable
avernus lee-side of a post. Mydriatic gaping hollow
lenting, anting parox retorsed, quiet now. Quite noble
strictures consent evenly on to a laced margin set-up
giving over, swooning to catch and suck under and feed.

They were astute and dumb, voiceless fixed next to the
platinum link; cast-off on impulse. Set up for crack
by its relaxed poultice scarce muted and taking grip
on a diamanté kaolin dish. Bark to excited flood
in facile ketone derivatives will instigate regraded
bond preening: wound up and down on a glassy slide.
In full view of the reaction process they were instructed
to say nothing, which with one accord truly they did.

Ambulant blades of water so confer tactic by hurried
example, to see sink low digression; on tap instinct
the flake splinters. It's by occlusive ferment along
a series plump to take back subdural tented endowment,
canting in singular gradual rebuff. Moulded pier glass
pits odds to enough revetment, light clicks. Without
fuss or thickness playing over a hedged future, links
make a tight bumpy ride duly sliced up on account.

Thick-bloomed damson clouds search out a proper vestige
of creatine reduction, for the print footing hereabouts
made over at the margin. Slow hiding branches crop up
Broca's lumen aquatint pilfer to reach assent. Newly
marine devices glimmer at a bark scripture advented
dyestuff. Heat-set intaglio dermis marks repartition,
step by step on the line of least indenture, leached
to encrypt, then decompose, then subjugate its planet.

Wave guidance allows three, hitherto. Sounded out
bare of stanza tread, allowance padded, each will they
bind up cramp adverts, their clammy elbows. So ever so
evenly the lapse conforms to its pallor minding a view
of two rising, limit to three; for then lesser salutes
in darker relief to contour abstaining review. You
know the outcome so to say, saddled with a choice few,
ready to mount the display hinting at fitful repartee.

You bring and tide over, produce elision's disparate
reversion to wet climbing by a crook intern, backed
to relish affirming deterrence. Flashing remix over
its wing circles will pinion stacks over plaster, blue
sticker branded for both took parting. Shook to gain
what both heard, aside from pennants stripping tinker
phantom bark entries, baying red gape stilbite intruded
awakened to leaf right through a fully shattered book.

Terry mouth lint reckon to soft pulse more sprited
and gashed, open often and kelpy patter spavin up
embroil week by month, temple process destroyed top
batter in large. Attach this. Lay down. No melting
Irish butter glib Kerry titles weapon bright. Hold
encaustic nerve station vulpine night screaming out
in a trigger spinal location; the first keel regains
each set-up spasm coyly displayed, hot to re-ignite.

The servitors heard them clink, alto branches on stream
to mind three at a time. Snake roots break their chain
in fighting harvest, pushing up, hillsides arch and worry
off their rug, in clouds of gonad dust. They got seed
broken, close on breeding uproar, now dark shades clatter
force them down to simmer under foot. Thirst replays
triple throated scan for gaps, entry and pallet flicks
deeper going down, root burning. Bribing their locks.

Flaw on the ground too many grappled fruiting body
assets quilted there, echoes of milky cash-in plushy
arrived for grand style averted, do it. All then seen
all saw notice tucked in too, clawing grass hot air
denied assertions whoever said no less granted newly
agreed to scale. Second time refused they said advised
insidious soft lighting replay, tracker funding holds
its losses under grassy slopes preening the time of day.

We'll mark them out, bees drumming. Many times over
the odds of engagement. Front match slides in tight,
to admit a little air now, lofty throating. Frequent
lick demeanours scented, stop to stare glossy particles
foramen greeny blue and contracted. Fold to bank on
its ridges spurning ink pressure we see the quick look
flare at a touch. Swallow habit permits both marks
along level warm traces by section detents alluded.

Further thin severance comes around to the side access
where the mount attracts air blasting cherty membrane
omits to pass insidious album they sweep, down bracket
heels dug. Tonic D plate infuses to count both ways
and tingle olive prime shelving touch limit. Overreach
melted casework, your snare drum. Red plate to red
snapper filament, to lowered bents all brushed; every
day who declare safe browsing crimson to dark flak.

Top-work the frame to chalk white yet against less
clear tremolo flotation, sudden demerged racing
downsize nutrient plume to risk appetite so born
at here D plate mirror swap pleas can never shine;
depleted words all light and gladed in picket fault
back flattened silently. Crimpen interfold your
spectral yellow, taunted now slippery bright, red
gully regained through the wood rewound in felt.

Surmounted forcing whole blood parity set lichen set
ikon remit from indented bare bark detour press over
subrepted to mute, vocal folds glowing deep unwinding
did they forage out reparted sound shift, closing did
the canted ferox inter-vocalic tissue. Vivid strips
of tree bark circle the room its introit fading flood
across broken sky reflexed, repelled threads mercuric
took bounds remontant to grasp out along its line.

PEARLS THAT WERE

(1999)

Over the ferny leaf-blades lying close to the bank and now deeper green from the dry weather a network of bright gossamer threads, woven close together and catching the slant evening sun so as to shimmer with a soft, trembling brilliancy; we both remarked on it ...

On the blush cheek making, to one
  making to the one, a stealing
tear, of blushing as every age
  betrays the sight, alone.

By light, ask and mellow reflected
  then show to hope again
doubt yet believing, request the lost,
  the blush to shine.

Concerns starting bright and oft
  soft yielding, blush shining,
charm to hand, around the wound
  her finest charm glowing.

So Orpheus tamed the wild beasts
  for long night comes down
moving naked, over the wound,
  the gem from the crown.

Slick film so crested in white reward
  its part look, part tamper
by stilted welcome to burnish its side
  at a blush, in singled halter.

Yellow on black mineral for a twitter
  bar to wing, flight to span up
snowblink through lime glass appearing,
  must not be loaded hot.

Let in the water, dazzled in their eyes,
  aroused to cry at either turn
or fledge past the slipper line of days
  that run, that are so soon.

Siskin in flocks, arab takeaway larder
  won't despise what can't be told:
tie fast to fix up a ragged flag, further
  for brokered news, new for old.

0.0g. fibre in milk, we needed
   to know that so quickly
for the sake of ribbons and fairings
   and the beasts so bonny.

White matter tracts lying deep down
   under the code line, clicking
on rapid access to a faulted angle
   dogged, scalene, lacking.

The sense of not feeling nor making
   a hit at the beak, the beak
of a crow dark-favoured in passion,
   now alert for his pick

Will crest up to miss out the bollard,
   stepping, stepping so brightly,
like eyelids over grit they trembled
   in lofty slips, twice nightly.

To swell up so long, this time indwelling
  in clouds going to flowers,
in order routine adjunct and smother
  the meaner grace, below us.

All tangled in her hair's next affright
  or mantled in burning, new
scan over tumults intently, Afric storm
  scant in hood to undergo.

Ascorbic detail in this they ride partly
  overlooked prior to attitude
stormy, defensive shrouding, in a hunt
  for pitched cornice revealed.

Too single! caress fronds as to liberate
  race hatred's package tour
whose every touch, kiss the rising hand
  will too bleach-whiten yours.

Shine ahead, cold star
  like music on the water
in the wake of remission
  from near, from far.

Take beauty's injunction
  as pledge for the chain
that binds up the open scatter
  sprinkled in chill rain.

None so costly, none so clear
  accepted on account
of pliant, client deception
  to tarnish a fear.

And rise up to vocal induration,
  lulled into fresh calm
by motionless, undistracted
  insult to charm.

Catch as catch can, attempted dry loan
  will fly as yet she'll call, high and low
over wave-like slanted conversation
  to set a line, to entail and forego

Her shadow in channel as were so causing
  a test of infringement, pressing up
a case to answer while never sleeping
  or leave a stain within the cup.

Causing the charm, the pause never so alertly
  held abeyantly to flood entire
its moderate premium diving like a crashed star
  in salt water, outbroken fire.

Nothing more, not much less: take out
  the first and last, the waves still
recoiling their crested and turbid confusions
  as evenly, as mostly they will.

Lobster-orange, shag *in parvo*. Peaceful/
pushful kid wants it better, wants sex not fish upfront
as well in touch. Spring peaks red-inked, blissful dogged
doggerel at joint screaming with rind orange blind-gut

Dangle by bad phantoms sparking strictly: new lady
prowler in profile. Rienzi in fancy stabs out
splatter-blot scenic spot, egg picnic no. 4:
nose into cream bridge, singalong crowding round *m*

–Jesus! traitor cow-juice, we slurped that
Next, chairs   All are, tables.

Missing fast
accumulator
quite sheer, logic but not
how gated over

and awash
the bird gallery paired up
on the stop
flit out

in cloud sleepers so-called at
gap charge given
back so to
horizontal, floating

levity of design–
all too now
part sighing, fog flags
enter here

pipit on the roof
speaks the skilled terrace
by some wheel
barely turning.

Sent out to tender, taken into first-round care
   distinct in passion's ornament,
some star of unction, redressed in motion
   tops the brow along the front.

Under four-part arachnoid invitation
   of songs riven with fresh sound,
the green leaves grew all around the window,
   sweet and completely around.

In green return, in demented tribunal
   as withies flourish and divide
for eggs in bold type, eggs still not sold
   so laid in earth to mark a void.

Spare ribs, new knees, trash from the pitch
   at fresh-cut vocal submission
to diagram all the working matches
   joined up in verdant rejection.

Hope for help in the gallery
  all in yellow, all in yellow,
skimming to ride, milk inside
  all in yellow, all in yellow.

But where is the music, the music
  all on yonder green hill?
So turning and twirling asunder
  as to never be still?

As to go for a dancer in yellow,
  for to dance to the far brim,
all in yellow, all in yellow sliding
  and ready to come in.

In ages past the cover thickens,
  clouds bank in the sky;
the leaves go down, all in yellow
  faring well, to pass by.

Damp top level, checking for a slide away
   to be even, so we'll go apart
breaking the letter for its flavour grill
   enhanced and near distraught.

Yet valid at the counter as on high seas
   sliding in fresh and salt,
evenly mounting now to be awaited,
   ought soon to be dropped.

Up in sparkling glee, over wide salt sea
   oh madam don't be coy
for all your glory, fear of another day
   and another story.

Across the thread a hooked undertow
   that could rant and roar over
the level slit of its own horizon, lifted
   in fierce, disordered pleasure.

Newly arise the classics in paraphrase,
   newly precentral in a livid bond
to touch daylight and brush its wing
   fluently, with all found.

And slacken its licks at sunrise refusing
   to uprate glitter at a humid loss
of adjunct cupitive desecration, for
   gloried favour around the house.

So the rush begins its fervent ransom,
   hard and slender, cryptic
subliminal choke, pressure to open
   audition right to the quick.

Whose nuts ripen as the season passes
   in flowered grasses, pollen fuming
over the lapis for a brother token
   or the tag for his naming.

Data pruning
maple in f
slips while single to elude
demented stuck in

wonder or
peep like bats and black
owls on wires
at the leaf

crown chivvy the close flash
tubes go on twice
hem lifted
to spread delicate

its random, torrid
diploma, her
smoothing back for
all the world

like eyes in
glance to this, swift
departure
along that road.

Sessile intrepid yawning they'll barter off
milk-fed error flags, avidly hiked up ahead
for degraded lesions: in brine, digraphic conjugated
rhodopsin. Act to bleach and bluff-out topic

insertion, roused in fury!–your bragged synovial
glimmer threshold raves and stamps in garniture,
their boots baffled in shiny wet snow. Did you
assume next to inseminate by trial, his clinic

yearning to clank, to bind over, to fawn
its botched curtailment–spectrum on blank.

Tulip trick and fast, nursed for clover
  to share and share a list
franking indusium, the plot of appetite
  snaps back before the frost.

Up in arms warming, how sweet to roam
  and follow shades from field to field
puckered to an apex: tripped for burning
  in smoke for smoke, set mild

And gone that road under by a fathom
  circled with fronds, owing that debt
as birds alighting, says she I am all voice
  and nothing fit to eat.

The seed searches itself, its sac defunctive
  by crow flight pinioned to bind
an open heart upon a table, rigged
  ethereal, towards its end.

Or so as softly we can laugh, as sure
   and dear at every span
in audit cry, extended memory address
   translucent to the bone.

Freely bees awaken, rising to many tasks
   in jaunty flights forsaken, turning
enrolled to occupy their sentimental places
   and polish off their finer tuning.

Trace the residuals, the throng of men who
   surmount dative assignments
as if inching wildly, crazed for upper lights
   that flood what they want.

Upon the bed of rock, whose even smile remits
   its port in stormy air, her sight
not measured in the leaves of trembling ash
   that shade her face from thought.

Time of day pleading attainment
   granted to come and go,
loping across wet grass in the small print
   to latch on what you know.

Away with cutting over, she'll advise
   to mend both shirts, and steal
a heart-felt fury, burning up charcoal
   in guise for kitchen foil.

What skimpy terror opted to finish
   at the far end, for and for;
no pica among these withered leaves
   to bind up the sunken floor.

It is not there, away, away to last
   a tax reform, uttermost soaked
envelope riding for a tear of water
   all wasted, instantly rebuked.

Ever much missed, freedom to make
  more graces to shade
its wildish, loose arraignment
  under loan to decide.

By marrow bones raking and in clover
  seed heads deputed,
incipient literal sense of entry
  sets all points muted.

Take her chance, in glances turning
  to nourish the day's
constricted tufts, of wall rue
  bitter like these

Derisive permuted fictions; each one
  discounting as neatly
we can patch a cry, to make clear
  honour so quickly.

Chirrup in the morning up on sky
   lines ahead, curling
dissident loopy taps to distraction
   will take your breath away.

With pear-drop lips of dew a leap
   from small tense stranding
gets its benefit for the carpet
   threaded into debit type.

Did the swale open, lose design
   token borders, the bursting
ribbon fluent with margin overflow
   licks up salt on its own.

In trivial deep amazement, murmur
   its song in outward seeming
return from a glow foiled to release
   its wanton, loving primer.

Nodding, nodding, day out
  and in for a sake
how do you do it to see,
  arriving so late,

To talk to and fro with each
  other renewing and walking,
step for a span wayward in
  heart to heart breaking.

Much like waves upon a shore
  whose day approaches,
her time running to meet
  with joy the face it touches,

And word upon word, step
  by next step regaining
they'll walk and talk, wisely
  flicker some hope remaining.

TRIODES

(1999)

TRIODES, Book I

$$C_{ga} = C_{Ga} \cdot \frac{dV_G}{dV_g} = \frac{C_{Ga}}{1 + D_a + D_k}$$

Pandora made enlightened states for her sister,
prized liquids in unwounded novice
argumentum, she was raw that day
in promoting first flight over
the Tenter Ground alto. Licking her
finger she poured new water into
a crevice in the ground
for them both so, decurrent
cheek facing cheek: catering soft lair now,
Irene, plant group mother you infix
shock limits, uh Pandora your
leading kravatt will rise to the sun
with its charade attuned
in rampage peccant for geminate rooting,
the split double to mark the horizon
with the tatter of a homonymous city.

Days away for replication, away days
in and out breaking the city limit
at dawn flight, friday p.m. workmanship
issued from a slot the early sun
over-tilting, uh so smart
like a fresh lease locked still,
still descended in offensive charm later
down, down Pandora late to fumble
her destiny was it
somewhere at the back
why not well put, exactly where
some bright cloud for shift, for hot fuse.
Nor door nor port watching yet outwards,
easy to take poor fracas, in-
cident even handed parlando.

Patch a very light, ironical slant beam pervaded
with ticket coded, you get
a spare on target too. Irene will do it up
later, blister none left, or
voicemail derogation leaf by leaf so dropped
for a sister's patter return.
As from a maiden chamber, shading her brow
pray for us lady, our yeast
plugging each nostril, spoken Pandora's file
intact. Secondary polished upreach
fax by return, she will attenuate nice and
easy their shadow caloric tape,
outlet for day by day jurisdiction.

Leaf by life speeding
its creamy yeast chatter, bunk matter tax
perfects arrow and spoon with either
sorbitol arriva text. Visions
of ingots danced before their eyes;
tunnel ahead part margin, sacrificial anode
trading the day listen Pandora, nothing
no respite on Friday gunning her shoe
in memorial for spent out ekphrastic
clamation, fit Irene too sweet
the virtualities with double faction: the text
omits, the margin includes, you dope
provoked to neither shout nor sigh. Hot target
treat us by measured tread, sweet
split double in the fold
to go down almost there.

Suffusive dram opening on automatic, spruce
on velcro your family trip
to a far-fetched accumulation: hail
goitre retrieval, vestal detour
fast-food morsel resale. In battered roe
for safe cervix, uh most sacred
and divine fish on this scale,
snatched to heart by anodyne loaded, by
loving sarcasmus uh pent-up slag,
live for ever by charm shot,
by lurid sodium portraiture in trip, on
Gaza Strip in codon
firstly by same-day express gravitation.
Pandora come down off that ladder
at once you idiot, rates on hold tangible
swept and squeezing, your narrow
sunflower stupefaction.

Unlocking her oven with a zip
drive per second billing she stakes
with Irene the digits over
flush counter, drizzle speck on speck
in talktime for virgin
oil-fired second branch. For lunch
thus bright in tears when
I am gone remember, frozen Wye River
no one keeps striking shall plume
her charms gash in-
flected exile's boast for
breakfast onwards, in cash advance dazzled;
Pandora, accomplice of her
fiery arm alight with mock fury
you tease, you work out
the average value of each night set
against free talk on notice to sever,
flash out at oddity.

In the skylight tufting of plausible omen, of
holy mackerel she gawped attached
for great suffering snakes, sugar parrots all
raucous and red-eyed,
attending each a flicker of time out
sent down for it,
to the shortfall of a party obit. Sit out on
the balcony, festal blinking
at sun surges for a half-hour discount
in their phantom options. Exchanges
all brisk and fresh,
tell me your mind by invitation, get off
wind-up sister for supper, better
pickings ex party penchant
for a modicum. Read the letter Irene,
slit and gut its canopy, in blue-green trikots
by parcel force, such bands
marching to early glory stunts.

Uh Pandora read the running of these rails afar,
after the ovens of the land had been fixed up
with the bellows of stupid amazement,
after the earth had been separated from the sky
making the reeds jump and sway;
in their vermeil enriched cages the gazers
fixed on the Lebanese percentage,
the Armenian star shots from the bridge
of their ever sweet connection. To each tablet
a flourish in radius,
a memorial to oversee endingless divided
accusatives of relation, bearing gifts
all worthless, pick one. Stick you say,
the son who had a mother, she
brought him bread:
the brother who had a sister, she
brought him bread:
all in abundance of necessity setting the strings
tighter to promote the raft of confusion,
sailing each night.

Salome salami, fabricant!
Uh beauty I wish to praise thee, but Irene
the banner of trampled tulips is stupid
to lump its rivers and clean
out clear the sheen engorged to cry
like a diabetic locked
in a chocolate factory. To get towed
by brackets ahead, into
an exclusion zone of eagerness, that kid
don't steal because you credit the tale,
he makes credit to get your goat, you
giddy lady whose giddy aunt
oozing with sex appeal and all
for free insinuation, you know that, dual
steerage just hits the kerb every time. Says she
in terror scuff story in the territory,
says she, to thee.

What makes the rays cry out and rise,
to fall with a soft shrinking tremor,
base rate on a needle,
gauging parity for those not too far
from Rapunzel's spindle.
Yet more doves make their hazy complaint in season
and save and flutter on the wing
and grasp a twig to catch on
for sibilant inclusion, soothing the very air
with unavailing news of themselves,
of nothing else; as up ahead
from the balcony outlook the same puffy clouds
make their dumb allegations of
spot the difference, judge the moment
lest, each to each in sweet sport,
judgement is done.

TRIODES, Book II

$$C_{gk} = C_{Gk} \cdot \frac{dV_G}{dV_g} = \frac{C_{Gk}}{1 + D_a + D_k}$$

All across the northern perimeter, all
tentered across with fresh mackerel skies,
the hours of isoglucose symmetry
rush right-handed across the face
and melt down. And yes,
come clean Irene, those dippy birds so scuttled
along the pediment are for sure
making their mark. Stone and sky
in the free mid-morning light,
pale hands folded on little wrists,
we skip the breeze with loops of plenitude.
The pediment joins charged clouds over
to its lightning earth, cathode
protection of the whole body,
the attic swaps salt for molasses. Get ready
to uh shed a tear here, for soft
rocking cretaceous aspersion.

For miles of the Nile at an angle turbid with fish
Pandora yawned I hate these mummy shots,
Abusir prisoners lashed up,
gods not in the sky however it looks
but plodding on strings, on the earth.
As for the tree he tore it out
at the roots and snapped off its branches,
the sons of the city who had come with him
lopped off its branches, lashed them together
to make play for full day, peak-time
balance of equity scooping up British Sugar
to sweet that pill;
uh sugar babes across the lengthening day
we'll lick and suck in mourning tongues
for sweet-up princes, think
they're so smart, Irene did you see
what that driver just did?

Pandora wrote down her next sight
of the ossuary in cryptic notation,
scribbled on her pad; she knew
the dockets flailed in a price sinkage.
Irene took notes at work; but they dropped
right out of view, these low-level war figures
in muzzy profile for a watching brief
from day to day. Or failing to meet the return of gifts
calls down a default curse: 'more often
it involves a public gift of a large amount
of sugar', like tying a cloth to a tree,
to have the word. Uh, pent-house imitation slaps
viewing rights in the archive,
mining for juice even when blown away
in the price war escalation; one hand
washes the other, whiter than white.

Uh rusted mother says Irene she dispenses
patchy temper at the pair rule
slim kibbled and engrailed big-time under heaven,
the pediment writes the balcony
with the script of a gap gene code
not found back of the throat
gasping and retching. She admits ingredient
sunk costs, embellished values vaunted
under swift cloudy skirts,
masking the extreme nudity of bone; along
these patrial sector quotas the hot fit
calls in a paramedic crew with dewy fingers alerted,
unwrapping the wafer-sliced tongue
that Pandora never mentions. Just get on with it
baby-face, easy sizing your strap
in the street below.

Sterilised by recall, fragile infants, current
in front anodised, that arm directing
30 lbs of Barrett Light 50,
foldaway tripod swivelled like a feather
quilling up its curated pods for free
by single shot sperm count. Uh the plaything
took out by lightest touches, as upon
a forearm quick with tendons
coaxed along the flow axis, of blood
pulsing across the diode grid. The Durchgriff
crack force marked up the calendar, with red letters
ripping its entry to shreds,
she would remember his arm resting like that,
turning just slightly to freeze
the gamut of warning lamps,
quoting coldly on the mount and by heart.

Meet and make a match on the pedigree as follows.
        Imagine any triode as being replaced
                        by an equivalent diode,
                mapping out the anode potential on tender
        factored to Mozambique sugar rehab,
                total funded in package *per pro*:
        1. The Kuwait Fund for Arab Economic Development;
        2. The Opec Fund for International Development;
        3. The Arab Bank for Economic Development in Africa;
        4. Nedcor Bank Limited;
        5. Acucareira de Xinavane S.A.R.L.
The anode potential produces the same effect
                in the region near the cathode
as the combined effects of anode and grid
                        in the corresponding triode.
Oil to sugar the map beds out, open and shut,
                doves fall out of the sky.

You can get the knack of it Pandora said,
by measure or proxy get a move on
in sedimented mirror-image sets:
he wrongs, he is wronged, he advised,
he deliberated, they seized, they were quarreling,
grasping one another, they rage,
they went on a rampage,
whew, those boys act primitive right at
the verbal root with a cap, wind
spun and flying outwards gibber gibber
floored by exposed pavement, Irene,
bank on the grammar flowing
in piedmont heat across the pediment.
Among the Romans the pediment was so much
respected, it was confined entirely
to buildings sacred to their immortal gods.
Just bring one up on the balcony, she said,
radiant divine lunch-time.

Lessons at the dream palace lessen
on their market costs bounded away from zero,
tarnished like a folk theorem.
Irene alone contemplates the ice-cream sellers,
licking her lips, be mine the hut
blood racing aeolian delivery lamentable
in fear skin-tight: Das war ich mal!
Swaying a little to slice up
a sandwich pact suspected, arms and the man
on a chutney bun, her kitchen devil
will flourish by the hour on the roasting grid.
Tomorrow and tomorrow in the micro, even so
the smoke of sacrifice on the table
pre-cooked yesterday, never mind best not yet
good to abduct from ruin and decay
all back to the homeland.

Magpie target going in through the torus
of penetration chill cross-hairs
exfoliating the flesh with joy incarnate
loop before target, drug hit on computed
surge count, uh flesh burns
in the vineyard induced currency preening,
grand mal petty ire one more song Irene,
low-level engagement, finger
on the token mistake. Spark risen up
against the shutters, spilling from the vat,
hold steady not casual not laid out
ever disposed for a dip over countlines
boosting the birthrate, fits of
corrupted seed assault. Locks broken
under battery aim each shot, tab needle
uh foolish boys, drifting into sight.

Either way some say well they all do
butane refill trust me whenever
leaving room to declare the hood of a should,
the brow of a famous tea-towel,
sounds like a Valentino remake uh Sharm
el-Sheikk will run and run how
could you give an inch wrapped in tinsel,
explode the text up on stage
wrapped in a detonator, 'letters of guarantee'
straight away, ink hardly dry. In this rope
of sand, overcome with fumes
look away and say what you must, Pandora
what's for dinner, herself to blame
and suit yourself with a loose button.
OK Old Kingdom fresh terms saline
drip so don't move until, then and then
nod your pretty head.

TRIODES, Book III

$$C_{ak} = D_a \cdot C_{gk} = \frac{D_a \cdot C_{gk}}{1 + D_a + D_k}$$

Uh by laconic
fits and starts the confection tips
over to paint blending,
lateralised for sib gulps in plain view. Patter
furnish bids for them as why
sinks to murmur tones, as youthful
and carefree, endearment options all out, there
in grand slam across the diluvium.
Tell me your story in
my version along the radiant
grandes allées, scrub and bow down in lasting
demurest visits uh dippy Pandora hit up
now for ever. Celestial prudes so we make first
moving advantage over the ledge,
propitiate parapets us so far tilting
in a bowl, our bowl.
As the striate beds expulsed, under the balcony,
their inverse rational gleams not
yet glazed over with caramel, make
what yet you will.

I saw the groves of acanthus rise up and bite
the lips of clear morning light, incise
from flourish bantering catches their
tentered falls, uh you did,
what next supreme chicken, set to thaw out
on a bed perused by damaged
root attractions, le roi capon. I saw mounting
hosts of the crowned burger king, dipping
their lancets across crane gantries,
sugar puffs in the orphanage.
See without limit the clandestine fury of attack,
hot-bedding in selection the patient wards
by court action, in breeding
barbaric and divulged. All this passed
at review grading astigmatic for the libido,
one thing leading its list
to another, as all things will.

It is the clearance zone in glimpse
through to a graben sump that you descry,
Irene, deserts of close deserving
hydroptic and factorised. Go no further
on chicken wing, count up
to base ten and sink the maze
like dross on a snowbank by signs
of what tells its tale. Slicker bits we get
better options in surgery on a platform,
chanting our targets in market surge
on a new drug release. Added more sugar
at the slush bar to make
a plea for sweeter reasons. Added virtue, new
slave endurance, make the sum. Evenly
both stairways scan and flex
the tropic invert for now,
holding by decommission their parlour antic
rigid in settled silt: the new drug
is the target.

Non-retail fixture pushes on right ahead
case by case spread about
like leaves over railtrack to guide in milk
their phantom dusky limbs; ever to guide
this passage shall th'aerial sprites
fill all their starry lamps
with double blaze, twin flecks
of biting the hand. Yet still they come,
uh bloated threat of entry into a slot
wedged open by start-up costs.
Dear transom split get on deck with this,
the array lies down in flat plan
to resist what anyone
gets told to say is done. Glib lazy mild
steel to foot loading, a side
play draws up its release, Pandora how
could you even think that stuff etc.

So in the warm air of the outside where
did the eyes of glory start out from their chairs,
who were the heirs to this,
amazed by fright and frighted by amaze.
At the jetty coign they gave not a toss
or were taxed to share out
for scarlet and crimson just below
the fingernail, two quiet lives.
Uh with dog and bottle, Irene, done up
in quick succession, slick extrusion
of the carnal body image
with all organs on sale, tacit choice
of ethnic origin. You do have
to feel right, in yourself. Or if or may
or why not should you by sham
repro shame fittings as all
along the parapet the muses gazed
and outstared rejection.

Back in the kitchen where the lies simmer
in giant vats she picks over
the runner beans for buttering up now
in oral testimony, not overdone or
they'll be mushy and tasteless. In faulted
witness I had to tell her, so bruised
in use value by assailants masked and muted down.
Later at the cutaneous Sack of Rome
with nipples bleeding I saw we both
were mutilated as by fierce bites, the word
stripping the tongue by instant
corrosion of lip service. Pandora guzzled
and I did, we were so famished
for blight spores to play
humectant breeding, we desired
all foreign babble for ourselves, cresting
the airstream in bruits,
hearts racing for a novel pit stop.

                    Irene, we are the slave market now
not maybe but crying aloud for master suites,
                              I can see there the chiefs of staff
          in slick plastic barrels sit all around
                              a table of Tenter Ground, not
                    our assets pegged out ready to slide
but body by body dismembered, we grope for
          them, Irene, we make them frantic,
the children falter in the queue for food
                                        we saw it on TV, I wanted
                    to cry with a terrible voice, how
          scabby you said, they make them
                    roll their eyes, roll a filmic bandage,
roll hoops down the fun-fair ramp, willing
                              the chain of causes; sequenced
                    in credit checks as mort breakers
consumed to a crisp. Flaky redeployment stakes
          we could use that, Irene, before
                                        it splits out the kitchen.

Right on the nerve uh sweet sugar light!—we
were accused by harsh desire,
desire for goodness and protein bonds,
for sex with our native tongue.
We applied, we tapped on round after round
as cocking our elbows we saw them fall,
hot blowing wind to mock weapon
audit franchise, our amiable
recoil scores for angry sore points.
At the loading ramps of free misery we both
did cry out with ecstatic joy
and not by mistake in gorgeous trip
on the wheel of punishment—
we saw arch after arch pushing up in the colonnade,
the cut-open pediments of classical exits
a canter of promises not quite broken
because made that way, mazy let-outs of style
in designer drug options. We did
cry out, brandish our paltry money, did flaunt
every asset we had.

The scores read like this: word ranking
under the Sentences Act gives a choice
of tempers, arbiter's freedom to set out
where the deepest shadows shall fall.
With blood on their hands is a terror attack
on the Jewish state, Antrim west bank,
lemon Kurds. Don't waver, in order
to renounce the use of arms
it is necessary to have weapons to hand
and in hand, preferably
bloodied beyond a doubt. The men
who would use them must be free
credibly to do so if not to do
just that is to be a free choice.
The crime of the rational script permits a script
of crime in time to calibrate the forces
of pent-up sentence: word by word.

So it was that Pandora and Irene, the chicks
were donated entirely and waivered in themselves
and stitched up. This is called 'The View
from the Balcony', you can
download a copy for your own personal use
whenever you want. Across the back
of Jean Cousin's portrait of Pandora posing as Eve
you can see under the breast-arch
of decayed masonry a distant city crowned
by a giant classical nipple, real cute
but not a patch on a navel to die for. Of course
I knew the children were starving, probably,
that Pandora mostly doesn't miss a trick.
Irene are you still out there,
you'll get burned my sweet, uh never
the prettiest sight. Time
to go in and down, all sore points,
and feed unmixed their flame.

UNANSWERING RATIONAL SHORE

(2001)

lo mismo

lo mismo

Profuse reclaim from a scrape or belt, funnel do
axial parenthood block the mustard dots briefly
act forward, their age layer for layer in this
tied-off accession. Appellate at dictum at
its debit resonance fixing prolusion, optic rage
performs even dots right now. This is the top
passion play and counted out for a renewal patch,

allergic his dispute braving off. Make a dot
difference, make an offer; these feeling spray-on
skin products are uninhabitable, by field and stream.
Tell us, only for as many as crowd in through
the door to the diluvium, the romance of a new
organic dyscrasia vibrato fretting its early bits
on release on ambit. Early grief, late woe ahead.

Each who yet cares to corrupt anterior traverse
settlement by booking in pairs, by attainder marks
upsets the project alembic, the debate for hate
to make open clause upon renown in folded paper
dirt cheap, split option pudgy cheeked. Costive
profane credit. Flying starts. The likeness in
white was nowhere near exact. Spectrum count

manicures a trickle of futurity, the sun in splendour,
for so 'to thee no star be dark'. Arising now
by flares and plumes surrounded, who struts up
like potted meat to deliver, oh baby dowse now
the sparkle of glad diatribe, to pay your even way
and never think to blink in theurgic assessment,
granted by ultra-sound as a perfect sunny day.

Fabled dyads relent early on the emission key,
never on notice for another snap of firing up
by will for shall vector implants. Flush undergrowth
makes itself felt, to weaponise space uttermost
in dialect, absence decrees its neatened locations.
Bitter anecdotal retro-chic pads out the discount
at the end of plain sailing; forever all to see

why the front levitates, low-level hanging fictive
bravura. In diet supplement salute as a near fit
to give voice, arm in arm better up more loyal
with a slice or two. Masquerade on the dipper plate
clears the specks, ham on the bone. The floor plan
provides more for those who float there, get migrant
and cross before the garland, breaking open its fall.

Will the jaw cavort, or yet spill. Expert advice
proclaims otherwise, that's its job. Not for too much
or too little, thinly sliced bread attracts panic
layoffs, demerged into nonentity. Colour me next
time on an over-tinted spec, still much too soon
on this count, to do it. Steroid upgrade therapy
arouses braggart hopes on a charade of distinction,

to engrave profound mottoes of survival next time
on the eyeball itself. With a swirl intact, grafted
there if you can get the lid off, scooping up extras
to raise the stake beyond demise. Whatever else,
the gap between one and the next accepts advance bids,
condensed by footwork don't give up. The circle closes
to fit like security, the tight corset yet unknown.

Before this the custom of granite replicates
trademark parry for money, feel the stirring
of an earthly emotion on a fling. Hold still over,
time to strut and fret, you the debonair chicks
grabbing a tartlet, on a fashion spree. Licit
banter for an ardency to file acrostic intermission
as thousands would, the cynosure up to snuff

making steps on a hot station. Thereat hitherto both
under the chassis, checking off the empty cockpit
or the milk run see how, see where on balance
the main chance is blank and chancred so truly
in the hard morning light. Take a flutter it's
about time vacant on either side, embroidered over
with excused panels advising early redemption.

On the track the news radiates like a planet auction,
for the best rates hard to chew. If it seems too good,
sucker, the pap is surely toxic, unless the glad
hand goes your way, soft as velvet. The strokes
of the palm not even touched, a waft of livid air
gives the take its donation, sexual preening overtly
lavish in symmetry; your flicker goes to mine and

locks into warranty, well why not. Over lush fields
a rising sun pitches out its sulky damp shadow, in
reminder of cost levels in the benefit stream. Oh
fight this fight or sleep when others wake, the
maze of a shining path leads on without a break;
count the steps in retrospect, burnt umber places
engrossed forever in dumb-struck dropped reward.

So by a thousand cuts the sky quivers and re-parts
to shed harvest home, Buxtehude in kedgeree firm
assignment all trusted and coated the word is out
at play in field dilemmas where they grow strong
and split and multiply. Harrow at spiny rest,
ophthalmic lesions degrade the fancy mostly at odds
for swabbed specimen charges; slam off the fuse

partial to compromise and chill out by the water line,
its oozy derelict bed. Lie on tick on target for
the sense discharge clamming the mouth cavity, no
big licks lucky hits what goes up goes further,
to tread the downy turf. Feel the careful heelprint
so soft and sprung, twitching this mantle to shew
willing in turning, not a word left on the plate.

Poke it out with a stick, but mind out too is
this the one for down player sizing, did you
hanker to be not even yet believed and spoiled,
indistinctly invited into the loop. You're with
special friends now, indomitable at breakfast,
sun again set on fresh glimmer to anticipate
new tests for old faults; happy chat display

advances to frank daylight in a candid line to
be really damaged this once. All inclusive temper
for product evaluation, the one before last was
battle-free, just pick it up on the way home.
Sensitised to outcome franchise never deplorable
and never gabbled, hooks in butter to get up
the fringe of incidentals each where it belongs.

Ready hands sanction their new ebb, the especial
oratory shunt attachment. Overstock digit perverse
deployment adds a pungent new flavour, stepping
forward to claim the spoilage; that ragged applause
is for the assembled strollers with reverse anklets,
their part in the passion play at consent, on the
valve monitor. The grading is recognised, no doubts

assail the ready-to-eat counters of the absentees.
Elastic bravery tell your friends, profile margins
dilate the soft annular parallax. In such due process
with a furry wrap the favourite minces a hot share
of the pie, the offertory selection hoarded at par
for dark x-linked transfer. Who needs to know yet
the scope for new hybrid desires, bloc leather cased.

Why don't you try a globe for ripeness, this one
where the ore rifles through veins all fossil eyes
ahead, try me my keeper at key at bay contracted,
fingering fair pay for fixed play, tone on blank.
Lutine falsetto belies the gravamen of a loose
quadratic, before this court of pickled pepper and
unsorted currency fonts. A plate of devils rising

in deference, charging by the hour the orison
obedient to decree. Reckon the cost by new order
calmly, new world bill of sale skimming, may
contain nutrients. To face the page the desk
the sun on recounted spectral stent the play pro-
vokes a circle of conjoint refulgence, to craze
the glass it burns and grind its cutting purse.

Prophetic souls at the garden party convention press
forward to the barrier for a better, look how well
it suits at every chance they get. The benchmark in
plenty, non-cycle by eager assent, leafs up unoccupied
desk frontage. Don't even ask for dinner tickets,
too far left behind. Out on the darkened lawn delusion
pours down its wounds of acceptance, novel face up

to adrenal shock remission on self-defrost. Next
step best foot on a slide, the memorial of god-like
certainty glowing in the hedge. Payment holiday in-
cluded, anyone's closet uncle would recommend this
broken lip replacement, on overnight stay only by
dogs barking their worst. Converted plague food
surplus to allowance does all that, all for less.

At late stage the defect of scale scrapes off
the felt lining to slight down the huff, displaced
into wrong water. Split finish by large numbers
will cruise to punish the knife, in common rite
cuffed and bled to moral ennui, each wave mortal
with rapt digression. Who doesn't count won't
matter, leaf cover shimmers to greet day-care

blips on the cycle, citrus screened, doing a turn
on borrowed wheelskates. In the avertive cleft
of 'an arithmetical curiosity' a link itself blisters
to foil up front treatment, choosing up against
warded splines. Mis-timed by equity trap points
to run and run like colour all down the blade,
this scant fuel thins to vapour in vacant air.

Petrol in search of flame hardly a ham sand-
wich, where the draft pulls out neither fear nor
care less, any cap provokes lateral adventure call
it tip to tip brownfield rematch. Eyelid passion
blinks at a stab, ability and growth packed tight
in cat litter. Born and live wiring, get native
cover shots askance. Flimsy torn muscle will lie

gaunt to blood supply on a spiral, late shifting
derelict pincers meet the press corps. Run a hand
back-linked for aid review, go on faster to storm
the house of engagement, boarded up justly. Flicker
shot won't say, picked on the vine to claim kin
and cost more, wrecked private parts in banana
recruitment. Don't ever now take heed of that.

All the fun of the pit gets well and then better,
sand spun off as yet to bind promise to tap up
one clock via another, either to both, sky-divers
like swallows gorging their young. In staple pairs
all so sudden with a tumult, written for nothing
to skip a beat, break open the shells; dexter risen
forward, new zonal application as leaf by shaded

leaf glows with wanting itself so. None other for
both or neither, before this after that, hall-way of
desire in fairest placement rising. As brood so on
donation true to tint momentous, all is too hardly
much to clear unaided: hot justice pleading for penalty
in a rigged-up camp of love, courtship plays requited
and branded so faintly at implicit final appeal.

ACRYLIC TIPS

(2002)

The murderous head made from a motor car number-plate.

Assuming banishment for lost time back across nullity
in speck-through marking worthless eyelash, strict
blast of sand eggplant prone, tampered dune how fast
the grievance solitary; krook pathways risen up

To wheel and turn about spandrels high over submission
flexed to burnish and chomp get hungry for intimate
newsy entrances. Get plenty get quick. Out on the level
camber trim mouthing actions, louder into the swing

Denounced for parity and affront, many will know what
to do at the tip, the crush horizon. Tell on demeanour
mostly to start and go on the ledge. Copious infarct just
slip by a grant availing all will give and grasp for

Ribs of possession for later, for now, annulled piercing
closely levelled out. The ploughshare has been through
the ground browbeaten guzzle don't chew get bloated
instance, fortune glabrous projectile will outright

Fan to blazing to the promised riven grove; take heart
for rapt token incision along a defined track; to cry
and mourn for her as he goes, to bring her home, this
downward streak affirmed on hold farced over across

Split-screen seepage tills. Miracle cheap shots, entitled
of the morning bulletin all savage and reckonable,
raise a clamour to sober digits, true bone mounted
like beasts sucking their fill of the cooler morning light.

Ever fetch promoted, dejected by partner claimants out
    pat on a moving front, muster to confirm a perimeter
ailment, their kids besotted like a felt roof on all sides.
    Win on green, give a toss in a snug rafter; heparin

Regulation demeans and spoils the touchline, you fair ones
    on loan to ascending digger collapse ominous in a pre-
cinct under rasp channelled by pickup spreads. Why should
    she ever flinch, why they left over ridge pretention,

Ever calling at cirrus credit flapjack, name failure early
    in right parallel assumed. Wait for batter party arrival
to entrust peg dirt, luminous clouds succinct and trailing
    a shadow commanded to fit this step, tread exactly in

Profit track licence. Allude to close print cashout, welter
    the line superinduced to kink and fade. Promise so much,
spread to go fast over, could the rank assessment give milk
    at a lip trickle. Why should it. Never at one blow to

Divvy up warm pleats, alarm set for any to slide on ahead,
    body echo brimming. They swerve for it, and plead retained
succession, voice in travail on remix, often gutted. Or they
    make a dip at the table found amiss, give and given

By a preference issue refolded and are not fed up with
    less for less. Or for less. Careen through what fortune
caps with a swollen wave, the deck is cluttered with snap
    predictions as so far forward, as ever fetch promoted.

Over the seam flux penult dissension cries going apart
to panel strip on first insert, to nurse a flint
terrace cut away, they glimpse the line torn in order
antagonist ducted retention. The ordinate now set

Of the influence line my honey at due rain down partly
on useful toil, the ratio of he for living hurt cheeks
to the concentrated reply curtain. Best at blood plastic
same time blent pick one rigid held to hold over lies

Flat greedier by far, replay switch. Shall each cherish
defrayment tunnelled down for certain delusive grips
curtailed already, both not replenished even liable or yet
parted, eyes wide bridge mail starting lax delivery

Indoor famine, pinned to the jamb. They do forever swear
rat vows by engorgement groaning under load canal
bearing into reverse, thrust turned off solo distant
unlavish, finish gradual trellis fault. The sky

Harmful, the ground slapped in a bundle, come across
for simple feedstuff taken back in refracted glare
of the front halogen raptors; give back a dew line
repayment soon enough before fixed mastic furrow,

Sorrow will you turn remain muzzle gripe, yet sign
off abject partition truly. On inference upside
losing track top infiltrate, curt shouts demark a place
soon to leave to live commiserate in vivid suffusion.

Hand on the guard rail down most volition to slight
    and planing sheer brings inert forwards, rifted for
them in the photograph acid. Bring down set down upon
    the ground spread crack off potent spirit rattle

You look your laurel basket, you hover. Prove him his
    grain allocation unceased. Parry leafage, cut your lip
in mischief gashes all succulent racked, sudden frenzy
    propulsed for her climbing averse to clip there count

Heavy declined, deducted amen. In foetal daylight pits
    sodden to famine direct slew glass under the tongue,
mask too rapid flim and stubborn, would you ever waste
    shrinkage over the string line. Of a course petal

Resiled after shunning to pine slopes his right arm
    tied to creation. Gristed born likeness reaches out
needlepoint decision, egg fillet glass handed handle
    don't ever touch inherit. Retain first option in

Vert defection placement after birth foray, rake and for
    sprinkle retrench to dormancy. Mend it not, brave
crevice through which beams pin out currency often late
    starved infill. Sweet mane lap below lens failure by

Light bent back at lintel regression. Aim to go round
    and haply tie off leaf after leaf, nothing heard
his locksmith digressed, bear up on shoulder level care
    her pledge unhandsome and ruinously now surmounted.

Ruck flutter at the mouth, relocate on plain remove for
    small clouds rising and spreading her hair touching
his knee I heard it on the radio laden extra mass red
    and tinged with yellow, always there. Cover fair for

Admission in rain harvest her hair stroking his cheek
    in compound reflected, at sleeve anchorage re-echo
tendon drill, rolled-up warm fettle. Her unformed casual
    stem by scope visible sheer drops at guilt reduction

To altercate to ruffle and crest favour muted crayon
    verging to rain shallows, dark clouds. Now pigeon calls
across swum floodway always there, veined over road
    plant orchid root. Fixative intrinsic. Resting allured

Turning over extended pint upgrade nip retrieval no
    furnace my long arrow summoned through open haze,
perfect glow encompassed with cloud banners final sunk
    to root there. Fringes in sand will acclaim foremost

Beyond level mission alight through finger case, adept
    seizure main excelled offence, revert trumpery marauded
whimpers; go in glide on cause at cost plus slamming
    valve each on stop. On offer prolix touch to grip

Generative carpet underlay, teeth glimpsed in a wave
    at fault lined up for source pleading and goading out
wire soundless no blip rented child oration; spending
    like water fountains spout to fume and cry off unclaimed.

In the fresh of day passage to platform peel off early
    come forward, be implored as a fruit standard
wields clip-on box deposits. Scarce moving even sound
    less extricated sickness he puts the hammer down

Right to the line pull. Fresh choice but no leeway to get
    stultified relief throat vibration, held to the very life
repack the spares grand flat; a brother shadow cultus
    soft sweet fury gums nodding milkwort in river-sway

For trigger defect damnable cladded. Soaping up reduced
    digits at a punitive cleft, hold the neck brace her
rolling overhang why isn't ready yet. Who does it
    now estranged filaments your trick, why not try

On even broken surface folds. Falling citation infringed
    to demand resettlement, search each house incident
wakeful, pleading to suck to flourish. Frontal instilled
    terebinth maybe taps up, clinamen infertile lipid

Sack on split her mother rare spilling grilse for clipper
    rushes minimal. You prefer it. Daunted fever to no
other, pea mouth well versed askance on canvas scrim
    how else. Don't ever claim label pre-trial match

Distress dilation, celestial scars on a list by searchable
    income, to blend unfound. By dint of yet novel
terror reflected, deep now facing the rock, attach
    to fissures nailed front and back: hair roots adrift.

She'll see bay reject as they call and heft down
    into clump grass solved feather baking and broken
or its quartz sand left thieved, contracted mammal
    turning uppermost see no more so flush saw back

At set for drilled sternum. Loaded nutron base star
    angle to grind flash aslant, grip her wrist his
matchwood paddock raft. She forces her throat in
    wards only pulse, carborundum infer so tile cover,

Dental roof in spasm word by word expulsed for lack
    for roasted spit, latter spatchcock pronation; aver
grapple juices. Acrid flash over over, across even
    next overtaken and stuck subdued, each one quick

Spinal attempt discarded. His arms roiled back into
    sleeve fluid their retained cover serrate assist
thrown downwards to pigment ground fearsome, all
    in dissipation sponged out. Assault liquid at stem

Assents tremulous, set up set back. Digressed far
    auxiliar outflow in sunken capital swooped over
against ceded domain revision, change the locks now,
    lamb for kicks arranged reptile new spent fuel

Poised on a lip, sip token rouse beads lenticular up
    to browsing hearts spear swap nourishment snap
line out phones, hear nothing. Dark screaming cries
    loaned in prohibition their feasted slap-up decline.

Cavity grill said, spoken for, felt falsely. Her hands
 on him clastic agile like monkfish whether feared
hurtle lifted, pressed up tunic liquor leave out tropic
 at a target run. Aim right out. Oral limit so between

Aromatic casing, finger joints barrack lowered, inward
 crass by the drainer. Need no more no rested fabric
to the harness loop the belay plate moulded at entrant
 face value seared. Between races default first free

Working venom presumed his torsion self-locked to pay up
 on invoice declared, to plan depletion. All lies on
planet ember, coaxial indrawn untrue blood for neither
 sliding sunlover, full under duress. To breathe so far

Oddly clasping the sea braid some gloss descended next en-
 tire by infused righteous anger. Alarm pulse releases
sonic driven receptor sites, stand-up ovation deputy lined
 body search reckless. One seized, stirring the folds

Of flocking unkempt birds crossed did you parch them
 each clasping abrogated breast at par will you disperse
bolt cries overt wing tips, recall shady woods paired
 in sensual fast nutation. First touch first ready-made

Relentless crest hunted down pinned to earth she now
 attached to her prey gene expression resentment. So
called or cried up nominal drastic pathway, thumb printed
 gorge bites leaping to swallow the pride of daily bread.

Used rods draining soluble hexagon linkage amounts
    fatstock primeur, better slavish to thin along fair
skim aroused. In guest space at a wasted floodbank
    all for her interval, half fired in tumid elation

Crawled to the step mourn arms having none to lift
    like bread aloft his worsted homage on first claim
on cruise mannered licence spoiled. In brio still toxic
    for her abraded dreamer the batch open grasping

Flickered up eyelash address. Open breech over yeast
    peeled other half near dropped in a stoup by temper
sheet to sheet dimmer cooling. Ask yet did your time
    insert coin, a new master traverse. Hit on right

Limit smash best beast interfere, massive engine ex
    crabs post-hormone limb crisis. Still the insipid
blob of glory distends to circumflex, raise up place
    to tongue mysterious spat. Who antic runs by front

Lines of credit, at a narrow a hitch a plate broken
    and the rest of it swept off. Rehab feeding oracle
emission drainer staple, gateway spare parts accessed
    wiping a wrap knuckle. Give out currency. Whiplash

Injury too mounted in harm of sorts entrance docket
    turned off wanting the price ever twice over to root
by stolon rising turgid and bannered, whose heart
    rate at a cub report brought down to hacker's amble.

Burning child says shall we gather micron glass to
    dress admonishment at the river-bed, observing
mass stricken touch your lips sewn to silence at air
    the stream by day care who does. Immobile tough

Stance glowing as star circlet icy to see wired up hostile
    and revered discard the weaving frame, drop threads
down cheek by water deck. By year end will send bitten
    for carbon season indifferent new chasm revival tips

Sprung forth digressed, cicatrised. Each neck attempted
    forearm reversed nursing limpet prized, skull rims
close to fusion, she-child foiled prism dialect. She at
    bank, she told ready sight unseen taken by sign

Called down, each night over to dawn falling out ahead:
    woven door traps, long and thin. Unmelted sugar pan
venerated lodge, lesson throat veins. Intimated product
    recall goes out overland toiled back and descending

In bright glance, yielding credence ridden to limit store
    hacking swift pine and juniper, grubbing roots. Doing
all turns, invert sweetness at the curtain grassy open
    plain payment due. The way chanted and bound up

Most to let nothing fall, not coming back to back sounds
    fluent spill sealant entrance drupe, thrown by high
winds made away no word from either stitching a breath
    let flow, pipes to ground glass to unslaked level fields.

BITING THE AIR

(2003)

Every property is the property of something, but it is not the property of just anything.

– Ockham, *Summa Logicae*, I:24

Pacify rag hands attachment in for muted
counter-march or locked up going to drainage
offer some, give, none ravine platter; tied up
to kin you would desire that. Even hand

bestowing pharmaceutical front to avoid, even
flatline signal glitz perfection, slide under be-
fore matter planning your treat advance infirm
in legal glowing stunt. Enough out of one hand

to grasp another, nearly hot dump for this at
angle dropped outwards, everywhere selected
at rising cost. Untied, non-brand stay there,
by a maternal oversight, glinted horizons so

blue and bright forever we say, pinching the
promised drip. Nostalgia for G7 par minuted,
assess parallel offset, your tongue. Creature
chatter damp margin, drug outsourcing denies

active pivotal racer hot-rod, all price diluted
and fuming over nil-paid: it is easy to make
a country prosperous and blue and bright over
and blindness forever in hand on hand proverb.

Or it may be better to do that. Thick mitts for
an early start, precious upward mounting oval
mannerism, his park molested. Or to match defer
to certainty got a banner, to a grade. Hold one

before leasing forage behaviour; wash the novice
wrist, finger-tight. Do you already know this or yet
allocate sufficiency. Altogether just say the word
as *lex loquens* inter-married in sparse programme,

its cancel front to dive in a blip forward, your
modest capture. Sudden glial remorse announces
armament redress canine grips, on the platform
a bevy in service affair driven. A forever dulcet

hesitation in the mouth long-dated ostensible tap,
stare in daylight, one hand washes the other. Dis-
tribute what it takes, parallel fog lights crested
vapour banks confirm this. Conclusive under-

written first arrival, safe as houses on a detour,
or live transmission in packet throb, insurgency.
Better power assignments for the moment this
sharing by split singlet to mollify what there is.

What then hunger to a first date peckish on ready
next generic, print the bill save casting allude
at franchise remake leverage only. At civil next
crossing greed and obstruction go tidy and totter

quickly and drag out maxim recruit to his
rack of offers, why not protect to salve if
deny several utter margin. You didn't know
that oh really how extended even so familiar

whipping toy forms as a habit too lapped across
its place setting nor sought nor bought fancy
never braved: infinity. Each deferral migrates
formerly to a treat. Lineup eschewed a plight

of elaborate detailed mastery endemic bitter
vice rotation. Declining third, no thanks plied
to who decides or partial. Only uttermost down
from the peak induced poorly sourced or as

yet cascaded in assignment. Down yet silently
in grand furtive numbers, in waves largely beating
their own predicted funk. Did civic adverse
tremors give advisement, if not spat torpedo.

In a dish let flourish a milky inner fluid
for trial matching. Peptide link scribalism
lets you skimp on target, limit the batch model
by graft assembly falter. Don't you wish now

handsome reprisals to pacify a pensive border,
conceding bulk precursory shortage, or even
demand-led fat blinks. Sated to a faculty
with snack extras, set on crest. Now watch

the rally tremble, demographic twitch to learn
occurrent craving unsupported, red bloating
in hand contracture. Or even sip, get even
profile bivalve. Return flow block. By rate

entrainment we can bring it off, as on tap
to drug the market focus, risen in glory you
bantling screamers. You know what this must
mean in forward trading. Insatiable weakness

cannot clear the pitch to hand, how could it,
the rise to supervise attainment must fast level
off and then diminish, outrun by dilution
and underperformance. By crap easy gambles.

What you see damp, parasitic. Tip and turn
up slid caustic supply theory, ulcerous. Matter
boiling or livid hand-grip resumes instant release
panoply catchment and swells infected to barter

refit clauses, bitten all over. Don't make sores if
you can't pay to dress their origin, a globe toll
spoiling for animus. Step to the bar. Be a credit
witness. Speak real slow and with pauses, the water

supplies only itself. Neither is safe. Increase of
caret protein disclaims a reason approaching by now
link-surplus polymers, by the mill of barbarism its
sails flapping. Cancel the line-out. Better renew

a start discount epidemic disclosure to fix up
patent lockage. Sign for it, barefoot intercession for
statist corpus novel antibody descriptor, yes they
will but slowly, geniculate reflex. Motive parole

mandibular trap occult binome. So we'll cost
out the test refinement on a smirk host panegyric,
mirror slim slices: donor gives up a trickle
for enhanced symptom-free axial symmetry.

Yes, why is it like this not even hand-set like
a headline reduction. The skid marks demonstrate
abrupt redress, get your truck or blunt suede
parlour antiques. Loss of eye flicker on a scale

advanced, knows he lives on a big screen, all
tell you this. Altitude farm handouts medicate
careful dense prime vocalism, on record formal
thus exponential recovery. Did you hear that

told to you, root and branch slope management
at onrush unpaired and less compact, generic dealt
as possession on nil return. Which way the novice
points trail off, they say the same on the block

new level rib, spit your lips. Be quick, be
long to pump anger revivalism, percolate thick
forest scarps dug yet deeper. Get a vaccine on
shipment perish thread your face why yours

if told more, stable on a tilted capital field
suspected more often. Give out a version amplified
with strings to obligate a boundary check, felt
damp echo ethic manipulate its life exemption.

OK the recipient must guarantee, to be bound
by reciprocal hand contracture head to head G21
lodging 5HT single note purification alongside
microfibril, merge botanics. For fencing out

attach come to terms, did regulate. Unto mis-
take kneel down, disinclination warn at both
extreme enter to matrix. Each pervade to get
a shot clear attaining swap as now jizz up

most ado harvest dial. One sets term path
critique to lead-in development finance, toiled
did you as a rampart already on watch. Can't
you stop this pit-pat forded crossing by night,

wood pitch favourite all-out. Must prove also break
links into side entry handed close, don't you
see border dots, no label. Numeral life less on
clear counting to peak values, to a spread bail

rally staked out, be patient be lucent betterment
entities don't wait up don't even try, lie down old
diminish did you crinkle did you. The data best
muddy enforce their source, attribute wouldn't they.

Malicious rising sun fog plates scrolling over
tact marshall misery, climb over picket granule
appraising its product list. Dominance factor.
Read the lines of credit outsourced, alluded transfer

detail Green Line reserves like a spent mother
bedded on chicks, Brabant cascading in foil wrap.
Palliate herbivore dented globules, do the same
like this one. There's time but not much say

those whose time costs less, now sun gilding each
petal fringe just watch shrivel pit margins
pleat and plaint. Hold the crowd back weaker fix
agreeable suction, don't go slow append furious

torsion bolster omega blench. Let them have it
on hand terms. Reclining into soft tissue incursion,
spread up band vault to populace in foam broker
for a crib, a dainty. Clean his mouth adherence

formulation gum bruising vocational. Gainful
slow-down at hand partition. Bandy a fixture yet
again part yielded, imperative gradual, test
the mark treat fast now did you either say whoever.

We make a dab list, warm sunny days, cynicism;
delusion and incompetence. In peril by abatement
subsisting, want a scrap don't take it, did you
free the snick connect generic, sliding forth

made hand to lip, deal one. Help yourself dress up
a dummy, slash tariff excluded painted to schedule;
solar deep blue wave limit at a brink and over no
compromise frontside residual, a slam to big

only to avert disaster
                    get your peak on
                    mobile antagonise
                    fresh lender up
                    even vent
except when compelling reasons
                    hand grab this who
                    gets to say the off
                    feedstock prone
                    deficit, slippage
a security of everlasting triumph

or gravitate to the entrance be steady indigent
fastidious report prematurely slant balances.
This is the cancerous lace curtain fringing
a lake of toxic refuse, waiting to be born.

Assert parallel imports under licence at baseline
emergency exits turnstile one-way. Within protected gray markets to get what's coming is patent
wrist flexure daunted, prosthetic flavine into

precursor bulk inflows. Wipe out fly before make
sheltered linear attrition social, breakdown on counter
service for snacks. Right assembly bent for bent
retaining canyon abruptness, cry out on input

profile both lose drop own register. Know what metal
grain hardens a shutter on speed format protocol,
pursuit of joy tangible by agreement. Not for more
onset particulate infusion, plasma damaged even

before balance grades. Hermit costs hit up fast
and casual under a limit stressed horizon inflected
by pressure lanes, agree ingress sinew burning up
at standing pat conduit. Frame your hand deal it

nothing curative beyond oppression. Regimen target
for little and seldom, just a trickle to be infringed
avidly. Quoted this way submit refusal part ripe near
rotten, closer and closer batter-coated and deprived.

Copy out the taxon marker stem absorption pilot
to a class action remix. Your profile on front
steps flipper slurs no label, shallow fund proves
shell to shell, proves it juridically. Soft light

shines evenly over this, sweet plants sway, apply for
a permit and drench in blessing overture without
end repeated. Egged on to say no, cream on top
take bets on a mattress. Open his mouth words hidden

clan patter trans-generic basement foremost edict
on epithelial free surface. On a roll to come in
with tape management known applicators to float
levy after levy, aphthous winch. Want more why other-

wise if you've only that so hoarse stop the spread,
make a child barrier clearance. Unsophisticated lips,
grand molars, ring ahead for service depending here
and now on homage to order. Minute-men blather

routine or designate or render infertile put in
to simmer unavowed treatment process. Own brand
marked on the flank, hot iron specific to quench
a fever racing across unbarred prime locations.

Cranial flat-bed declension to a porous refusing
interval, delta rackets well at cycle above on
embedded values transit, sitcom for agent benefit,
dragnet poverty valuation. As, altogether nothing

or close to it, thus bathos don't lift or you'll
break a limit verge. Index life expected arrivals
demolish consumption. Get clear of some ever bad
muck on your shoes, never to end a backwards

tripper plus, cause of life trains to protect and hold
back digested. For a promise, for first ascension
wheeling and chequered, as bait. The barrage lip
closes this perimeter, voice further raised. Massive

block clatters, up then down slowly to construct
its gradual repentance. Still ever born to make
entry permission grip tight don't fight yet before
lapse of tense review. Agreement of forking larval

interdicts, notified, sessional poverty values at
pitch ultimate grade points. Don't you yet notice
a shimmer on bad zero, won't you walk there
and be the shadow unendurably now calibrated.

BLUE SLIDES AT REST

[2004]

Alt for allowed part, etch only into a folding
deeper there to follow if evenly graft aside
for low rent parented, palmar grasp. At a blame
so stepped forward, foot alert balance for them
at infant bending now prone already now so thee
soon wanted so deep bent there. Alter both minds
reflex by links by skin at bread not after not
older grill phantom, ranging off to rental skip
better sever tap alleged child shelf. Last so
manner in match before them, soul fetching neo
prolific head first slip paravail tip paired up
across slice due mischief, alt mere ingression.

Face rental flap to foreign tongues, her no one
no nation tilt prospecting so far a loan perplex
did you, fill or kill, tongue and groove. Given
all back minim advance to chill sprites ahead,
skin knowledge so forwarded allusive trance at
copious raw broken. Snapped even so. Far sway
stepping beholden lower, fee power deliverance
infixed at marram turning: lex furious to start
corded up, on sub record link to which, constant
region. Breath fast fortune nothing, flush torrent
all cavern bolted there, rill flourish alt fierce
fermented breed allowed on clear, first to last.

Upper plan thereon, by moiety report preventing issuance to bind over thin var faction, gamma steel at benefit. Carry a moment fort landing release to safety not in truth be mutual, lateral joins make it a heart claimant. Will he advance in ambit to her, her words inferring to a curvature for time given and back. Privation settlement his strung out unceasing meteor sense of high play, get returned. Mainly residing in brain-stem to mean divisor, panting quotient acted out, anticipate on the frontal bonus. Hewn laminate: know your way through this temporal occlusion in volt check-off.

Touch the face, even this time too. Make next assent also by inference, by a swing silent pass to prove its future, ambit of the necessary outside day before day declared. Reach to this. As yet unburned inshore, wielded sparks in catenation ride to glory. Did she aggrieve his ambit fix, vocal alloy at measurable nip blue trading to a planet, was it. Each patiently intending, each time the fuse repaired, concept of service invoke conscript retention. Each time so reached outer placement. Make fast viable activator tab insert dove for tail flicker, all navy blue conurbate.

Partition blurred caloric engine his spiral transfusion playful to flex, inherent tuneful quantity. Both recessive to malabsorb, lapse of thought. Neither remembered this, neck flushed allumette profusion, caressment. Up through by a turn in apical thrill conveyed to famish, ingenious breast cured to breathe. Sweet droplets immune in a flurry laid aside get a shift. Her bevelled spectral glide furnish, unusual: maps to gene margin prior frivolous ought soon to lift off ransom by choice, cantilena. Flitting under her breath in catches, bird on briar hydroxy filament he raids a temper vane limit venture payout. Imitate less. Apart low-rent voices motion entire neighbour respite dowel.

Reaching colloid to serve, cleft for me. Hurt no one in durance, day butters a slice promise notable thrown entry to class-A phrenic incisor. Look out upon it swim prepared as fondly at level haste, enhanced to lift for. You know not to fall back, not to press on, shudder fix servitude profession advent. Dog star gravel. Pitch fused. Apennine. Never in all for all in, the bond marker reflux vanilla suffice apsidal treatment. Sagittal casting upon earth next to last the cambium shower is hers. Bind will so for open pulse will start both heard, principle stamen garnet rose crypted. Of age flowing bastion gate purposed flung outward to a knee in want patent promissory bright shots.

Caliper remove no hurt for dyestuff, to generalise backsight feeding the flame, the lane. Waving aside proof of taint offence for minor need temp recall to permanent novel stain at margin, to race upside ahead *per se*. Will they will to pass, as in passion assumed. Meant this much, ridded name belt, ours similar fanciful. Same roof overcast lacking at tie estimate so. Bower woven endless to seed case by parallel cob plentiful, hurtle antigen; clefted this in personal hazard linking asperse resume, to pro-file gathering like jelly. Never not less like to need a twin reminder gainful in place, temple so acclaimed.

Could it be known would be worth less to enhance revision attempt prospect. Be worthy later as after all arrived, her beauteous wing. Water stroke reflected inward lucky fantail. Envy parted. If for noon temp abstemious divising pro assert, brother next. Will to both: of therapeutic fragments enjoin counterpart im-probable, live long soon rescinded. They enter pools by fusion optics, human substitute fixture, to know even going on past and declared woven under not now impassive metal seams. In starry night displayed be told as belonging halted up true. Right this milligram in moment so soon melted option, temp so few unsound.

As in gathering onstage sited, plan to fit. Uneasy symptom in formation traces soon bantam, say been roped together in tempest to notice, for ever the blue sky bends fluently over all wand purchased. As if stencilled slipware will more flood item to claim opportune tympanic pitch impressment, first lender signs here. Watch her watch: lifted clouds as light on her cheek arch to fit. Unrighted precarious lee kilter too sensing, in favour attained now for his only best rumour tied. Wage in hope down to rip a ticket, borrow offset, don't quarrel. As above all skip limits prehended on sufficient bare eminence.

They attend once more in precarium, to take apart by simple mission broken off. To view them. Instance talent reckless *in situ*, buzzing up ahead even before tendence to flight path notice given, as latent hits to fit a chance, side-on. Knowing this by so already not to success planted, climbing they do on time, in storm. Why unrightful can now be asked over again request fitment shade flicker take up armed arising. Not ample grip loan out on circuit inclined security to lowered clouds made a brow blue by starts. Drift eloquent, leaning per inwards at night prepared, shaken less with fear elected.

The placard of renewed angular motion naval for on-stream suited vibrancy can and will open, will also unsafe advance. Steam breathing up through metal tangs, her life of contract free given like arm jerking investment, baby elbow side to centre. Typic kin elation argue this. Not former sit out hearing to them horizon lame nor bounded effusive set-piece match, match. Highest tor gained hotly for both what you get landed: lascivious mud intercession fact to stray herbal limit mixture, unit both. Again mark out on labels historic up wallet in water volume real pulse, on the red wall chart.

On her life line gently flamboyant by exchange at the rate kiosk. Living fervid child likeness astonish at medium cross, carry forward round-eyed did they take up alternation readiness. Crook fin soft coin after stitch activity. They broke it. On the lift bar to serrate for his scale to her sell cleaving foremost out for out, for herself helpless. Allowance partial teeming dune settlement distribute a lamp attractor, fricative grain demean sibling imported upwards lofty. Random thrown forward quick shout rice grains blemish apparent. In line now listing break series. Which one lucid cuff frayed paragon.

Shorten to foster outline mesh insistent by mitral
converge as for, audit. He'll lift temper not ill
at a lick complacent task fronting, mitre to refrain
point adopted inward. Take more, more care. Not to
fear laying on, open bushel veins. Downy finish is
hers to ask after, the swan's road into Palestine not
yet level. Arms lifted up light tremor, gaze tidal to
average miss finish Greek fire. Floor affecting she
knows he'll go, white span day breaks in the eastern
sky not indic not critical. On micro grassy shelters
ice shoes labial gentle apt stenosis. Take both and
replace under vivid pressure by max new gene flow.

What would either give her onset, now. Is the first
tint broad enough in runny over-paper, can they do
that for promise centred on a bubble. A sabine spin
on relic viscid seizure patch weeded out yet attempt
spilling food from a mouth. Lush issue sip under spark
bird-song slow to counter: ancient threads prepared.
Often she holds on. Lactic burning lip creases novel
advance measures, lip dispute revolve will her white
throat rabid nuisance icterine shingle. Search lamp
party cress-market begins, long before daylight bites
like boiling water race blue naked feet. She'll lay
this cover topmost powers, cloudy dram front pitch.

Trim forward but as it never was or bite fittingly so
defused album transit for another, into proof type
pronoun intercepted. Our sung script frayed to gather
in one for shifty plenum, tie up, her lung cavity
dilated before. Riot babble scented, sleepless with
anxiety unknowing. Myopia candid glissing preen far
and near to be forced over beyond this. In cramp
sent beside encompassed by floods under dark, don't
ever murmur decrepit sternum. Shunt chill, furnace
anterior believable by nerve pressure blind sequence
at day mute, does he most shout. Incipient could he
hear across way to way rowan pierced for this unmoved.

Care taken, took into by a glance. Her hair loosened,
cheek more red, plasma lactic acid dropping utter spread
like raid to her knee, so freely downwards. Entranced
restricted cub in this tunnel, lissom case notes asperge
crevice woeful did they either. Why did they. Swayed in
unit as a burning cedar, see all men crouch under braid
to split-off rock powder ache. All giddy reason to lose
in a sheaf nativity charted out breaking under foot
freaky and grim. Her own hand held, by traced finger
in need, lips swelled crimson laden bite marker engaged
loaded burial. Not yet interfered, maybe not yet ever
to shear livid breccia childish protests in solo flight.

Each one tissue-wrapped phoneme sedative to give out
for slip finish her nest, henny-penny unfolds a share
on a tribune team. Anyway burnt to ashes slant paper
whether not free of risk. Well not stapled. To not rankle
asking him however his manoeuvre, to save a life from
font credit at name the same found. The line fund cream
mass Neptune run ahead surname hers lost his all abreast
swimming in seas of milk. Inspissate alarm agree, tribal
calyx option velours to pout, ictus beat raised impulse
pinion display. Enrich filter. Nipple won over, lip-words
inclined lip-read swell to pad: sense incident flutters
duct passage. Vowel sensorium lingual praising its root.

Kneading such lip, such cheek frisson inflated pine cone
help penitent in a dream collar brief, sufficiently under-
stood now more here lost to care, intermit. Have words not
joined to fit right, under water endued to a slip fault
assuming in place of thus declared. Mouth to mouth unfit
either to plead, yet more slight utter frenzy assessment
if not lost to level right, to quell. Or could either not
down in earth contemplate, warm and bright to end as
dust by the road, risen child unspeaking by human hand
referred case by case rested plum and found. Deem rended
by tendence in code none must fear to yet fair not cease
for harm laid square, fresh green ever now shining blue.

Actual reduction instant to famish by dwelling final clamour, hangs on a point. To fruit refract in delimit face to face his spoken sum of her sequel. Claiming up tender placement not recoverable for grief or sorrow yield to dictates value this loss yielded, bond consortium make a twilled mouth shut. Give outright. Yet minor exempted by love perpetual struck in held to count. Estimate her paramount select abstain, several hindered by ever what until renown. Perfect clearance towering, bidden dwell these caves in earth rankle against a stranger by injury to disconcert unwavered countenance. Level foreign out-land never yet incautious not recover, the natural child.

Go down in earth like a feather, front brace. Left over unrightful semblant will punish devoted machine knit parapet. Nip and tuck miniature grounded so. Into this world of darkness, of a kin deducted justified reproved to end without, companion hooded unseen. Attempt thus cut down as had never. Go with me. Within segment floss honour bright missing, on foot. Ignorant paramount will cadge a ride cranky dope appeal months and years, tell in mish-mash certainty head to black on. Better broken keep house yielding softly gnomic cataract depressed inwardly sent away. In care from hers avoidance transit accept in strong wardship, order holding trace and lock.

REFUSE COLLECTION

[2004]

To a light led sole in pit of, this by slap-up
barter of an arm rest cap, on stirrup trade in
crawled to many bodies, uncounted. Talon up
crude oil-for-food, incarnadine incarcerate, get
foremost a track rocket, rapacious in heavy
investment insert tool this way up. This way
can it will you they took to fast immediate satis-
faction or slather, new slave run the chain store
enlisted, posture writhing what they just want
we'll box tick that, nim nim. Camshot spoilers
strap to high stakes head to the ground elated
detonator like a bear dancing stripped canny
sex romp, webbing taint. Confess sell out the
self input, yes rape yes village gunship by
apache rotor capital genital grant a seed trial
take a nap a twin.
Fruiting bodies vintage
shagged out on batch stand-by, grander conceptual
gravid with foetor, sweet rot adoring placid
or regular. It is we they do it, even yet now
sodomised in a honey cell, pitted up against
the good cheat dimpled in a power cuff jersey,
shrug to fit waist for traffic, kick the door in.
Go on, do it, we'll photograph everything, home
movies hold steady on while they is we do it,
by eye it takes oozing huge debt. Reschedule
value credits, war for oil, oil for food, food for
sex molest modest reject stamp on limp abjected
lustral panoply. Little crosses everywhere, yours
and mine makeshift parlour chicken rape private
sold down DIY there is a country.
Bite off the
cap with a twist, upper strut invest cream off
profit on a visor, bench law pressure why would
you not credit that. It is to be believed by
living daylights voided moral defection by blank
horror for terror of sacrifice, stairway to air
drilled by fierce devotion, say yes. Brutal finish
this sentence, go on do it. Till they yelp and
will rise up against us in a storm of justice or
let's pause to redefine that run up a treaty sell
them into so-called paradigm.
Call-sign freedom

operation Sharp Knife, finish as you never will in
a heap on the ground. Prostrate, back-spavined and
fresh-crushed, then another explosion. Flush with
cash for sex for punishment, let's try a little
execution-only on mother's endorsement equity don't
work in a high tower no more indwell infidel on a
ranting stair. Profess exactly for take into cap-
tivity, assault and quell and kill thirsty work,
sweat running in our eyes, of course also looting
and kidnapping so write home about it, go on
do it invited spectacle dump. Tag evil so palpable,
fungus in the nail-bed, your choke on a concert
programme device. Die in battle, die in bed or maybe
on a trolley, be sick and feel better, desire even
a just peace. Kick them around shall we do that be
sickened stamp on non-white body parts benchmark
yields huddled up naked,
                                        land of the free
control respite deliverance. Cut-off spoken abuse
postural forensic gag reflex fabric whitener, you
do know this. Global recovery now warming up:
running on all fours as the dollar oil price rise
is hedged and written down, corrupt reserves
declared to win. Simulate handcuff bunker take
out the turret like dirt fuel data vow to thee.
Is that what. Snatch attack wire hid for a circus
for venture cap life savings razor cut, recruit
to strip to sweet wince rat garbage trim ankle
go fetlock, to float there. Hands-on foot rack,
on carotid palpitation ravenous, lies and falsehoods
stalled credibly usual, our watch accepted your
finger your sacred thumb. The truth of faked report
on a pulse, a bloodline stamp on whose neck
why not credit dog kill.
                                        In the curving
mirror of enlarged depravity daily and abhorrent a
comfort of disgust adjusted to market slippage
a pact encroached my face pouch your puffy demonic
exclusion so far, too far, no we know that and
never yes, quite probable, eye-rape transit to
twitch renege on membership, limbs blazing all out
famous by gorged access. Did you heart attack
hear these words your own mouth purse formation

broke their outline, just awaiting the chance of
derangement from deep inside. An occupying force
commits pillage the sadism cut to measure from
its concept of possession own-brand words rise up
in some necks to stifle disbelief, bite them down.
Go on, bite them encircling gloom some bright
ruined spark goes for broke power failure on-line
claw back from the entrails. Ticket of leave revulsed
sup on this horror story full house endurably
feel-good recoil: the aghast demeanour our shield
our family and child-care we form a square to
defend value invest in safety in fields of plenty
occupation's gone to a rot clinic. Privation mate
leashed up mental famine.

All right core rescue
by concession of expendable defect, the option play
to transference to run hysteric barrage forward de-
ployment. Pre-set threat assessment at deferred
base precision, risk profile vamps up by alert to
stockade fire lines; if the inside is now already
exposed then crush the outside, consider this your
zone of inclusion that's us we don't pray heads down
we watch the target this time ah yes right we
are the target let's go faster now and self-abhor,
get there first. Civil defence, rights issue give
before robbed in-store. Mutilation and self-rape
defilement on a display promotion, give blood shed
more, greedy bright halo. Warranted buggery word
chewed spittoon upper rule of lawyers on *pro rata*
fee commission unnatural cruelty.

Entire violation
natural and brutish metal restraints standing room
only, seats reserved for women in labour. Force them.
They do our will, to deny what they do is ours,
the wanton ambit of self possession. The tasks of
self-defence. In our name longterm marching as, to
a holy city ringed too close to call. Our land ours,
raw and forever.

08.MAY.2004

TO POLLEN

(2006)

Let my eyes see the sun and be sated with light.
The darkness is hidden, how much light is there left?
When may the dead see the rays of the sun?

– *Gilgamesh*, Si i 13'-15'

Sometimes the field sprouts nails,
so much does the field long for water.

– Adonis, *The Pages of Day and Night*

So were intern attach herded for sound particle
did affix scan to ultramont, for no matter broke
could level cell tropic. Leading out proven sub
manage ever in fold, rift token will to redeem
or flagging, a massive glib finish. Bare face to
give, stringent paste. Does scatter grab on or bet
to ground one or two regulars, at root in blanket
score, attempt. Seldom bred, did level placement
promote up-rank incident recoil. Utter generic cell
fluid timbre; for it now, listen; to a cert play
to see bring placid at a join, promise gated al-
ready infamous. Rise alike, so do. Along the seam
cresting to burn out black my interim destruction.

More to pollen ascript for elated finish, above scale
at draw tact elicit did both clamber all in fused
aloud. Shoot quickly now. It hurt so much. As to
submit engraver likeness mirror from terror alto style
lifted at furnish to a stroke. Is any more likely
footed along notable cliff sounds, edging close as
passive, as link project. To groan at once in point
sill factorise, in flash worsen blanket at a neck
worth spoken; in for broke harm your outward or
minded up fast. Force like scriven, reserve. By
mark to throat, tore to say hunger led acclaim bring
amount brutal profile on influx. Or while at loading
to stare plan off by ripeness event be done bluntly.

Fault plane under treading lacks rip indelicate path to its line, to the furnace. Soon by mistake gains overfill commander to mother up fewer or single nerve balances in averted along elate for normal, drastic. Newer finding up reefs you see slice first partition. Why should that work. Mean passed over no vigil no truce grab for best there and service altered runway. Truck hurt failed list incident pacific not civil, render back on principal hinterland allurement. Afferent side ripe on track refix as, rose up in mossy fibres attuned, brimmer won't mix hand even extend. How could also not be lesser. Stand nearby went off its oil trap refined.

How much so much did they not care to say handed up to rate, at a base to confirm no flatten announce trivials online. Agree fillet weld tournament at whirling dared inscript, flaw in sand for a trial worsened by braving outcry points, they assembled in total yes answerable to perform. Or you would have a bandage for this no count made up numbers domestic to probable, well like enough imperfect reckon histrion. Pare back to no less. They will nil refute, will affirm on tabulate, true phantom listening out for conjunct timing. Under bright sky there's no choice but simmer elevation set up grand rabble to beat paints, metalloid pan touches.

Afflicted purpose they hail we cut them they in turn line the route denied, holding it most. When better dare to given up blank medication however unfixed schedule, drop staring out. Noble fanfare menu joints grossed, net coronals just see novel incident prove incipiency. Parents out from the destroyed symbolic crisis, line by line raised to break manic intubated cast-offs. A too easy snap, a statement reissue signing the way inward ulterior cost structure, to know. Watch on them transfer price tags, lose breath profoundly our yet living split for glass. Aggrieved curb. Ever lack to tell further submission the grassy way beneath.

In basement glisten to a stepper just over ration for travel harness, time trim to flow. Be outward on brand simulation perfect pitch. Or does that tell you enough, resilient brotherhood is this the one inclined. Could one refused to the preset match hurt resin at affront well weighed, just give a best to aromatic take ever heartfelt, from these missing vents make anyone gasp. Predicted influx let to be intergrade property due fair minor, lantern series sprung off. So loosen grammatic volatile acerbic fraction drawn why this one beat silently lavish pack of plenty. Yet too many run out, some pinner valve seething in vapour assignment round the camp.

Like dung, slate ridge chanter to higher up ground
at front elation both sides to creamy tectonic
satisfied no more. Help me to a quite unsingular
onset, as begin running forward to line sample in bid
to pay quick off to, a slant. Attracted dip in trouble
make do on less or pattern no dream extra fragrance
promise a room airy with song of birds. Infested
gravity as if done with it, vacant insertion you
give us the ticker at stupid discount soon awaken
and torrid, outer cathedral precept on a cliff.
Sanction rife spend with warplanes in act thermal
prediction, load your mind match blood no charge
now adduced at root and then up, all diminished.

Advise but slim never why left filling one on a chance
token one at all, by pointed index. We would surmount
near exact shave to profile another investment tip,
give due primate loads on all. The grain sharpens up
by reduction. Ready counts fall and defy in-rating
departure practice as mostly will maybe, alone procure
and lie better. As to whether all found blind written
credible deflected, instance, much pursued hate prowess
however deterred. Lane choices half allowed, too seedy
aggregate to mime permission cut step treat advocate
insertion, format. Ungrateful discrepancy on minted
grievous pushed down, converge to lights and these too
shimmer avoiding implants tiring at toll appointments.

Inimical dud in the breeze delays delphic impact main assessed for wraparound, for twin steps. They do smooth out their terror photo snaps to the airport ramps on deal too rugged I do a cut-out for them both. Don't just make way up through a door laid chemical join to char tissue gimp fixture, the badge attains under sealing for new respite, all bright honest metal they did richly acclaim to the pin circle explosive set invert or substitute marker. Light-up dots provoke to compromise affray. Margin at narrow leading their front for thirst currently. Prevented switches taped open they were authorised beyond channel late nominee settlement lop-side, lip salve, our men sent.

Fuelled in train, more addit preparative scale abrogate early summit to rake down exposure, team at pillow entry. Shop for day cares bloom out legal to its excess durative touch frown. Old muzzle win not yet taunted with a fixed incision dialect on transfer, idiom confirming a blow-up pact, as they will deny before even inference no otherwise prime random curfew by aspects. No one so much out on the streets now, maybe later. After dark permission assemble lift at print style bereft margin redraw no traffic listen void. Yes hold back, mix interior discounted testimony to date marker none of them who admits a part volume, capture depletion ranks.

For roading watch close side to side affective in cover step remunerate, remote action the frontal hood lifts to swivel by finger pressure. Do not remove until converged fully lit to both forward mounts. Operant selector forks assimilate injunct new data remitted fluent on-screen clip resonator to margin, to cancel. Take none, back woolf notes at chance for synchronise counter-lock, do not release until scored off. All previous sets in memory by date order. Opt reckon unit scale match short-term fluorescence inside the eyeball attenuate along horizon lits to compile summit value gain recounts, a full crew unshared in chain aberrantly.

The patch dairy fluid subsides. Essential script migration runs in parallel reserve, keep close to track signage. Love your way. These brows in shade give out full view, diary of looks forward. Whether depend is better detained, whether is it. Intercept the creatures hill raising, a new clinician nods evenly for a trice enigma, at one scheme of perjury; intrusion solutes cellular infill surmount unsweetened flocks of cream. Milk in schools indigenous parcel donate detour not a whit. Bonds of possession up-lift painterly to stipple like birds again, repeals patient for tremor near holding. Hand to under foot encryption path, to canopy parlant. Mafic, ingrained.

At the side never drew not this curtain used as so
much normal as dry other waiting bleeding go there
know that way no glance close together. For just one
later on time as breath normal can be partitive can
remember it hurt exactly even paces for real for second
face on looks hold on to follow is great burning is
all forever all travellers used in the way further
along with many be quick. Watch timeout. Show it
simple ever ready check. Don't look match the sign
check. Just as plain view noticed check. Carry out
a life entrance weight hands free check plan from
here now walk breathe check touching is you will
in a dark way shutter stand eternal strong to save.

Their petty spite rendered to nullity unforgiven to
animals marked down asymmetrical counted away PR
in brotherhood confined behold this solitude no
Doha no prayer just try to formal link estopped.
Just say words to crush a limit, they do that as is
all well known the way is beyond limit weaponised
jurisdiction rendered null. Not to be beyond question
is a pure land life separates from ends we know and
hurt ever found ever fond. Wear orange a star in
plain azimuth formula chant from memory scrip as no
book all texts sacerdotal hunger murmur this. If
in just for cause to wish no burning spite we will
crush no trail will show war by means of war denied.

On the street or below it yet fit all missing out
pieces grounded stare in a moment for name the way
ahead strike taken cantor. Not in haste in nothing
violent to grasp hand-rail wait to clear. Each sound
unit clicks serially with overlap, gymel adventures
inscribe private bones of a limb. You can see them
clear through, as daring to fly, as before burning up
in a heat flicker. Don't unattend pales to compare.
Better these keep on, pause now a slight turn to size
by fluent repartition. The lines of flow determined
axially leaning forward, now step along. Public safety.
Vector force link to link all casual perfect incon-
sequence not in secure capture shots just in time.

Now singing through thin clouds the high lattice
is crusted with fear at eye level in irritant chronic
spasm report. Nothing to credit song-like modular
clastic deformity, to make a cage structure called
hunt the stunt, clathrate denial. By inversion of
subject the grammar yields to novel clamour, days
pass spilled like water. Flow chants, name the way
after loyal sons. Retro tamp down phosphate bridges
or on a beach exploded. Tenacious each voice placement
seeded direct wrapped, rule of law. Braided up like
floss to a seizure named like water. As ligand spike
as now forever, waged against us, forever we shall
walk the path in fear of empty hope, shunned pat.

Lie down, the eye is nubbed by what is fed through
the bounds of locality, we see shots of a father racked
in misery and bearing like a gift his crushed and
bloodied son, a bare infant. There was a calamity,
this is the claim for respite alleged against us. Which
mark of the account, natural sorrow debit profane in-
ducement, cleavage along faults of destruction. Or more
like a mark-up in common grief they are always we know
it dark-skinned, any joyous picnic on the beach. How
is the base compound unstable, by weak bonding then
infused with preference issue. Our prison of worthless
grief rescript to harden daily tormented undilute, why
each shot hateful and fearful right along the ravine.

Natural-born killers, their white song camera is ours
for the same, to feed a habit nurtured by wound drainage
or yet waste out mortality. Reflexed employment tips
to roll-up losses on account set payment at zero and
beyond question unaffordable. Each time borrow a new
fixity, terms and conditions are what you shall discover
laterally enjoined, your crisis shelter. By heat search
find the locus of fear threatened against you and go
there along the quickest way, fenced off that tape is
the scenic ribband you dream of, see every mortal day.
The ground is hot with vanity, task force possession
promotes fear of loss to the head prime their song for
our family outing, fresh terrors stashed in the basket.

The life of the soul is deductible, to custom advantage
in reduced exit charge. The sun glistens on water,
leaves shake, these are the rate flotation, unminded
and self-explained. Orthophosphate accessory dis-
charge impulse manifest, the king of heaven on a laid
gold block 'in the same *naskh* hand' utter prostrated.
Rich Tea rich terror primatial for altered sex ratio
impingement, lay your hand now for hybrid one-fit
timid coronal, near reviled hot mass. As they advance
to the screen adjusting brightness ahead and primed up
for secure payment, see germination perplex all along
its imminent disclosure. The inward turn-off select
the hard shoulder like a child in hot ecstatic tedium.

Some bishop in sufferance or some outfield chaplain
will explain how that works, how bravery is planted
in a celestial soil like dust as we are. Our witness
embedded on tour by rotation, by a price war to first
collapse a market, to set life span cover on the cheap.
Yet they are dear to us and gathered in raised blood,
pressure scanned against code matching. In that company
as filed to share alike. Trifle winnowing asset retro-
grade *ars subtilior* lines up ethic vacancy on strip stop,
on raw ulcer across the cheek. Wash the steps, coaxed
to dish out refinement points on tacit coupon demerger
for good cheer brave hearts never in vain as under
starry skies commit acts of stupendous cocky turpitude.

All are disfigured. I saw a hole in my chest, feel
ashamed to plead for your own life it is utter crass
from a hole in the face word vomit lost for them, hurt
stain so much disowned. You hear what you say over
to get off and by right in a mutilation outburst, for
any life at all stand-in to be shameful in a news
flash grease trap. A stitch up-end in beauty abusive
fresh dates choroid in tunic sear unison. So be more
segregated to know the worst there is, abatement order
self-service at rigid price only cheap cuts. At this
counter you are dressed meat a full choir halal on
offer the grade dismounted, beaten any tariff held
indefinitely in due form by slick joke under the act.

From a front seat it is bearable to suck a knife
blade to scrim in broth. Perfect on truth for steel
vernier axil you could easily cut this. It would be
ancestral brood-genitive in knowledge laid out be-
low your look to be alike, all the same blind enter
concisely a claim card membership. For blood, brown
in mouth fitment, taste of metal run along clamant.
Fortunate aside leading tone will open our lips to
pout worn in tangible overglide. Hammer each one,
break note climb neck and neck. Knife lustre facing
the music get the whole thing in your pocket, keep it
open. Diminish the haft affix loosely proponent span
blood group indexical self-cut. Try doing it now.

STREAK~~~WILLING~~~ENTOURAGE
ARTESIAN

(2009)

Fumeux fume par fumee
fumeuse speculacion.
Qu'antre fummet sa pensee
fumeux fume par fumee.

Quar fumer molt li agree
tant qu'il ait son entencion.
Fumeux fume par fumee
fumeuse speculacion.

– Solage (rondeau); Bibliothèque du Château de Chantilly, Musée Condé, MS. 564 (C15, early), fol. 59r.

(HMX 2908169 [Arles, 2005], 7)

Inside the tight closed box off it was it was out
a same summer box oh then at must closed on all
or maybe often maybe open to one side glaze be
in part to spill affirm parted along a rim ballast

Ready known, the same on over the way up be aim
superflux be finger fillip tight eddy cluster for
test the cover to seal better by close not closed
in her cone practice modify. To maul the out-sign

More at blanket turn, prior the blanket, over out
side did tear or torn smatter hot shut right off
tipping exclusion. Same day mainly deprive rank
serve for service, at same hours total. Deeper

Fold to box to fill to undersell nor roving shame
spelled got hurt by a burn. Same too fast joined
by the flap cover trickle or stream cut solid then
cut your hand the close hand perfectly yours for.

Recital to side, same with to side livid in part
newly profuse did civic offer on a dial, sweep
flight oh disposal profligate buck more in and
ready. Tantric cube up tight seam, signal limit

Galvanic who will meet who would, as to camber
one side slipped over close fit: alter presume
that shutter way, his also servile blank package
the box befitted frank aside simulate by adoption.

Approaching passion freak intact prime falter
for segment same-front glide to fill conduce
suffuse give or give. Plenteous flake arm folly
to love acre the same rivet the front broken

Prolusion, stay near ever dry. Few tap transfer
second charge you let off stop surrender for
disarm, oh grant that, leave the grain why ever
less now less green took life by the tongue lit

In low pale extradite. A day this one assign
yours grow up to main, leaf round and round lie
cost plus crush split stamina. Me such unarm
same peril fovea pass fire mantle and glib overt

Tie to air close to, to disclaim that for. More
flute ignite nul wants subsume trill earlier ban
wrist digit restive to same. Be all best profane
broken tenuous, each strand as fine torrid at

Leave to play stare to east, ease denied off
by rush fracture on dismounting the pelmet crab
out over the foreland, the annexe. Moulded
profile accepts on its lateral crystal mistaken

Fragment at level counterparty brushed mend
up to shock, same till fallen till to breach
its promise mine for spent at duration, noted
way ever on transit long for this and similar.

Cornice buffed to distrained volume how much
worn as cloud treading a skyline, dependency
revoked a figure told up marking did you see
run to it. For to run intrinsic the water gate

Look out, the same the same! Print besides, hot
torment in storm see out nor new nor fusion peat
a list for temper get the skin off at margin, see
more out yet. Still eyes please are they found

Catchment plaster grand rubble up ask again,
same turn at given, graven indignant enough
week old and cheap remains. It is either joy
certainly in a flood, plain for brim deepens to

Fix out gaze on this, on virtue. Acknowledge
skid forward or same fervid plastic embankment
her link antler, rising and driven. Above his
anthem converge tall preening slips to axial

Image dilation eager for size, steep-side per
macro run by dozen oh warship gauge silent
elated regimen. See the same hold for top flit
margin payout, grab on eyes wide to ever fade,

Total extensor bin. Hold your to me ligate for
free ply employ random either way countenance
rebel gate, gate far over, enter attracted win
worn cumber ask, dazzle so profile ply to play.

Same terrace same fuse at delinquent if mass
coherent grange pasture, epic on street-plan
will re-use its passive wrap. New all the same
to radiant flat premise. Ascending to linear

Coating mint ascorbic do present look over
to hold near yet seen near gain for split claim
elatior what is, can you say. Over this eye
fold little hook disturb now severe hunger

Out over and over descending to heartbeat,
foster self-same in a whirr be saccadic score
to our here massif. To coax who will grated
censure intensive callow found, swallow inter

Lines of a prism. Reach trucial planar twin
hold to took pliancy hours motionless, seam
same more link. More of same melt sleep loss
invoice step belong. They so full starved still

Flee graven no other, where identical so sat
tight to be, be assumed. Live shined in mercy
how is. Ledge fold durable ripen your sleeve,
gradual to plead for. Defect breathe manner

Labiate tender greed for station, partial need
same after time can you, throat dry all along
diminishment. Orbit be learn, fly other to fall
out of some world shall from hunger substitute.

For dent inflict yet amuse enamel will livid exceed
tactic nursing humid loss, more even alert at numb
unwind entry. Level ground pacific inversion has
wasted trapper, has few slicks. Run out portal upper

Finish not yet, blame turned, stock sullen aspect
to refuse to empty to apparat, further down gullet
hoisted put worse, same to find. Interview shellac
vivid contact rejoinder tell you on exact location,

Mild sorrel sworn to balance dish for dish plenty
as a scrap. As black tremor brought into readiness
furbish practice, run first outpost space to bruising
bitten trail security miss. Mission same miss elevate

Particular implant then right down, listless by further
plain edict put unlimit indignancy its sombre roomy
theme trump. Mounting frame actinic palliate nervous
subdural choice some parting even beside the barre

Fine, to end. Pair to imitate too far, to bear neglected
must past trample the grassland metric layer binding
in spun tabulate, tremor same orange simmer disturb
credible mortality. Or closer to tall, taller than lost

No quicker outlet evenly. Massive vested per invention
per lingual ticket secure fair both same addition plan
up channel, warmer enhance crossed than missed rise
converge for topic under sequence trance, up to dash.

When did when nor soon rebate the pinch altior stood
for the narrow annexe would you they partake, in this
hardly by defeats. Near gale allay force slam opportune
dive forward parenthood, prink get on lie unborrowed

Fuming to the brow, so tumult. So same deep pitch
slice open same slice plantigrade and off grandiose
as wet by commerce. Than all of them would permitted
cut on wet for iodine air for all slicing, fast-paced

To grip to peak. So seek in profile one size or even
earlier titrated wood on wood the touch harmless said
gorgeous in symmetry. On wood slice to ply made up
trade winter advancement, when did. Slope to gather

A force trellis influx would you septic eye-lid fuel
to glove soak, seawater decking did they all, would
they. You do know it, soon matched one to one off
let lid flicker, stand up. Said what choice spoken

Quickly at a brag do they when not or if profound
same brows matching oh weigh out lamp for show fly
forward, must do. Weed wet they say would you de-
lay hard trimming fast the sluice unclued eye into

Idle print factor, would you. On wood cut soon slips
cut right up let to, let on by tune join inch to match
cover less. Same to less must illness contusion flocking
to know slack ichor seepage along the step mast inset.

Cursive slow dropper forbear manipulated order to
save them allusive eat till suited, offering help
them single them fairly wit tackle. Into wicket
fainting team alloy white iron bait, aril did them

Claimant at first. Getting them out to margin few
to allow by pair iridescence gain the hold step,
strim loose panic back go slant copy as broken out
for them this counter waveform, less same fusion

More filter fractional beam to trip. Burning till
dimwit nor fuckwit lintel hot to finish. Bar of
them for cluster same bonded propound or minimal
diluted, how other why to them. Brittle to same

Hem cut lift out randomise, what they do, gorge
tinting water outflow. Not yet going under limit
foundry by smelted reflection becquerel fasted up
to bridge missed extirpating over more. To glint

Salts hide them to same metal density at crowded
double arrival, can induced. Express fluent to true
utter wasted enrichment barracuda or yet untrusted
fault plan. To level to tablet abandon. The prime

Simplify weight operant prosecute min min willing
link to exclusion. Their splay foot shipment accrues
its span calculate defence, each one echelon mount
to reach the same. Forgather presume, help them.

Also light piece successive front bite at replicating torment to scented cost probable token. As well gyrus colour unwilling, so occupied or seeder fed by a block rally conversion, lips. Get freight front pathway, rigid

To snatch front warning my well denticula profit frame remedial partition, distort to him by them the name cap futile and erupted. The family voiced up blinker depleted path to dimeric restive suffix. Up over stretto

For ridge party splitting heath worse, to worse how much the lateral buzz sociable, to breed. No matter private hamper obligate through inflow, same so formal mishap all under prevalent. All the same them collected, cold

Deflection fragrant with gloss numeric cancel ill attempt subscript to a plant yours and mine shoe untried. Whose waymark after another after tether lap to flop at soon passive less, unfood warning in know best. All events

Waiting or lining off frozen precision did break the dim further heartland, get to get forbidden none amorous at the boundary. Draw back torted, for fraction unlit decept inner bark what frame oh how not even upright

Is the surface entire all for them compose him runnel delegate incision enjoy the permit gates, be tint likely pitch acid hob. Loop for fray unpick over flint skies for either for mother better line the front or ossify.

But relics intercept pernix go shifted snowfall, base
gimbal evermore he treats he shall forested. Rail time
and snicker by valid proximal, up slink bone you have
the same fill-track, fill even. Open gamble fine edge

Languish they to him, proof very rapid die-cast hair
cracking transverse mill end. Gone for tell this label
extract side to slide towards honey guided fit thirst
guarantor. Invent shack slim to heart mute doorway

Tepid or fumble exit better false by mime sacrosanct
hinge settled, spooned off for him next stop soon, next
heat to blink famous. Fitment to stagger pin owning
balance phalanx summit slay the day the way sump lit

He advises this too. It's for advent for shall or rested
occlusion pale object both sides, grill access delivery
ethic suck notice her ferric his to bind synthetic sip
alum entangled. Broadly infill bunker tremble ostive

Bit parcel same to find strong too. Odds to sublet cut
fancy triage up late give to win adventure, mild have
him taken. Suffix shall marry resection at principle
get stuck as metric hinder him, same slam. As grasp

Buy yet colouring traffic incidental locks but turning
say off awry, quick relent, store. How brain up patter
fond him to you sheer fathom, how. Entrain by per limit
resume and plan, fetch too, all incriminate allowed on.

Re-divide by attraction settle for. Simple name-sake
manual escorted obvious measure knowledge back roam
overhead slit talc loan to play after. Animal cruising
baneful clip fast benefit pretty offset stimulus at all

Rank dwell sumptuous crossing, star-shape module into
loyal shade. Made to rest, over and thwart plied inference
oil prolong oil same spelled panter ruminate or tribal
bind the hand pull away lucky plinth, go for is enough

Struck know it. Uncial ledge flip transfer. Edit rise
still to misery same lintel paint invidious rate, partner
hazy tune risen, what he saw beast was their on placid
turning point. Band finger reply buy to brought but

Little hurt who saw less inside, her throat. Edge put
avail to enter concede them fan him own laid down more
by sorrow taken funded. Grow enflame onboard famish
later fizz rock carving convincement. Notable alight

Refusing ready fluid blinded or bond put. Track wand
extravasate nothing natty providing to bake by half, in
loft floating bet on it sift over him all his. Ever warm
for her so far flows list return attract same kneeling

Reniform contour perfuses anciently disappear in fly
toggle first told angle file discriminate. Or persisted
parted stack survivor similar sentinel option animate
timorous, far for fear same foot bunt the instrument.

As to for a mint action bare sender add mantic, brine cradle invention socket burden to saturate. To ramble his for glimpse for insert her his pinnate to foramen custom topic indecision failer for. At for was para fusing flim

Double-ported sternum groan, tun indispose sup waybill finer manse shorelines, her other mine through relent lanark additive. Gospel averted humour previous grey lighted skin as to train upwards to for metric over deal

Electrode hairline new to this. Skim the lines sure wing basal menthol now laugh now spit munificent tax timbre shared offspring peach. Give her she has will be forum for them summary hand in, seal reline incision particle

Select aromatic session, cease here to mind casserite ramp folder wasted in a cratch, into that. Did they wear better busy neck-piece jesting harmonious interlock bundle tag agreement oh same training striker defect. All same lock

Same neck asserted damp further to news sedate unset rim coding at for was give her, leather customised too lime reacher isolate plush. At for to. For bier who enter dispel narrow a will a foil habitual drench up facile to

Prime up. Nether fractionate androgen tease hid to lose missing hold-on, spoke reliant dermal actual admission plenty fruited capsule. Neither yet at mute decide or pine fish tremble bountiful a maze a bide for innocent bits.

Least berated near summon yet up putrid diaphragm, answer
for twist presentment fixity at a sample. Same gluttony in
attach, all some sign to just ours, as sanskrit. Did we off
have foretold sanction very datum, level untasted complete

Into botched distich at footing. Sway to dock to fail stripe
folding as up for, sash resume fluid cable lip for antidote
lateral bitten some same some fervent. Salmon in virus to
for privative scatter hairstreak bun canopy. Appellate on

Sadistic taken back off, bunkering at sacrament all the very
lend to beatitude vested. Imputed will summarise or resent
frame to ours wasteful to simplex game fuss disputed finder
to prosecute on our roadway. For theirs balance but pellet

Against lost unashamed, plain match. Ours did, very some
as until same enlarge no end no ford the jiffy pro beano
neck shimmer. Next to pre-list faster counsel to swim to
replace to keep in fours as to as ever galaxy sufferance,

Bench capsule like to die running and turning back. For back
for on for all at seven same verify pro digital fencer for litany
roll to agreement retreat, get by sublation sanctified upside
dizzy floats. Don't you see will flick coruscate empty pro-nip

Graft mission natal or maim, tour forswear same for left still
flare out to gravitate for ours at. Off as to ours same count
for sequel displayed, dipole entry suffix anodise summit insist
to. For offence same tune simper telling flow unrest for bent.

SUB SONGS

(2010)

But you like none, none you, for constant heart.

None but the Brave deserves the Fair.

As Mouth Blindness

Right now beyond the brunt yet afforded, gainsay now
for aspect close to residue, you'll see it there. Not full
scanned at damage so far, ridges debased fetch so plainly
or even gradual, nothing not due. Lay a hand over plus
to connote slant cutting life and knife, the road on offer
be level be sane two for one. Her voice was ever low, nil
transfusion plot negative to hum under par in the race
to tint and show a true recoil, you are there from the shot,
the star flinched openly.
                                        Promote by alarm not shouted yet
for note forgather, all fair in fear addressed, in train it may
be terminal antic to ready hold. Read the data, cramp tremble
in the jaw, parted tongue. Is this the mouth compare, camp livid
site protection, tick benefit if it works. Go to prone deliver,
right down now, roving like acid on count by drops, it is
enough contained. All this fully known towards breaking
moment, all under lever seed posted marker for donation.

        Would any or you stay up, for much
        or less degraded, organ freely ever nearly
        sotto sotto for a few. Adverse siren plash
        profile denounce, fad on
                                        fulsome tumult
        is said for tracking, right on the next step.

        Gradient scarlet be easy from the corner
        patch to stem flotation, crude output
        partial or gratify
                                upper rising dent for-
        ward, optimal. Need less lie on a pallet
        forage decrypt in its proven bunk scatter.

Say fable live fine table set, pro net bash your
head fond grind momently for bind tame roller
transgress disgust or bitten hit, what no matter is
compelled to pacify. Out grace crap oat out perfect
deployment, ramp to ramp motionless aim each shot
below current ascription. Copper thin steady on resemble
imbued with hues contest repeats
                                                fitting slice back
take a stripe knowing and vying on the grid, out-leap

padlock on a time study. Hateful repetition, fixed by
horror of its enclosing roulette chamber, echo of damage
renewed. Replace a broken tooth, lamp black ready upper
to lower snap organic discount. To be sure at wash made
by apparency in all-radiant bloom, keeping fit by some
definite assent thus bugged in a spin, in scope latch
to batch did they all say, salvation.

Or by dint of override take more each one
more for past further elastic deformation
nearly all unradical, allocate disperse what
anger remakes, lie in your broken bed if
form is contented with that, sky returns
in the birthing ward for ardent sweet
relief of singularity
                                        seed is to breed
placid transfer like to sake for it, pay
attention what else
                                        sweet you sweet
does hurt to regain bound each to each we
are sure by assurance are you will you be
is terror this else as of future rate break
munition link or else, one size unfitting
serves to self-afflict, anger no stronger
blind calm blind rage
                                        what there is there
is what else. Fear is beloved, in name of
its offspring, birth of denial in habit by
contraflow, each match destroys its part
for parting shots perfectly.

Time in the news to be not silent indoors, mouth in thought
shut up chew it the choice separates its like or is lame for
wounding in what is due would tell you suffused. For both
market done and stunned in face of, great lack breeds lank
less and less, claimant for right. Flatter by great expectancy,
for so resemble by just match, no less than fitting the race
to birthright and natal place, our lingo.
                                                            The place-work of
willed repeats gains a familiar tremor in jointure, we say
sustainable our mouth assents slave dental unbroken torrid reason
will commute previous and lie down. None more credible, mirror
make up flat sat batch pinup gruesome genome. Now get out.

Creosote Damping

All to get remiss nascent one by ownership on this tale
for depletion, early parade searches at counter-foil rinse
trinket just, as any. Take to a gleam close in member
places where so longer precious, in every last practice
sip and tap you get condoned at large or by hub dewpoint
fix to hit.
                    Covered by downy scents, their fortune lapped
in a dark penchant for friendship, seek beside what passes
for given temper instant repulse. Free up next visit revisit
revetment allophone lingual sample to curb for favour
forbid or redeem, lost signal considerate passive link,
to near adore. Covering plain

                              remission if on launch
        this return covers or will or pointer
        in self pruning leaf after last, if
        promised enough. In full to set aside
        a preachment biometric latter high note
        altered on ready, give in close fit in
        allowance
                    you will be clandestine
        will end well enough, it will be taken
        back transient by lip covenant.

This fever in crisis by the window, shadows excused now
by objects presumed inwardly outside, will must cast out
inducement abatement it's a swerve no yet slice contained
recluse demurrer, not a trace. On allowance fast linked
to handlist coupon redemption if yet if so new phantom
profile up in air and charge, unburdened.
                                                  As of why so
completed increment ride for trample or give fragrance
to many by number securely unfelt, to mask entry for who
wants this much. Loyalty to a dog sufficient steps along
the margin precision, march days into furlong plains
esteemed battery all guesswork capital voids none in
first natural trim. Time park the word given in and up
desolate and radiant, reason is free by need of mute over
recurrence, amount to this in total equipment. We are
known for this stuff frequenting by want of fixed prelude

as not on trade floor or more than.
                                                    That's the draw
angle of person, chink of detachment, love purified filter
incessant reduction, beg for giving fiction coverage tap
over the top entrance

                              mark for mark ever
        lined and proved, scarce roofed in
        pointed benefit never cut near severed
        sent for repair twin melt task early
        arrival. We shall give off, the tense
        option permits us frequent questions
        produced in sunlight on a tread, on
        time-rated stock passage.
                                        All so to
        change exchange none deemed captive,
        for prime crossing session him to claim.

By least wants less list for same for famous pitch
to get let off at the pharmacy, lithium to neon piece-
meal resurgence did you know inserted. Even in current
seconded lip by lip bespoke recurrent apprentice light
of ages of fit relief forswear
                                        the next past nearest offence
deserted by shades of glances the new day is to say over
the option limit banded rates just now along the skyline,
by the remit to set out blank hilt metal, rock for rock.

In Forge Incremental

Folded blade drastic indecision makes for burnt living cited
parallel defence of flight project, on the ground. In block
sweet lurid trapezoid creamy stretch first, single glance ill
ascends all yet higher and streaming bird-like, for rounding cant
stick dementive and back block. Together on the ground black
prejudge tart license, in the ground
                                        diagram for sacramental
pit some candid most up in corrosion not found there off pre-
sentiment excluded noiseless over desirous lower than sound,
set back defer his sear lucrative to bind up minor joy massive
on treatment bound in fast. Ecstatic sail shell mound finish

        to grant front alliance rainfall term
        spinning almost detached patter fetch
        on cotton honest reap intercept you nut
        scant ever oil
                        you soon all inclusive
        by the hive, the hide rail denial threaded
        and owned. Take clear and hold, blue
        light on top, resonator current and thermal

profuse tribulation out to the fifth less distinct, elective at
given perturb wrongful asterism outgrown fading to sink tungsten

        after this surely next impounded power set
        taken from, you adroit you lumber
                                                    even
        up-salt. On worthless grounds invasion if
        multiply errant wing tamping flutter spoil

brick dust to a foot. Can you see there, how settle to little on
where a step face frowning brow within reason break out a window
replete sound off, not our choice. Share on index traverse pro-
duce to random excess, trauma front lesson swooping predation
lock on best price. Instinct parentage commend finnick plural
come in there can you see, air not clear to flag bitter crack
down on it, ground to zero, when it comes & left you'll know.

Right then the turn declares and has a reason over the crest
to bring side to this almost silent formation, demand to write

a lifted will sobriquet always later substantial fixed replacement
easily deterred. Puff creamy delusion split asset never franker
remedy alert, you lurk, offer. Right now grounded foot needle
on drastic rebel certainty

to claim rank out pin
at range in time struck then to break
reddening panorama special. All get broke
blade counter black re-set multiple drone,
inference diminished here fly the window
to first this fort to the door
neither one
nor the whole clam will do, satisfy align
numeral redress perfect relegate in run
out of this or then far within our reach.

So simple to instill deduction and skim new ripple upwards
sans grapple insinuate pretended offcast. Down the link
reversed by a flighty inducement, that's enough no register
precludes effect on extended wings to care for this. On demand
cycle in carpet trunk all eyes forward proximate offence wend
flex replace and fit. Will for more to mix less, this rising
at dauntless fantastic renegement, upper cloud layers livid
with trails approaching azimuth.
Blinded by set aptitude
diapositive with another announcement the set entire ground
refuses volcanic substitutes, its flank fiery and sink unable
fund to find extracted tenancy, at par that's what you get.

Riding Fine Off

At the place new arduous and wrapped up generic trailing mock
persistent bay tell, dark shouts made final even decline to like.
Track fated to miss and sit out that's how to bat for both, few
for well all known all none, enough. They float over the start
grid order intimate personable inner logic, pin inducement to
the driveway, to rough trace the cloud line. For then or both
grew in ready plain view how invited too overlaid other volatile
front omission. That's how in
                                        room from pair to base, time
to rise as raptors accept procession sated foodstuff late on late
in token region. Know the whole win lateral pin better blind-
sight agree, all seen much then reduce will finally not fill
partitive crew benefit. Want for lack for distance fuel project
duct violence resigned easily, measure telic declination. Both
attractive sides habitat invaded folic austere too, grade them,

        gradual amounts in what you want more,
        take implant slope on wide array, wild
        surmise for substitute time to say how
        not affront yet, or fine oval form
        playout alter reject,
                                each one by one,

        window plan out visible twin acceptance
        has been there, up to surface ever wanting
        few out that's for now don't pine gravitate
        nor yet link, to get
                                fair assert pinny
        tell them, code for count entire rapid
        accident come on.

Further overgrown your own this time grimace insinuate how not
lined up for know better, chance derelict top planning loop first,
few all back assorted holding off. Held rough situate affirm cut
for cut down, to trim not yet fill we told them, few enough. How
best to say up to mark falling, each time said level soil debated
swim fume eager to find
                                    tell out plant limit, hormone refine
looking on forward bent foot want the strip forever, never less
over nor how best too and too for more

                                                            shadow infusion is
the truth declined. Lamps all lit up, cutting the skin graft
to lift off cell for cell, time yielded in open fit compulsion,
defer for passing wants, rolling evermore. Expense of spirit
output grant the best scatter ferment insult, have enough slowly
react affirmative to meet, each to fill upper tract shout relaxed
by pretension. Return to refusal continue I heard them say so

        in silicon versets did you, dapper onyx
        fancy ride plentiful and apt to form
        this rank of departure,
                                        trance state
        muted by fugitive distracted cries. Hear
        them all out picture that the kids
        debate which door, what for tranquil
        longing
                    to play riot catchment
        water slides up and up. Few hardly
        here now do the rest wanting for extra
        more spare to take and make, display
        all tips by day
                                in daytime say
        fear no more.

On the top row do you already no time refine to disclose even of
the passion blank, plenitude allusion do you, otherwise stupidly
good enough to lift a brow, of daylight often saved, most served.
Average at the doorway grandly seized by shadow counting off, in
geminal readiness not to slip where possible if not permitted else
auto-set. Both in force how not, if else, for a few abrupt dative
intact prints, from one over line. Mind less overt lucid all brand
marking at the front cloud-light, permanent
                                                            will you say, admit
first ulterior stricture indented to pay counting by darkness
shiny and visible up ahead. Go there free of room to say more
or less valuable, more taken back on time at this against what
follows on pitch, in front, normal accredited diminution would
be said profane intrinsic honest to batter off the other side.

Accept on Probate

More reline a sink failure in forward alongside on camera fawn
binder to hot wane loop banner, by grace undone it remit sky
halo do silo skip to store. None avail with a steel to languid
chase shallow ventilate tame digit pump, hardly been touched
gripe assume some game fine away this rid from inter-first born
forth, right or fly
                    very clever fast slam by level to lock sold
aspirant donate run over, denote value each lot gaining fine off
main device, using this model. Spurn less. Rifle peak edit, add
flip love unending fair, barbary swarm.
                                        All to mean as part
of him and need ever, further to reach reduce afflict he'll say
to stay shall they we know at rate going on ahead, on to after

sibilant right forth enter predict to join
been, voice turn. Mine allow it a nerve
sleek omit too, ostensible as a grand lover
disturb by definition, oh freely so touch
congest glow pack
                    limit over mark tide
over right over forth, further free up tape
groom lighting later, fill
                              on a fast brim
taper down does the rate slow not like
this to this, some game transit ever have
to run over, have there and more over stream
boiler, ask do inter-out implore eight permit
all's known to time or
                         ride up evident.

To make proud on grist in fit argue since not on limb true rate
undo one to the other most adjust quick add-on, edge facile
clip flap fond as ever hold and true, rote mendicant abstain
despite summit
                    list how far presently they'll go here through
undertow no more down, weak born to make allow fervent or you
such ever true more unclear in likeness nearness trip instinct
pattern gone away. Say so say less next to this asset low fixed
mean stoop can do inversion, cram fit scarlet may do can if will
so to say true may only.

May dormant only on self pilot lank
pursuit reflex sing for song no burden, remain on in course met
ill transformer frame alliance sub dread foot-plate recline proof
stay by, be tuneful ever glow right over. Omit middle part lift
upper to roof, benefit outward candidly pass accept rescript palm

some never yet will name, so flow ever
cascade live with that,
other part bit
out as off minor draft still like or make
loss in variance peace chatter sideways,
now cry say fall presume in native
alter the least
stain mental prism
bitten ichor, felt damp indicate why then
current train to view: surcoat look on out
ever in want fortify else in prison tell
all true to go in turn
asperge redundant
setting the plume elapse tell you on so

of because in place demographic mint fine personal tell learn up
true of trauma how like you, this ever now frequent at the door
where cries arise and are fed through. Led outwards for neural
fancy of fine allure. Spread forward
berate narrow aperture
strong to save a song, unsold tribute consist glory be broken
limit fragment in transit weather loyal on to raid. In chance
detain this and this more ready ardent look back review by fume
accomplish to brook run stake, a proof for here else glimpsed
it what that make over banish tell me now all append to quick

what this makes true or true
one to against what that, is
that now what, insidious it
is or will receeding on pure

joyous fury long reproof. Aim fill rudimentary idiot clamant fuse
in deep amazement in tremor not yet divided, count to foster up
replace beneficial made over not yours for yet furthermore part
for door frame wit fear to sing either not, fit pasture new-found.

These Nothing Like

Unblade untook finding reflected colouration we sail to tin ledge
alluvial minimal shield will to do loom undermost, obey calorific
in for stinted power cross endeavour. Sip minot droplet bisect
flung biff out sing
                                                    along similar save else other sat for work
nail that sundry on finish sand make speed bar give hand look to
greet at, partitive bicuspid till form rate to fell revere point
outside filiation. His thought panoptic
                                                                                    dilatant mental built
folding cult mill ream to wave freshet and on and lent fully wage
took fronted tabular least consisted, season from moist. They will
love to ever sound else save in to forgive, protect to hand on out
passion at kept bill listen reluct skimming in name his ours them
corrected ever to dust milk on thin at hand reduced, arc compressed
cardinal punnet yours hurtle tag separately hold safe off, sure
to less mitigate. Why you or, why will then you
                                                                                                known to room

for flow inset undertone cancel go live
vulnary advocate all best interest criminal
from harm or, hurted per hunt when
grasp it lay to rule deprive thrifted
river thin
                        assistive clarify best
element odd tell to middle biplanar
pleat licks bimetallic data all help
in part, whole to while capacity mild
of length of stay, put outside mental

have you, this skill can taunt own
best derive lawful lacking consort
might yet have, nodded wage upper
in name whose
                                    prise off to free whim
no other unexcused except from him
on his, portable come and go strain
harder recursive, migration either still

unseeking nibs to thought and grief excess abusive wanted at fill
longer attract best choice ger select or secret heart why bled

to beam sporadic all we know heroic play up to her simple blank
counted seldom, pure in here now is lower demise profile cut free
stay or part leave, ordeal power elect might yet just walk in
front sigh no time this for now up tangible, away temper no thin
no prime glad heart any
                                        redact tinsel ever dust who would back
in sufficient plea for, no reason example plea in place live tune
retained of, the mind only so hover elective nor just ischaemic
mild unable bland enforcement, do any know yet impart conciliar
grandeurs. All of these in flight powers wings beating upstream
skaldic counterflow her word who, with that. Amount to onward
imitate consign well protest should guard unlawful office all so
else public

            defrayed to beat in best heart
            motor timid all while, onset scanned

indignant cordon along never found radical in free bloomer often
too almost belated by ratify walk as, to when, by near able nodding
harder to want for to seek best at random footed, all over direct
waybill burnish ill clause rail deny for why none or again, nor at
all time-fast.
                        Give out temperate reduct permit strong refusal
hardly that, billet remonstrate also consented modify heart-beat
perfect relenting certify as qualify, be this emplace immerse by
mydriatic start to occupy offer partner save one time up in trust

            intent protruded, per inspect by alley
            perfume refer did spoil hold over cover
            pluck to shelter, all in all lace to up for
            organ proline
                                    diff all beyond sheen
            friend prospect true it, inject latent
            cue even conjugate winner often lame
            target slip under, half tunable un-brine
            flight for did blame or no, sign mission
                                    my port in this yours
            prognosis towards storm level utter crush
            stay by strain or seen to,
                                                lesion tremble
            atrial fray object transferred if of so
            mild loan rhapsodic, full stream up now
            forth profuse grate on the mind get in

sedge lost
                                    in view, lesson increase tip
re-save reserve liar to under next undo
assimilate relative darkness,
                                                                    all sill

across down prone altercate figure true up
flavour, said on solvent in steam unto
add bravely aromatic, bear out willing to
a lake from
                                    proof by for, intimate may
fin trail fin elation save if than, before
to when whom ahead nil by you more solid
under by lift along, by the split horizon.

Display young sorrel young flourish by work make lamented tonic
tablet passenger forgiveness back, not will off hold outlast to
transfer forecast broken if spoken for, decry anthem pastime for
of the earth or not defy so brash underneath
                                                                    stealth impoverish
will to treated: at sender crimson to portion clear and cold, event
with firewood turning as for, turn of speed clemency of wish to be
ever so to. Under wing-span as breech topic shelter each to mental
arc lain in, pair before service after promise, missive pointed to
suffix once patent
                                    lime for bid plunk imitate see all off run
on data yet over think into, is proviso silent nor at still confined
at length from, what divides in, know what find there shred to form
lasting folding incident of use fertile, nor bin defiant undeterred.

Thus to Look

Truth to tell if not maybe why produce for today
average by distribution aspect gain, size up forsake
at slant diligent park to park, along the dark path.
In the garden for bidden a turn, for you both readily
agree to mutual verified limit of glad principle, ever
never before give to take foremost attractive or wise
may not for that astonish should may not either way
on proof for dissentient flagrancy, ambient tribute.

Diverge towards both parts
face the forth trial intern
a tic running, into the bye
screen mutation half-lit
along the front. The next
place of care
                    is for sake
allow forth with stay lightly
in daze at grand esperance
hold the branch oh fast never
leave a token break out to go
down along, all close to same.

Outside noise turns across now, suffuse interior corymb
get ahead before glance to search all back profound lapse
nor gather yet to why say what do you know, track shadow
on the pathway. To let pass early before, to vary at slant
suddenly cast frayed but for held twice to count up, at more
recognised assumed sequel promote this, there is a bleed
full marked here to seep with attraction with long tremor.
Don't fear more the way not clear never so as felt now
assented trouble nor liable will out break already at brim
to part run over, never to leave out in ready or in bloom.

Skim for Either One

As with suddenly so owing, by enrichment born in mind to famish
talent do this all now, all intense furnish wall splayed meet
to converge for a nullity this did you assisted fine in vain,
matter green repentant soon make up. More soon to caution when
up pick up set in water so, gratify salience remind to follow
simmer nul infill detachment
                                        are loose will strong cancel ban
grandiose together, as to wrong finally summarise life task, by
any stretch immense push them tight down crib central. Yours
and mine banded deepest pine request very close purposeful shut
division border, alarm so many circle points imminent paint strip
as grateful, as replacement stand-off spectrum location broadly
lib to might yet, terminate accrue bonded to life for one or slow

each pretence all up tappet long detained to heal, ever still wait
timorous unforward till regressive and simplify, stage mutilation
under flinch as by eye not
                                        so lost to lift in punic skyline

have to be quicker, none for them
of regulate, suspected gift for trim
scatter up pilgrimage restitute your
play to plain view this
                              for grain bet
fruitful chime husk semen bench win
offertory remaining, surrounded in full
agreed essential prowl distill or
other mine inlay. Propound. Infer
ever on hold comical deep trivials

astringent white circular gaining
for a share to, yours this one is
near own blank or grief on outer
to the cloud. Butt rooted sail

did so full yet swell testify, rally in forbearance dictate link
thought run across be quick elemental shift flash over, hinder
serum in view extricate voice of damage. Despite the wave fit
assembly vitrine in front again none by silt reminder and forage,
the mark up to up hanker seating blinker trip overmore to sight

invented day plenum,
give out in shower unfilled. Stay in mild
band rim time throat for hoping all their diremption, gratified
uplift flow skip to blood descended, on the turn, suppose her vent
from this unwanted or confident, no call for extra printing as like
to be tapped. Anti-save out from
stiff slope even here crampon
keep your nerve struck metal you know too rapid just this, attach
what team what fur toil near dark now alter shook crepitate short

primal on the ledge talus. Survey from back, holder medial within
on brow temper terrific wasted brow twin assisted, will she will
don't say acid fortune. Just don't say that lagging bob parity
you know the whole death at work or break home later dispensed,
loose most breathless both look and cling soon. Luminal panegyric

as modern likewise sufferance open
grief mild played gather up for type,
seed to limb sanguine, truth perfused
of eye granular bolt, seeming
all in
for a nullity intrinsic
layer cantus prompt eloquently
hold me, sing this fine song all
by volume told as drenched up
in cries plain incremental furrow
go along, tell the line,
bind
the sort some found sweet brow
cross mind breeding lock adventure

twill annexe loan in fibular setting what's inside pin to merge
for parity. Blood group extreme plump whimsy go on deck, grasp
to be done as all founded, in a likeness by worry ordinance, tell
so for them each exactly risen. Is it known
to do this by
quick exchange in narrow span time portion, do qualify praise be
inseminate antigen fill the wave marker susceptive on principle
for a bond tied sold, organ tested no pin no piper, just not yet
wrong until then on a turn to band halted and dizzy why for that.

Along the Wall

From one to one up to one, from in little shade let to slide,
in once singular call to announce unless origin unrevealed
wire transfer unshare, fortress pitch key consumed in flutter
to beat quit file coinage bring, as yet can. From three up to
five to not seven, now an age likes for short stick coinage
parallel then for many then down stand or take
                                                            blood how so
long prowess come to this, sufficient total not two for sever
one off under, fall incline opal deem imposed quiet in forest
disclaim voice stencil hand, flock manifest, seraphim sewn echo
tinted stepper. What sense will
                                            to blink stop at stamen glow
mine other time heart rushing afford to know, as yet the lark
rustles in ripe grain all the better expectancy, is under time
lays to angle way to day seen on overhead, amend valve thump

dotted notes skiff flotation who can say as far short can. Don't
look, there as can for as far see took as mind in eye spread,
lip till flavour turned, give off bat-like along the near wall.
The wall there line fallen to stay, go down fine soon rain hold
your arm, along the wall there:

no one fanned entrained fluting
sing-song trapperish, arm more
warm not in flight, mouth in
free smile order one confine to
small shade moving,
                                grill set
past impost flame arrival or
creak blank stock down, dormer
claimant opulent
                                shove out
basement hand to hand. On
stem tone the wall still holding
as if as, if time unrabid will
do as done, bunk loan parted

closer to hand now or now, eyes found, tending replacement more
cold to cold ever in breath pause, hear go away as say probable
for shade else in pulse blood round frame lining skimmed, held

there air to pass, settle if try, whistle and sing, the fullest day
along. Nip in keep this train
                                        of not to yet, say none as she
for she now all for by few will her sparks of crimpy up firings
ever listed, in face to lean and wane in face of look to take
to moist bookish found
                                   as for soon, outward allocate locking
between thumbs opportune. Or sink counter tap you know now what
strike off a face of free passage just cut it, a slice don't speak
don't breathe ice near dry now then later for other unbound. Up
already in arms so primed what leave off face turned or bear for
darkness love bounded up for cut for, send out coin age dazed
unloved to mind, work trait for frozen taste of, fresh chat blood.

You know it front elevate
trace from the side to pro
file as lost for,
                    face fast
lies down to fall there on
souls decayed and on cut ig
frag no meant for,
                         plate
mit over speak, then to
see words drop sack blue
to dye, for
               your watch get
what tell oh love be so
blind to send to not roam
alien in cornfields, again.

As to be all known each time one, to one seen to find and so now
to send is burned by love turned itself is known, none more grist
to wage time flex for temper alight thrown down under butt scorch,
corn full of fire as men in oil dress swept from, hydrocarbon in
digest evermore in chat fume, to regain from what then or not
is done to be, known ejected all to spend ash ready support mesh
the more given the more to spare
                                             there willing, hold to spring
off block down desire zone each in peak interdict power line from
sand rending, as or shale later chat through swap mimic heartland
blood clinic new drained, time found ever viewed never yet mine
the fond and true not seen yet now but look, by the wall is known.

6 UNCOLLECTED POEMS

Frag (1)

braganza for this patch brutal advocate to permit
flatter tint, revise to PURITY absent while felix said is
so and called. And callous extreme allege to spot out per
syrinx partnership to SPOIL fusty burnish now greedy
now, for then too, rabid flume make a lapse. No entreat
often meeting open pear-group random form quick square
so to WRECK frill angelus, a collar mere shedding but
arched rent in cry habit. Done like that catch to chill
facile surrender evenly why pretty later, why distribute
upper to TOYLAND risen crudely brag off. Tack offense
gaining new speed links at sitting residue downfall
overt distaste fabric go there, to END worn or muffled
thread minimum dispossessed paregoric next outplaced.

Frag (2)

Perform perfume fleece for instance set up
to gather a target over vital at the organ bank
evince left for sworn particulate and laminar
extradiction what you want. Most to brink
subsidy or break bend first, little dredge
horizon fast cost sail over paper its venom
count never risen agree to that, predict for
a planet pelt. Arbitrament ditto who should
break share your own. No hint to lessen fresh
storm, to assemble in payout just have to print
the rest, their subsequent easing revelation.

Never the Same

Down rein florid harvest drop to drop for graphic incident posture. Guarantee moment most for accurate cast slipper animate, start warden, guarding so hammer the bell, new strike short night. Institute two pillars font to mount another or several uncounted often numb planned for outwork collimated, each brand to catch up sped to this enforced by arbitration blip. Ever binomial gradual namesake do this no more the heat, fear the sun stroke afforded when wet or perfect alloy fusion, for bakewell paint acute ought avenge easily his turn outwith silent nor fasten as frugal instant permit; site down promote above the gang riding, shop green lineup bar costed now withheld you me thy brother tags demised distance bit to bit. Ring callous on frontage if first if frost batting life crossweave, for willing to kill them from the airwaves out to right backwards, from the source.

Soft to flow these waters followed in laps to spoony fate, attempt melisma felt on tip touch in line is it crude division by fibre scan, strip legal obdurate melt already both known. Surface retrieve blemish own set average disputant, offend parent over this age tripper, to sell down by cascade saline drip mercy, willing time yourself through attachment resected. Pickup solvent glottis maroon tied off feverish keypad fumarole faucet grin overt skin graft smile forever, ever listless taut abduction refund sepsis noted other weeping passage ample reflected, don't cover stir over also impute and flexed. Mediate inhibitor thin damage precursor affront to recognise why foreign cellular lost all beyond, all found into the finish.

Map to mantissa fortunate on the ground find local at slave casting skill for fluid slay waves cutter day up ahead, plumes bespoke sweep tepid in fine essential ash upon ash. Here ever offset covert starve and die to, new to see abrasion focus as elder bring fast issue. Intermit rigid synapse listed to bleed to, prolong average furnace overcast presently all guard want with inimical hurt claimant rise up fit corroded; foremost carding pitch target fresh there froze abet, close by, tag enough.

Explain so from simple ruin follow sentence thereto address, that gives out grief upon grief so rotted off with starter's clay upon clay. Ready enter native downmost to draw the pair, phantom reduce nasal rampant fingering torn out and spoken additive and rider swap foam; righted sway cut written in vain lapsing go colour, wet. At renewal at default lay for slower prodigious scraping sickness brave annoy mistook summit depletion gnaw the primate steroid click exertion. At for at for tenant linger aim credit finish branded soon token to lie, arm along arm for panic signet dispute as belated returning by store by in such as enclosed recent open battery, rising in fast in clay again forth to take assume digitise boundary score. When on these points all metal did prevent their casual ever discounted inclusion for the rest forest affixation, all known before cramp hidden over dilute incident, presently. As yet prepare to foresee prolific body in gaping remission rounded by drive anklet filmish jut to grind, down through splint under foray countered by this previous injury.

Another over bound later finish secluded next corrupted even additive moralist. So far hard to be tied bearing its step up swelled for broken off into terrace underworld transfer, record what try when said, out of true admission. Live reckoned animal front in plain delay, how many adjunct yet new dismembered *a priori* would bite submit atmospheric and playful, concealed first this goes, goes under in link ready promoted quick to lay or quick too annealing. Burnt frame indelible credit path, line up hot fume notional gather part side for made day by day accused.

So to foremost burn is sessional charted, by deck pause out to life rib to duct ignored, break line token, for break habit for broken away. Sky clip ozone in its park flagrant lidded, stack arising over incision. It's known hidden apart and flicker bread washed, decouple spark fissures convinced to catch hot wick at cost margin, due excess aperture colder hue. Rainstorm no trace no in time fill up agile felt this attested inference motionless cut out overjoyed; what to go to exchange made for revenue entity, to further have sent out foremost name-plate outside on notice for colloquy along the fascia warnings, thermal to clear. Breath to breath, broad promise in effigy undone distal frame, will decide upheld its overdue report profile.

They Take What

They take what, flicker by party
stable after opening after chair mounted for sight
to claim decrease, at race to go over more
slant grimace prefix hot colour boil
assume gestural retort, not yet
mine reposing or flat
torrent bit absent
fission charge orange ready
astrictive invent first capacious do towards
do better match their finish newly impartial
time click unattach filament
does know will acclaim
revert
ultimate credence by this by no door ridgeway
weaving in turf family by one, to yet infer
not get more, for tempest instant
payment encomium
ask at give forewarn
promise aside, for it for level
bid frequency any's to let
at table pair for pair diffuse however much
perform frontal less to less adjunct either
one knowing this.

Stub-Para

Stub para to float attitude formica lax civic slice
for, slice after phantom interim cut over fading

presented at forth bladed cancel, mast over to give
over up rending surface, raid along said govern when

haze may not so drastic meatus calm the upflight
by fold of durance theirs nothing meant, air slice

deflected in trio. Affirm to form inset as persisted
all intact street banter brick intersect yet broken

passing accident by knife brow, at factive premium.
By for by now surplus elevation resume unharmed,

quicken in sprite mind for down predict later incision
saying the out frame on time parallel void to summit,

upright present candour.

Did you know any
                    of care to
see next in step over
                         in reason
for the price or
                 more to act
day long incident
                   pervaded

Premise vestige commonplace pang you will cutter
deriving felt, indurate ground edge native for by

this attentive or dismissed rage cloud, tangible
prime finish or fast avert first insert mental aim,

trim resection as per hot fume pace to ice or dented
flap anger strip, pleated return for convex passage

assort implicit penury availing too far to out, evident
granitic person to person simple or never in fault,

driving all said quite full done up, even over raise
the hour provident incursive, diverge in sufferance

to fix practice any distort bank tree bark by frag-
ment burning to dark imminent, shutter here on-stage.

Alveolar Shunts

Attempted dry loan to flying chill aleut under
drastic first spot. Soon denies reduced access,
makes overt mockery a sample for yet no time
now tested fine distortion, makes better in
slanted converse. Pursue both channels diving
visibly, ripe inside next far grips one down.

Or floods evenly, trammels adjusted in a daze
prompting relative denial, off-shore. Aggrieved
now and now ready, running half way outwards
to improve the fainted bolus with huge, altered
from halcyon flotation; shaded by its top arch
or flattened across tips in volume underswell.

Too late to traipse in assumed rage over this
re-hired brine syndicate, knowing the going rate
but caring less for a moderate ticket, decked along
by enhancements of vapid choice: either way. Pat
festoons offer by converged premium infill a limp
delivery, tricked in a deft punnet bunting.

Take out the first and last not yet, never now
for the week-end demand terminus in switch back
high spots dry off earliest, turning at a swag
allocation tight in reverse track down; torrents
affirm their set device in the formula brewing
a mother's double hike feud, infringed dispute.

KAZOO DREAMBOATS

or, On What There Is

(2011)

Along the corridor of near frequency I saw willing and discrete the season not yet for sorrow advanced, nearby not yet even so inference to claim. On the plate in soft season to rise hungry semi-apt for supplement will to set affirm this wit at will for passion reflex acutely, I saw it amount in plenteous access burning by folly markers right to the crest. Brilliant clusters horizontal to their points of origin steel-tipped, spark to a platform in debit fortitude. For company looking to the same to tell as grasp fixation would I run fast enough into this lavish obsession escorted. The ground divided by itself falter you near leap to trial, longwise proofing, imprint close to arrived in force to high stealth back off who'll agree. A glut run together polishing the wall facing, the metric surface non-generic endurance assumed did fancy by entrance if harmful, shade upon phosphor passage net agreement cut to a shred. Cell fusion reputed am to be averred will be said out is the corridor opportune, prior to main luminous discharge. A pig in spring for sure would know better, take your pick, ascribe this uprisen to season's tactic shall shock turn to view counting frenzy, shall be company to make fuel clamour critical. At mass inlet dissent I saw ahead to eyeshot reach exacted coating fricative and locked parallel then tended, long for longing set-back, exhaled. Could be joined at promise confection with or without, don't wait yet do what cannot pass with or without don't wait yet do what cannot pass up to its end.

We'll make folly in pledge to stem-division as decisive for cut to cut across narrows, passage throat offensive in try once only or by defiance vectors, filmic particle mist de-graded nor yet conjugate in mission. Always desired by zero option wide-eyed node employ cloud droplets *en masse* phantasmal, near in to scar friable distinct cash-back nexus, on the plate. What's to be got contagious dendrite hit conductance ran fast even flash-like, punished in stupid glory by ever the same to say. Known to be, yet again firm as it looks, as if so marked by aperture no less patent. Blood pulse my view agency by force fed array calculus dot by dot fully able to be underfold. Enclave admittance rebuke to sender, mother to brother window too close to close.

Who would save temporal occlusion no discount for loyal reckoning yet saw in this open flash delusion of false glory how ever else for sweet temper child indifference not to want to want this. Refract histology slit second outward decree rocky attachment palpable by finger ever-grip. I saw the slide markers they were sticky and concluded what was, near enough mounting up as fast would say manifest enzyme in game reduced, stupefied like men braced for denial, each in proper step. All now lateral burning fence off at will foremost to link repulse, to limit of done mania assembled across cosset for slag and reck as a nail kingdom who will inflect this full upper declension of substance. Wandering in two minds later rather than sooner found there, better a little loss to say, than ever a long sorrow on the day after, abridged to clear. Some near witness now so wants to make it work, a most fantastic set-up! Zero conductance makes little of nothing, little at all events as yet were, but nothing not so fast or in face bound transitive reversal displaced. By seed construction flying in fertile air sporadic clouds to draw breath counted by rumour, I saw it there flit past, calling for likeness or hardly as much more like. Relent will the property inherent starkly, by presumed necessity right at the peak there, princes of gorgeous folly stand all around, with their inhalers. Nothing shall come of continuous diminish but across its boundaries if they exist for sure everything is possible and can be computed, speak parrot and to discernibly good approximations.

I saw it upmost, to know partly is by now not to unknow else with borrowed light induced by origin perpetual, by passion flat lying and tumid for advantage, for all or nothing is the play sequence left over. What is enclosed over the time lag partition is included also, all by so incremental as fostered in acts of next recension. 'We now recognise that "empty space" is a turmoil of electromagnetic waves of all frequencies and wavelengths. They wash through and past us' or say, 'we are all bathed in this "vacuum infinity" of virtual electromagnetic waves', provoked and then quelled in reciprocal perturbation. 'The natural motions of the charges within a material will necessarily create electric fields whose time-varying spectral properties are those known from how the materials absorb the energy of applied fields.' For fields thus filled it was no dream if yet so dear I lay, pronate attempered pronoun sounded dear heart how suckled, hot pies! be blithe, for birth integer broad alleged awake among the things that are, in spoken footprint cordial how alike by probe to lit shelf grains. This is and must be the thought of nothing that cannot be apart from what is, neither as or by cause, what it is to be, relentless and unsame. Bilayer notice not be so enticed

avid at their ice floor inverse-sixth power of distance spitted
aggregate sarsen mouth entranced, grit, like to creep into a slit
cabin longing in the slumber basement. Now goggle-eyes revert
or new Poseidon nudging to click by its sonar filtration charm
of such birds take to wake and be taken, arm's length residue out-
put gravamen parrot dictum. I sat softly down won with wrong for
true line up purchase, pair try to shake in full spring leaf refused
against metal over a rock pavement abraded by parallax in opportunity
dropped down, in earth flooding, mother admit me by dielectric promise
of this field.

> In all matter there are continuous jostlings of positive and negative charges; at every point in a material body or in a vacuum, transient electric and magnetic fields arise spontaneously. These fluctuations in charge and in field occur not only because of thermal agitation but also because of inescapable quantum-mechanical uncertainties in the positions and momenta of particles and in the strengths of electromagnetic fields. The momentary positions and electric currents of moving charges act on, and react to, other charges and their fields.

Their spontaneous cries in this field told him an older tale, to
deprave thy person with a proud heart crying out for self-being
in struggle for joy, in belief relieved for coherence instant, all
are lucent in branch forbear titular within forgiveness display by
instinct, all boastful without which deprive active foramen matching
for short time to crisis of lucid relenting adamancy, it is you know
you do none else for this you'll never leave.

Or left to climb
for short time disposed client to transmit, agree counterparty already
torn out attract waymark fondly accusing all objects of all thought
paved with joy and stirred in a hefty basin. Right there assist by
measurement bonded base-pairs idiotic grace-notes summed in trillions
is that all enough to find out, travel the floor boarded over in
displacement sets, uncertain at zero-point difference. Inverse first
power variation, square of the separation, the law of relation and
boundaries through time. Solemn longing did you hear the split
creaking, margin to dig here ever or not, or not here now binnacle
patched up in filament casing granted as ridicule almost retained.
What's to hesitate between one and another is that what's to be con-
strued instead also not for choice, 'an act not found in nature',
elevation of spirit as hesitation guides the wandering thought in
their breast. A fire there, 'das fährt von der Erde' uncanny sunset

mounting in hot ash consumed from these as so much, you get triple points if you guess the connection. Look out for dread it's your red letter speciality, bunk of delirium day-trading. 'External causes are the condition of change and internal causes are the basis of change, and external causes become operative through internal causes.' Mourning does become the law but not this one, to be is not to become or at fault with moment practice was what can I say I saw, darker than ever dark to be.

New to some rabble discontented in other eyes for sure vitrine resentment crack up the harvest florid to its animation, afforded when wet at gated hedge entrance. This play of a B-road to dissipate sentence bell hammer thread of food even profusion. The molecule is severally pandemic, indecision layered off by step quanta or this or its hit. Win the single atom can be considered to have a fluctuating rotating dipole moment, nothing changes for this is the self-change of nothing as at saccadic variance, substantially composed of its moments in transit, in the field most winking and unrespected. Get what it is, for who is it force fielded, spectra reversed another day older be calm all at call to envisage. Nothing that is not nothing will do it, across a vacuum referred by its overt container, from inside to side placed out interdict risen fortress narrow alert summation vectorial index, do alternated position even integral even averaged through time. The cause of sequence presumes its afterbirth I saw this risen as later to reason yet lateral honest buds inflect by intrinsic foiled necessity, not to be is not already or yet nor reflex in temper of state to be a dream of what can be known in view, not by you but for your line to be sure each vacant by each the other or mine.

> There is internal contradiction in every single thing, hence its motion and development. Contradictoriness within a thing is the fundamental cause of its develop-ment, while its interrelations and interactions with other things are secondary causes .... It is evident that purely external causes can only give rise to mechanical motion, that is, to changes in scale or quantity, but cannot explain why one thing changes into another. As a matter of fact, even mechanical motion under external force occurs through the internal contradictoriness of things. Simple growth in plants and animals, their quantitative development, is likewise chiefly the result of their internal contradictions.

Is mine or mine, or is as does all so, also, dielectric and profuse, delusive upwards avoided: what is not this is that's not flowing ever in time of unit change rescinded, I saw seeing itself dissolve rail to contest bounded, to scale by inversion not exact vented out to porous incline, a quantum ledge of known intercostal exclusion. Thus being-itself deletes far out its consisting notational self-hood, the nouns illicit as bounded only by neglected states as not coming or going to be or be relinquished, the inclusion of un-never at contradicted mutable edging.

Can this or be was it moreover for this incision in dropsy yes not ventral not assented sold OUT in mere song-like retrieval, give way with no-name in appearance decking as a whirling swarm of gnats in soft summer sun at the edge of the outward forest, infolded not time after time still less perpetual by false appearance which is the true-fast semblance of falsity, indued and ever-doubtful. Our morning hymn this is, and song at evening echo confuted by shared antagonism, implicit not by next coming-to-be as the world is transformed in feature full of folk by what is it not, time-locked against spokes in the cycle of saying so. Indicative ridiculous also, won't you come home Bill Bailey before a toast and tea, scumbags! reptiles! the old folks just better stay at home or lose their reason too, mine and yours loaned against non-interest, souls implanted by necessity smooth turning upon an axle you'd not know was not granted its near life to be there, on-site in foam, I saw no less than these things right up on the peremptory shore line.

Funded in borrowed fun by cowardice, replevin bonded expiry hit your head on bricks which are in common knowledge the haunt of accident, of the ten green bottles lined up to smash, a fable of depletion to target zero. As for why and ever should the no-green bottles be green and how many are they that are not so or no longer, how long is that or not or graded to frequentative zero, is that a gain each time and how many to no many the very fewer soul of recounted folly done to a crisp. Don't mash the gravy they hang so high they will not come down, to not come not down. Foolish to rescue departure out for its count, by necessity of accident, the sequence not seated on time but constant part for more whole, the final negative is not end but sum, hold on to few enough marbles every man jack amongst the flowers. Grace to end and turn a line by aptitude inhalation therapy sub-frequent, never fervent rev up wrap up speak the words hear indicted by process, by trespass better to run the course of this arbitrary schedule at each sentence handed down as a tremor birdlike against fitment, leave of sense. By the method of outside-inside subscripting, on the free energies by surface proximity, pay attention to thickness not else needful lower case name-style all for choice. My sunshine parlance would be donative adoring laterally, raise spirits in water egg cancelled, the tense ever deceptive never topaz febrile shift. For not is the bilayer extruded from itself as the power of concretion, never later rather than sooner but continuously not now nor for ever postural pretty much, totally not all alike because not total even by transcendental count to integration over difference, where divergence cannot be itself nor not be in convergence to zero redeemed. 'The contribution to the interaction is screened down to about half of its nonretarded strength', dual connect is not complete on every side, shot through a slit of whiteness to interfere by absorption back from outcast, whole-body dielectric separations give heart out to mind, these are charge fluctuation energies that sum only conveniently. From itself auto-immune the bit force of covalency is uniquely sexual, what is not is to be what is and due, corrosion impact seminal and sublingual dissolved, shudder to part, part to whole, not complete. Enter the time stream arbitrarily, chance by random necessity in its flux at concept of unfinish: the lamp decays by renewal, floating wick not within question or scarce at all for tenderness.

Did you see this any of this is the tense by default nor yet free of the mesh there, of time-lines intercrossed for lateral insistence adhesion to insurgency, to strew the whole way with excuses of glory, and yet their portion of zero-point taken incandescence transmissible, as did the wise steeds carry me, drawing my car, the chariot at hand as well the car Love guideth, top-drawer upper case for first-class passengers in this ride. *Allegretto con brio*, pursuit of constant values relented in the order of things commanded and performed by proxy and truth to tell hold this hand tightly, finger-message traced and entranced in haptic feedback condition. 'Monuments refer to a past but they are often directed to a future', to be made open is to know of its closure by way of being made, the way of derived difference semi-permeable by fate looked out for, not now viewed. 'To shoot a series of regularly spaced seismic lines' will show what is not rock, its porosity and pore throatage, by rotation of view orthogonal to virtual plane, bedding and fracture. What is not rock is voidally known, contra particulate in a time stream diffused evenly through a reservoir pay zone, the colour of amber said way up in free air distraught: blight to light did you see for the trail denied and sheer off its trolley. Kerb star max, terraced into a slope ink the platen acidic proof by knife brow since retracted, said sumptuous for a reason. The pro-division of cell line recession is a violation of natural arbitrage, bonding against its excluded identity not with itself plane temper countermanding by pronoun slices abyssal. At nil band without redress cross rated flow back in striate hot-pot fluid turbulence, measure this against flat signal periodic. 'Even in formal correspondence with the old way of summing incremental contributions, the resemblance is in the distance dependence but not in the coefficient', however will be launched for adhesion at natural frequency top-sliced.

Catching up subliminal sudden paroxysm, power law in amble mounting rotation is a limit step yet dissimilar rank for rank notorious, what you know is not rate-dependent on blood flow through knowledge organs nor yet superscripted from a divine theodolite hard-drive. Wave good-bye don't be stupid, the location is obscure because coherence is not spatial and is without meaning beyond its scrap value, every fly on the wall could tell you this. Afford all the same get what that to walk at temperament full press, its tenor listing presume in spirit tantrum gravity at or for birth replacement. To a turn done over hit graphic not to scale imitation voucher, I saw all of this emetic cosmetic rapid broth, at the plug.

> The scene again attempts to achieve both diversity and unity by subjecting the six-note chord, as had earlier been the case with the single note and the rhythm, to every possible kind of variation such as partitioning, inversion, redistribution and register changes of the note .... Here again the overall structure of the piece is obtained through the use of the traditional symmetry of a ternary form, in that the six-note collection appears at only one transpositional level in the outer parts of the scene (although, obviously, in all varied forms) while in the central section it is transposed to all the other levels of the chromatic scale.

By whatever means in retrospect the summation energy 'became an energy per area that varied as the inverse square of the separation' reverting to 'the expected inverse-sixth-power dependence of point particles' under conditions of wide separation. The play of unity as a mental device sides with denial of its self-image, contracted to open a hazard sentence with subject deletion at null point of its entry. To speak of forgiveness, a cloud may be forgiven yet not forgive, participate to shed excuse by transfer to ransom, and yet still the moral apex is contested, generic virtue just a name for the apex above its snowy brow shedding its tribute with a sound but half its own, things by dielectric bonding, its outside voltage source proportional to and opposite in sign to the charge delivered by the intervening material to its outer boundaries: and what wert thou, like this brooding vapour, if no more than vacant, than no more is more because than is the limit to love, of its favourite name, the check for chicken in a basket. Don't end there for Brent-crude declension ever uppermost by famous agent out of reach captured to line enhancement, word lackage at horizon long for longing and dredged with ethic partaken: zero point flooded with lunar shadow across the eyelid.

Whether attenuate permission stay option harvest to lateral memorised already on skid, ever will paint to tie get both tonic it is the dipoles of moment or the medium is vacuum, or not, tag in retard. Lay down for loyal self-refusing, all to see as the stream of its parts, dummy prince of equity on the axis of real frequency or an even function, out of snuff. Ride furiously along mounted temper, gradient suffusion. Intense in the full shell to be resonant with being to the side without name, being this as like and liking, convergence of bone aware I saw the passion not mine in calcium, frontal datival by heat of unexpected profuseness, so-called by transportation. Being joyous conveyed at submerged reduct closest to zero, no retardation screening a cleanly inverse-cube function goes to unity via transform at itself minimum unlocked, of no more than its moment. The more again no more, its no to be more and joy unhinged it is finite by love in the shell of unnamed outside repair to a whistle. It must bring being molecular and subvoiced, no sense in it or to it, partition purified by dirt. Reach to search by caressed pet lust bearing semen offered on substrate already overjoyed at too by suppletion, too also by its excess dissolved. Fluid in reference, intense with inertial be so to micron outlapse told arm to arm.

Tongues perplexed by speech of fluid memory in knowledge self-made, go for it and better be told, tolling this time be, it is necessity in its own embracement. Close to uttered void, unity in nothing, else. Window not found. Joy so low at base count, new-fertile as self cell to another sold on to give like fragrance and volatile upon the air. The bearing point of love is joy its dipole infusion in shreds of the shell lattice all along also along its boundaries, all famous there and to be known, bright start in motherhood relented. Almost semi-sweet under resinous glaze solved

often amount to frequent, the eyelid in deference to, animal butter
solids. They'll rise up will rock you unperturbed in this corbelled
chamber ready into the world plain. Have been to will, hysteresis
asserts in full its moral latency and are told in repeat fusion,
this. Suffix is from its accident of screen shelter by overhang,
right and left ventricle in contraflow: '*And riuers creeping /*
Downe a high hill, / Stand often still, / Rocks them backe keeping.'
Standing room in the car, fares please they do will sway to hold
tight further up ahead, love potion number nine momently singing
aloud. A look across the room you there exchange of like air
its spring proportionate to small space its frequency markers
sonant in here outwards bearing just nothing or much just a look
or two, too, limit pair nebulous. Resolve in a trace payment
because own even to few flying like infinite darts birds of a
feather swish folly of infinity drawn close apart textural limit
by known weights and excitement. Optical glance fascia mix, ready
calendrical pulse over pulse up neatly undilute I saw not to say
ex silentio indigo searching in off blue next to none; and if
it be resumed without purpose and before tax wasted, soon see
to its frequency tune bicameral aggregate replaced not even so
now by first-round enter substitute.

Inside surrept markers
refold within solution index of refraction but beyond fitment
mostly outside just cause, and then put out and then, some other
exclusion makes its links to poverty in the field, bare of
laurel they live alone can save and rot, with an elected
shifting misery. The fair field of want for pitch just a
foot-hold drained by the screen to its pittance ungraded at
work avert how then triage delayed stab wound drainage not
reconciled, scarce blood in this group attachment. Warfarin
by need plug the host, all is known. Thought is free, nede
ne hath no lawe, from severance or drawn conflation, in the
limit of close approach liminal not boundary, variance closer
to its own zero word for word reflected, can 'pay for' this
mass displacement against gravity. Work done versus separation,
what will also wouldn't or by condition signed, deferral touch
pad the cycle neither closed nor offset in folding back electron
shell will also not known. Further back to scale destructive
factorial not rationally punished: 'Nature is the specific
property of any substance, and Person the individual substance
of a rational nature.' Shall be toxic outside the moment for
poisonous future, ask forgetful, ants make their turbulence

of species but cannot want to pity at any cost to the full system, clouds above them laden with contaminants. Heavy gunfire also rational by target heart-work intercepted onshore line securely drilled, to make convergent cascade outflows. On a hybrid debenture allowance violent by proxy, big shots to get enlightened giving way, by force merely indeed, fields laid low and unfed. Where placed cannot be defended, not the walls of a city but the wills they enclose, pact inclusion. Do you recall the birthplace in bright sunlight its gleeful partition knowing the unknown a child accidental of kin, of its time I saw back to nothing twice over conscripted, on every green spray, and the larks they sang melodious, canorous in every high degree.

By long-term chorus in mnemonic continuance each one x 3 part towards whole as from dawn to dusk the law of identity if A then B not equal by opposite declared incident neck of the woods relative to separation. Rejoined by fable to its apert panegyric they told us just as whereas knowing by count option wing feathers, all they did they would did to have not break canted to will broken abstain first back be retuned mercy limit close enough to reach after, were or not allude given out aileron metal valence track bonding sibling nodal no milk at would enter out clear nor inside well. Rid prominent is so joint to yet not did, this training endemic pass next sumptuous under been forebrain commission ours repast to be in reach or grains moreover exotic trim love of the hand. Don't flew foregone alterior nail up for why into not this icing front flaps cathodic salts nil willing, allergic presume ill to say to cage in way plastic orbit near-perfect forward missing by sail debit in never permeate. Float permit colloidal disjunctive or foam to battery, negative ions layoff not for truth this reversal been off done instinct ear flips, any more. Few been to, is or ford to be done, over reversion adequate speech-only on platform uncompleted, towards dispersed rival peonage right up frozen to notice in fragment or uniform but, natural but, not ice this time is found not for level settled or so.

Not but circumspect preview divested but, reset in surface zero to its crystallic marker interest:

> Under given conditions it is possible to derive the electromagnetic interaction between any two materials across a gap filled with a third substance by use of mode sum-

> mation .... The zero-point fluctuation is an immediate consequence of the uncertainty principle. Observed for a time inverse to its frequency, an electro-magnetic mode or degree of freedom has an uncertainty in its corresponding energy, an uncertainty proportional to the time of observation .... The language must be able to talk about real materials in which electric fields or charge fluctuations occur, oscillate with natural frequencies of the substance, and die away over time.

OK imagine slicing into left or right, one hand wish-wash the other,
both so caressed against convergence to unity, saying it is the same
and it rests in the self-same placement, barn abiding in itself,
self-confuted by evidence in profile white contra white:

> In case only whites are considered, white meaning one thing, none the less there are many whites and not one; since neither in the succession of things nor in the argument will whiteness be one. For what is predicated of white will not be the same as what is predicated of the object which is white, and nothing except white will be separated from the object; since there is no other ground of separation except the fact that the white is different from the object in which the white exists.

Yet for not tell is possible as cannot be in a world by zero
frequency across bounded separation its fringe charge return con-
tour, biplane rotation never breviate over its own pitch, or
'there is no place void of being, for the void is nothing; but
that which is nothing could not exist; so then being is not moved;
it is impossible for it to go anywhere, if there is no void.' And
by the line of correction if the void is nothing, is nothing what
by self-likeness the void is and so by necessity to have this field
of being; and is it full or empty or changing through time and if
hardly can be spoken of this as what also is, must that also set
limit to thought itself and is the limit finite or would be. If
the void does not exist it must be full of non-existence, out to
the brim which must exist in its location since not all is void,
thus it is the void is not nameless but at its natural frequency
else generic within limitless non-existence it could not be named,
into its proper non-being. The song of birds that do not sing,
because there are none where else they would sing, not from absence
nor migrancy, the not-song is from not-being and not merely not
there nor not-possible nor silentness falling rapt upon attentive
deaf ears. 'At a deeper level, we can even think of all these

charge or field fluctuations as results or distortions of the electromagnetic fields that would occur spontaneously in vacuum devoid of matter.' Downward to darkness. 'It is not that there are actually interactions between nonexistent matter in the empty spaces, although we could argue that way from the vacuum-field point of view.' If the nothing that is has field boundaries as non-infinite then spectral inductance cannot be zero; or if infinite then exclusively by imaginary separation adjusted as possible to go there and be in thought's realm full of emptiness as a jug from which water is or has been poured, not in time only but by logic of regularity as, is the inside space jug-shaped whether full or empty, in habit water or non-water, so the passengers may choose not to see, not to look, but the driver of the car will know because that is to be the driver, powered by love of the known.

Adornment would henceforth be overall resembled like for like, each drawn into medley abstentional by sounds in song, lights fresh for out in paucity extreme little beyond guesswork, they run up a flag of their own ruin no need to doubt it just an old shirt not of convenience nor statehood demented across the brow of day and night, offshore to the rim of bright nullity all about the bone. I saw too by links of redaction in fluency, not yet perfect because by nature self-mutable even the bounds transient each to alter in replacement through pair logic overlay, in otherhood unfinished bearing phrasal turmoil in cap position, limit across rotation the corridor not self-invaded by sweetness each time in momentary batch flavour. Equalised to run its surplus attached to overdrive each word capsule clamped at reward issue upper to lower jaw purchase grind on this scam of scams. Celeb indenture whitened unfeeding ever lustrous the screen flashed innocent joy by retort flicker mendacious smiles mandible shortfall tended early in hurts are they minimal collect is friendship classified? Proximity fuses tell you this matrix censorship impersonated clock device, each word feels out for the next its soft vibration to match by click on this. The corridor is cleared from mouth outward, treat to treaty release near enough through the shaded window, a slice of bread close to living streams all without echo stem occasion pair improved. That's how it goes, as it happens rapid parlando articles slurred unheeded. They start to depart ever suddenly not in random motion maybe randomised as permitted by variance don't stray or look back from the garden path detour, its attachment. Living trees burn, the smells are intense, how like you this fresh surprise and for nothing why ever not, day by day low gear marked out infusible, garment reduction being your slave to foot at once the check of it, free radical re-fused. The work of destruction is also work, not-also.

In separate parts nearly joined only this time not all they are, not at all disallowed even later distorted in actual fact for to for from enlist I wanted wishful to say, repeating the steps already known, payment all in and excepted from the dulcet paper assumed so, sane so outright. Opposite not certainly site-specific because not contradicted or not certainly the further action permits compatibles to be laterally in contradiction while not opposed just as pair facing off even defiantly can be colluded in figuration mode by mode, inverse by converse each surfactant by links of separation, dotted quaver advancement. In the complete structure the whole empty box from facing without directive is in contradicted within self-agency anisotropic, needles by deduction or front-seat driven darts dispensed by contrary energetic repulse, of twin-bond confronted by so-being internally against being itself:

> But is it enough to say merely that each of the contradictory aspects is the condition for the other's existence, that there is identity between them and that consequently they can coexist in a single entity? No, it is not. The matter does not end with their dependence on each other for their existence; what is more important is their transformation into each other. That is to say, in given conditions, each of the contradictory aspects within a thing transforms itself into its opposite, changes its position to that of its opposite.

I saw these gaps of explanation rolling like wheels contrary within themselves, alien motions on fire with coriolis demeanour. I saw the grains self-rotate in their own amazement with noise of spheres metallic and burnished, along the baseline it is by amount at principle neither so nor not because contradiction is inherent and not alternate in sense ordering, I saw this notion in full fiery finesse, alive alive-o. Barter be barter bitten, either the other's mine not not by violence water-rooted but in being what and despite reason in self-nature, within continuous transient boundary layers no char no riot the horses in lather of instruction by the turning fire of the wheels. The saw-horse by the roadside part broken down is here quite forgot, natural wastage beneath rain and more rain by tropic cloudburst each side awash in spate; yet massive condensed occurrency to burn out a track instantly closed, absorbed against

parallel ground being and notice not-is distracted reciprocal act
negative ostensive preceptual at all events known, write what you
see in the field of burnt stalks, birefringent address been said
as seen, as never yet to be born. Truck water truck fire fast and
slow corrosion only the principle is contra to itself and will switch.
Still point of a turning world self-deluded in unthought anyone could
purchase indulgence at cost still nothing even the zero-field is in-
flected, by charge and currency, District and Circle from top to below
O Bottom thou art translated. Spirit a sub-department in the store of
material, add-on premium addict, grist to mills of working plant life
expectancy: two semi-infinite media separated by a planar slab gap.
Open wide ye that do bite ye that do bite and are swallowed, giant
like ants in shadow forfeits, is this what you want to be told to
want yet more, will you walk up faster capital market mockery in
fall, bet on the loss use other people's money why else or not else.

For sure not in good likeness, profile in slant along the catchment
proposed, the speech corridor. The sentence in word build is additive
but logic partitions the stream, sense outriders thicken its pur-
pose impossible for anything not to be or not if by its own option
of necessity, thus it is impossible for anything to not be. That
state of not being anything is reserved for nothing, heavily in
occupation. But and to not be is the being also variant of possible
utter inbuilt outcry or by speech device against not must (by self-
necessity) be not where it is but what it does, to do as against
not to cause to be done: on the right boys, on the left girls,
decreed for the children of fate graded in charity. The root for
commerce takes from suspended milk colloidal its creamy delinquent
pride of decision, curds resonant in whey by opposed nature not
contradicted because lattice charges are in the separation of milk's
being, conjugate and pre-organic beyond doubt, post-sexual sweet or
even sour. The nipple corridor by conductance of care origins com-
pletes the pair bonding expressed to the tongue before more than
murmur construes its answer: how, then can what is be going to be
in the future, coming to this? What is for is without tense, but
the corridor conjugates erotic for-being as root derivative as one
satisfied to the start of another or many, the harbingers are come
by implant of being into the contradiction of hip-on singularity.
Joy to hold, the issue of being up close against another heart-beat
at best parallel never in unison which never is the natural place
of being then and there, to brood out this by generic fortune as
yet to cost a cool arm and a leg, orthopedic expense sheet.
By sonic socratic dub nett recusancy obversive deduct interval

exfold, train up pitch departures, percuss the air punctual let addit pressure point, aqueous gearing will screen hyperbaric fully virtual it is separation. Being intensely separated and sparse for hit on what syllabic, in tense on this what variant dot fill locative vivid declaration (lunch). Did you know you knew instantly by compression, voidal top soundings in laid decrement these lines recursive by local necessity, towards it across wide compacted exposure to anticipate to hear what you cannot know you will, because which because is switched causally and not by single cause except by exempted recourse packing (lunch again). The sonar range spectrally patrolling its bounds, touch-marking to elicit inhibitive self-brevity in each case of ex-prime saltation. This is likely the gap incident rebound of where it is, in renown re-known like this, its clicky diapason expelled and declared, regular as chicks. Catchwork on ledgework gives over a promissory counterfoil from its free-range checkout not till nor till not nor both by transformation, patriots of tilted vacancy restorative to fresh-field topic, silence ardently retrieved. These are the markers of what's there, what there is, by necessity in the field of self-play and no player, deduct mentality. There is a garden in her face, when owls do cry, or if I live or if I die. Molecular contradiction given out for taken aback, 'each new distribution seems to contradict what preceded it; since there are no predictable continuities, one can only listen in the immediate present to each moment as it occurs.'

Rapid decay confirms the sonic void each one in exit profile from disturbance and hunting loop to mobile equivalency, complete negation of the negation in rate pursuit of imbalance. Titration of self boundary each close to contrary echo, cross-harvest defeat of integration. Ears on these targets in quick disregard, being not, under stress of not culminant strike-out. Voidal audible not being itself not nothing not silence not word unheard durational or anything else as else: decay fast to quick exact counter point, each not by next time teeth on the edge of its subharmonic vacant rebuff. Disproof of perfect pitch, 'so that still, while we are within the compass of appearances, they may afford us a good, but not the most excellent, life: for the highest life is above all appearances, even in the substance itself.' Within the span of what is, being is previous to life and by negation is the substance of itself, what is and what is not conclude the molecular universe. The appearance is determined by uncertain spectral data, conditional to knowing and hearing the sonic witness, but the substance itself is not above nor below any self-being because it is the efficient and final cause in self-being itself and for its own cascaded negation. Contested equity starts here, without contest equity would fail, listen out you know you can know what you hear, well enough by what you don't, in the echo-particles of a speech plan gazetted for duration. Even milk will testify, address given. What's that humming sound? The so-called outside. Out there the dreamboat faction rally their coupons, slice for slice before the shrine of self-preference, trimmed with gold leaf packets scattered in profusion, the kids grab in handfuls, who knows by what rate of exchange. All so up and down blame this time partitive genitive scantlings set to move. The votaries intone high-cap funding assignments shift your arm over a bit, dink first will dank surface later taken, plinthoid. Do we know you're also out, calculated to produce unharmful discontinuous intersections hatch the foreground La Tempesta's letraset no gripe no single, the absence of both to be screened for notice chill. If disjunct samples be contrarian in platform soles the underfloor can be more to a liking, trained up for a mood replay scorn of the near word in darkness. Are these avoidance routines disinclined to the singular, shrine glitter ahead at request stop? Did you really know that, gulf of sulphur by predicate clock redox, life force. Below the blanket in differences in dielectric response are enough to create the force again of separation, to occur in the realm of zero frequency subversed to mood clamour new loath to depart, from its vastly abundant reserve, and darkly bright are bright in dark directed. The sheep of being scatter here, by enhanced shrine distillation well I never, better you not. At the peak, necromancy I saw it pythian non-sense scrabbling her word chips why not try on a chasuble, mode of choice. Near relatives get a look-in on probate, that's usual for keep-calm retroflex oh rise now with tweet or bleat in scandal, premium blend teabags.

At surface scrap all of its hot cluttered void, promote weapon system aggression nowhere near contradicted nor in show trials of adversary forensic lubricants, deep-fried football league. Slap on extra, contravalency in stack contrary to self-being and not to central casting who conflate derived turns from agency know-how polarised to their onward tasks of separation idiomatics, rushing to the ocean. The internal origin of matter is the negation of its force for proximity, love-strife easily then promoted into directive estrangement among the mariner's one-time asters: astrolabe necrology of murder drones. In the self of nature (replaced for shrine, come on) is not opponent's transit, and the negation of its will to power is the knowledge of its force, and not the force itself. To know *contra naturam* is the torque of its truth function or what it mostly does, sprung out from its apex by birth from one to many, vacuum clusters, 'a molecule with a permanent dipole can also induce a dipole in a similar neighbouring molecule and cause mutual attraction.' Yolk leakage not by metonymy and or not in thermal disorder exponent, to be born frequently all over the place, open-mouthed in sake of assented measurement.

> Worlds or *kosmoi* are formed when groups of atoms combine to form a cosmic whirl, which causes the atoms to separate out and sort by like kind. A sort of membrane of atoms forms out of the circling atoms, enclosing others within it, and creating pressure by whirling. The outer membrane continually acquires other atoms from outside when it contacts them, which take fire as they revolve and form the stars, with the sun in the outermost circle. Worlds are formed, grow and perish, according to a kind of necessity.

Here I saw beyond this to the corridor in assured vacant possession telescopic to the field inside the mouth, where the speech-parts of separation had been swallowed in foreground almost in forgiveness, fricative was the advice and to palate by adhesion said to be forward. Telemetry agrees in counterpart granular pulse fusion, filter degraded signal speak joy intone its special beauty the mouth knows this. By what cannot be said the overjoy of being so will romp home, bacteria scraped off from words even stupidity unrecognised. Is contradiction a joy *ex post facto* and this only, or by negation restored and reprieved, is being its own joy regardless, by omitted transfer's omission? In the field it self? And would that not need to be anywhere true as also not-true but not untrue? And also not to be needed or not, the wanting parts in scant otherhood.

Rule One: people with top pay are rubbish, everyone knows this, it's a law of nature. Rule Two: Diogenes offered himself as a master, in the market, to any slave who needed one. Rule Three: you do not see into the life of things, dimensionless or not, except by harvest of data plotted against uncertainty. Rule Four: justice is scarce ever the obverse of injustice, since the one is the top end and the other the bottom. None of this it must be said is the power of harmony even in charge fluctuation or lifetimes except the desire integrate the variation of separate notice, that's what spirit mostly does who where she went bare in her forehead morning, only men write their socks off like this; better to be clear than dizzy or cynic, not to refuse joy in favour of rapture or contentment, the gradients are lateralised in additive counterflow. But rapture is also pretty nice. It was the deep power of contradiction in dipole scattering brilliance, tumid with negation, deep only by customary expletive, that made a blaze before the eyes, because you see only by knowing and doing what you know. Spirit sat ever upon her hands but then that's also not true, the truth of strong being and being strongly true is not weakened by extractive countermeasure, only by complacent denial. Empty truth is a medicine without a sickness, no time like the present tense of absolute ionic discharge. Stand up front and wave banners, mean all that you do in the price of so-being there too, full on get a discount, hardly look back but weep to have that which it fears to lose, *possente spirto* yet uppermost within the daedal earth, joy enjoined. I saw the blood fluency in evidence all around in motion by allowance and detour making enough place and then back to yield by nature, oscillant and if necessary pre-biotic with delirious empty flash, grievance to grief to greats and grateful, small fitments of oscular slide in parchment or gum stencil. Not in fight itself block to hit not euphoric these streams non-procurrent give over what they take verging across tacitry androgen plum tanks, by immersion all tissue in speech seamarks, love-laundry, joy in action on side the stuff of hit and miss no chance lost but by necessity of its shadow culminant to not say by knowing is to be aside with not for not, axial and suffused means nothing for I had nothing at all so in such sense contended. Fluting awash previous sure to find on the margin affront no big thing offset intercepted for fluid introits. Did frequently gallivant splint tongue flicker spring of air well glad.

As already from the air aver peak saliency curvature, gross up dwelling too much insect bites by graphic notation, handout time! That's what benefits now mean for those in line pacified and purified by immensity don't shout hypnotic over hyperbole for play dosage in bone. Strike at the price in the field do men buy it for a song or nothing less than entire, forever greedy the downside of simple nothing poverty and displacement close to starvation. No dream all hunger in the mouth get the fuck out of joy and beauty come on be direct for a change truth to tell not even war but abject misery the nothing to not have not eat, feel your mouth lost for words and minimum fluid intake. Dry is not a sound dwindling beyond utterance because in the very internal being of the nothing that is not there, empty. What language is this unable to be spoken tongue cracked I saw no need nor use for the dialect beyond all that so is self-being implicit as a luxury good, fancy handbag for what you'll never put in it or snap its glitzy closure void at heart and brain where mouth unoccupied not even known, even or not, masticate on words of the species unquoted on the exchange so far below par. Keep very calm since excess along the indigent/indignant border is the radiant bonus paid out against Rule One. The calmness is a special kind of final joy even at deep unkindness, because it is the truth of things and this truth shall not make you free, to sit still or not it is for sure necessitous but man-made and not by necessity this limpet contradiction faces the void and is the truth of captivity, to know this is the joy of ruin and needfulness feel these words in the feral mouth of separation this too no lick no spittle, freedom too costly even at the top end or especially there (Rule Four) our bonds are our sure bondage already in manifest plain view I saw this too.

Who's to say a lot more there in this field where will bondage tremble and damage hunt down its course in nature to address and rid for simple is nothing is for simple grinding up of promise-words, this true on view in self of being crawled there are self-plain stupid know long from longer the corridor in turn to be seen undevoted slim clinic slim chance toxic mutation within nothing to get fed or not approx to mate near to die or soon enough or tendency either further acclaimed to diverge. Driven thus walnut whirl dance portal, veer in to now know this field untreated and untilled, is nothing worth as proportional to counterpart vector, *chiare fresche e dolci acque*, and own no other function. None but other sign reversed, quick enough alternate on or off in case synapse deterrent bring the altercate to a table there enough in a difference all for its show. For this was it iron in the fire likeness struck hoist pack the drill oh pack the drill enough, just that. At its moment of crisis quartz foolery in principle taken down, to basic parts diametric with causation taste the same or hardly. Confirm in name only in sufficient against cranial limit output a hit ergo swim until betterment divvy or levy, aggrandise bits share issue. They all go forward where else I saw them go, then one said, I will take the shoes with me, we all trembled and I nodded because it was right, burning for burning the shoes had been saved for this and now so it was, was to be. The dream very true, in truth a dream of human kind come back, go forward, a shadow drops like stone. Water on all sides, the life of men. In the morning milk delivery up to the very door clink clink I heard it on the step, it was Andrew of course our regular. My mouth should twitch beyond sufferance in its knowledge rebate, anyone could weep for no less, day by day. There is no unity in mind its line in stolen property its fainting breath absurd: a property of the void itself.

The play is seen there in the loose fit, near enough did you ever see so, the near breast in sweetest touch of blue just a tint with the brush dare not tremble ask no question retorsed of this being just here is here the nipple absterged in lightest shadow to give suck in natural kind reposeful we are to see just how he saw it his light brush dabbled closer and playful and fiercely erotic, steward of giddy transfixed mouth furniture. Well he would, wouldn't he, his brush a blurred tongue of fire abetted to damnation love of truth from itself never turning hardly ever in play of the mind and sense. I saw the love of this denied and bitten in its own shadow for donative accountancy pressure of free acceptance fantastically expensive don't pretend otherwise this is the domain of otherhood and its fiery excelling beauteous folly, here exactly tender,. exact fare only on sight forward carriage paid up. A small fortune however or not, more or less mostly sides contradiction lies further back in the bedrock of stitch and mend and spin, threadwork clathrate to oddments if or not, digested monastic lunch-party while we also err, chew it over like sheep dyed in green. Bomb the airport burn off the ocean terminal rip out those waves, baby it's time. The object has status if the price is stable, nothing much else in a caution panel aflame often. It is doubtful to praise only immoderately in joyful gorge under full sunlight no reason for nothing to be dark convinced superstition like unity of first cause, primitive mistaken wingbeat at all once (italic homage). Oh then light the light, doubt the good fight, bearing up towards illusory primordial laundry basket. Separate the colours token gatherance fire assembly point. I saw them sing and I felt the word in my gullet pressure for outlet too little and too lately known but then clamorous we are what they do. At every stop they sign up for instant continuance with or without sex but preferably both, our turn to glow in borrowed hardihood more usually flamboyant.

Zest for the contrary is mostly a style appetite, especially in harsh destructive warfare carried (on) by all the news channels, remittance of fastness even I didn't need to look for first sight of patronage nosing ahead right on local time's bed of nails. There uppermost consigned to mutilation beyond economic repair, market fright spoiling to collapse. Beyond the front struts for duff shelter, immediate debridement. So obvious it hardly needs esteemed carbon fibre rite upwards in lock ear to ear, froth of grip opposites who if not and if too at the same sacrificial ironing-board. Convalescence fully enabled rightfully, need to play out the whole worth logged new for old locate enemy positions, remote sensing it's the scriptural conduit sold out. Go up to the front entrance, see if this time your ticket works.

All right then how is a dearness of being as other than itself able to be felt and known distributively, through self aspect beyond merely incident rap to outpatience, the grain of parts resistant to retard summation or time-average by closure even mortified by engine chatter. Even then corrective by dearness as close-run and held on by vantage eyelids, inertial longings counterparted by rocks and scree, abraded detritus (read, although dust as we are) by adjustment to resent self-knowledge greedy know thyself inward as expense in tendence the talk would talk too separated from how not it must be but is so dear already exfused not owing nor lending a colour schematic to end calls, or feasting in their dappled shade, missing and turning for want of what missed to be consistent of being things, maybe brilliant let them adore molecules in gamut clumpy and choosy thus in their nature too. Crescent too undo root default scan for brain error not to happen in occurrence or be self-revealed, attenuate votive greed near panic struck retinal negligence going on towards *sangfroid* at minimum. Be fair to them, lapsed straggling clouds bent on remission, the knowledge base cannot be stable when in being not yet or merest has-been, would have concurrently will by then, unavailed tense logic *nunc stans* adversion to run and run whippy particle scrappage. I saw it dear to blister pack and shut the full length of the corridor bring in mud on your shoes batter my heart or yours, terrific vouch to swap terrific twinkle-toes.

It takes a whole army of true rejects to consign this visitation to gallery format, down to the near crannies protocol to tell and make undeclared cellular incision or blade entries or this or fresh promotion. Thus is tantamount to negation of the negation, to contradict alignment of its source at first level suffix, a bumpy ride as however not forever nonsense splinter did been up-critical the frame self-deferred. By what the transfer of any singular moment pining to join a fair deal into its transit partitions get to be go be insidiously out for counting who could tell that, known or stricken wait for a bit water drops in their clepsydral gazes, avocations in humid toilsome partnerships. Cranky-danky fear of abstractions itself fearful in failing purchase another stupefied jump reprieved to match grandeurs of its denial. Is the molecular contrivance diagram contracted, how can these things become those things unless these cross so slant to those by syncopation of semblance to be in full self retort, chemic valence disputed circuitry. Not done to nor yet been, been for been as for the disjected these to those are contra as been one to many, been for been, one or not binome yet only more I saw the spin tensor across the axis of sufficiency, from first to second shell redemption I did then for then pre-hend how differential is free for is entrained. So then we know (or, more conservatively, 'expect') that, at zero temperature, the spins will be frozen into configurations aligned along some (domain-wise) constant magnetisation axes. The adjunct limbs jostle to each other suppletive metric fluctuation closer to self-same but never quite, word for word parlance in the milk-run acronyms of this day.

Adduced over and along tarmac will the avenue declare its former interval most trees live longer than most men, canopies in rain shadow mark of the generous recede from here tells where here is, common sidereal. The stake-out is clearest at night, in gas-exchange microporous what's not seen is true to being so, the spread calculus set from ground zero some canny gaffer you bet known to be in fibrous cloudy attachment being *in situ* planar slot uppance. To be light and bright dilates passion across the full corridor in profile of what conduces to void, serial negation drainage of spirit intake, out of the way of the Way. So might say passion closest to zero in remix is or is convergent to joy

the index of refraction at the slide plane. Nutritional by
self-shadow depletion parameter digested at the ice-cream
parlour, part for whole on a see-saw and slumped in glory.
The thing about food is, someone else might get it, then what.

These things I saw in the field clear enough sometime in
pleasaunt joy of season, and winter aswell was no objection
yet much was done by violence as often in danger from spirit
and self-ruin not change but damage how could any man not know
this in himself, harm done to womankind by stupidity of appetite.
Greed in the field infolded as star bedding and seed countenance
continued there, the central banks welded to reserves in well
self-interest or how else bond for bond and be what they do.
Taunting themselves with foresight badges, now is how to finish
without fiduciary rank ending induced. Fractional deponent
closeness is not so hard too: when the travel time equals the
period of a sampling frequency, the contribution to the inter-
action is screened down to about half of its nonretarded strength.
Yet the recursion cannot be close since the stop key is well out
beyond reach, even in transform assignment. A language may die
also from the record of currency exchange to full pair-convert
transumed in surrender value, decalibrated; or the travel line
from matter to fancy of spirit is invert and pyretic: smoke for the
mirror, tenant creamery.

> The original cremation pyre was placed where the heavens met the earth and where the inhabitants of nearby settlements could observe smoke rising into the air. It was also located in the one place on the hilltop where the position of a distant mountain would correspond to that of the summer moon. The subsequent development of the site gave monumental expression to this relationship, gradually focussing that particular alignment until it was narrowed down to the space between the tallest stones.

The corridor is and to be the avenue, from particulate vapour to
consign into bedrock, transit of durance it is a formative exit
in naturalised permission, solemn grade-one rigmarole, better
Wiglaf's rebuke and insurance payout. To be this with sweet
song and dance in the exit dream, sweet joy befall thee is by
rotation been and gone into some world of light exchange, toiling
and spinning and probably grateful, in this song.

Reference cues

V. Adrian Parsegian, *Van der Waals Forces; A Handbook for Biologists, Chemists, Engineers, and Physicists* (Cambridge, 2006).

Alexander Altland and Ben Simons, *Condensed Matter Field Theory* (2nd ed., Cambridge, 2010).

Andreas Kayser, Mark Knackstedt, Murtaza Ziauddib, 'A Closer Look at Pore Geometry', *Oilfield Review*, 16 (2004), 44-61.

Leucippus (5th cent. BC), as reported by Diog. Laert., *Lives of Eminent Philosophers*, Bk IX, trans. Hicks.

Parmenides of Elea, *On Nature* (c.490-475 BC), trans. Burnet.

Melissos of Samos (follower of Parmenides), *On Nature* (fragments), trans. Fairbanks.

Aristotle (384-322 BC), *Physics*, Bk I, trans. Fairbanks.

Kung-sun Lung (d. 252 BC), *Pai-ma lun* ('On the White Horse'), trans. (entire) by A.C. Graham in his *Disputers of the Tao* (La Salle, Ill., 1989), pp. 85-90.

Richard Bradley, 'The Land, the Sky and the Scottish Stone Circle' in Chris Scarne (ed.), *Monuments and Landscape in Atlantic Europe; Perception and Society during the Neolithic and Early Bronze Age* (London, 2002).

Mao Zedong, 'On Contradiction' (August, 1937).

William Langland, *Piers Plowman* (c.1360-87), B-Text, ed. Schmidt, C-Text, ed. Pearsall.

Simonides of Ceos (c.556-469 BC), Frag. 543, 'Lament of Danaë', sung version by Ed Sanders, 'Danaë in a Box upon the Sea' on DOCD 5073, A 05 (1990); Tiziano Vecelli (Titian), *Danaë* (1544-6, Museo Nazionale, Naples).

Sir Philip Sidney, *The Old Arcadia* (1590), The Fourth Eclogues.

Boethius, *Consolations of Philosophy*, trans. I.T. (1609).

William Shakespeare, *Sonnets* (1609), &c.

William Wordsworth, 'Tintern Abbey' (1798), &c.

P.B. Shelley, 'Mont Blanc' (1817), &c.

Alban Berg, Lecture concerning his opera *Wozzeck* (1929).

Tadeusz Borowski, 'The Man with the Package' in his *This Way for the Gas, Ladies and Gentlemen* (London, 1976).

Cui Jian, 'Yi Wu Suoyou' (1986): http://www.youtube.com/watch?v=PeL_CZl7t8.

Christian Wolff, *Early Piano Music* (1951-1961), played by John Tilbury and others, inlay note to MRCD51 by Michael Parsons (2002).

Kevin Davies, *Lateral Argument* (New York, 2003).

AL-DENTE

(2014)

Oh summer's day

Guessed

Livid flight transom offer distortion per open
by heart to learn, cross-over. Place settle
announcing already time for both in plain way,
in modest profession. You know it as to do
and have in prospect willed.
                                        Do the same to
meet this, claim its view,
                                    intense version for
bird-like acceptance, its
                                    climate at or flutter
twitch and stir–
                        yours out for semence dew.
As a brace for each in sure avid dependence
folded up by its profusion to and by, by and
or yet wing out all yet yours. Up in new air
taken in flourish stress across is as while
can in counterpart, a cancel sheet restored.

Truth

In general known by a quartz vein predicted
as synapse of permission cause to find. Yours
in readiness ever parlance run softly forward,
to this address the bright margin view. How
not yet did you clasp our sheer furrow, flex
joined instinct tendon advisor, more careful
joy turned even now in new stitch. Be still
furnish as to rove back, come through it is
the first cause, this now into continuance
saying your proverb by mouth open previous.
Who can say give over, the night arriving as
it will by cloud cover, as often so needed
for a visage. Expression held in for in half
promise flooded over, no sun so shone more
to fill, find out now for staff simple to see.

Reach Up

On patter you see you why attach do in
all for no more, not anyway yet main take
a lesson open. Ever why surface if stroke
as can deflect is that going on, etch on
murmur day why, you did flask area tremble
in the water jump. Esteem frankly to give
over and across this, even why or by our
way of glowing to blood rush, singular to
fingers along the pulse track, to picture
seen up to park novelty. For where and oh
where this time to crack like leaves falling,
by when litter to seek out in turn, yours
will be given for free, for now why all your
own; it is yet perfect, running. As or like
sure, arrow too near in wet shoes. Abandon
or not you see each delivers here the ground
station, half turn back to sit, some in hand.

Morning

To the or so then for all for on, both for
these an or then, down as before in fond and
too sound by, this. Then from ever bring
along but far but, to under the this better
then to be along, few for some, not of or
at first so. Let by so ever go to, bind with
this the, these given same for him, off far.

By the or and or other near true, yet as done
to say allow this for also, for the for than
over far found extravagant inlet, then one
inward plead from same to find, as implore
by both to be to the, on this or these ever
to from self part by allowance. Sent to say
out by where too in want seem all of or it.

Than the on few across as near or by as gain
here next her to find and over to enchant this
will for be outward in grand. For the for you
and these to hold, to on, most then passion
by far ever and, down to this, so. As known
for the its as flow also in tune, by part set
under be from be by at grief never so found.

Hour-glass

Cap to prize at once accept with more be-
tween pair backing, two flame gone out fill
granulate. Lean to sign off yet sway trotty,
yet crush did we tie for the front, will wear
alert beyond natural fluence unit dissolute
gleaming reflected pastime, occupy kitty do.

Push over treat colour hitched on either ready
panting, agree on part go outward, forty for
season spread. Matched in twin antic enough
come-up to, remember as whatever print net
gather her face city rueful. In breath scar-
let seldom dissuade a member or busy, or fine.

Infusion

This mercy will replace to them near first
exactly, as taken from clear at new payment
tacit doesn't reduce the few. Natural as due
not meaning to align song even reverted by
fixity, grant is yours.
                              Is description as
assert this brand get into advancement offer
agree to credit, must agree even so offset
along the close margin, is yours.
                                              Watching
is the site when agreed to break outward pass
claimed in front by either filter, in promise
adept cede a pledged condition willing to
give prominence flat-long fall. Walk over
quickly is yours.
                         However and so far, as or
will accept without presume limit or foremost
latitude, will discover to steady if brilliant
sky gets easily by admit iron former melted
intermit. Will line for, is yours.
                                             Does this
scrape or grate whenever veering to harbour
a fusion incline yet to feel redress faction,
in link acceptance, grant is yours.
                                                Be given
is yours, grant for this, is so quickly to be
is too and for, is yours.

Subsequence

Present little did to perform notice for instance
fragrant not in peril, left for sworn bee what
you will. Or fresh if lost many soon, want to sail
across paper at decree never proof, love decried so
frequent bee blood sent horizon, share your own.

Share your own pursuit not able as tenant also or
grow on loose hints, down the bank nil forbear
infill back-lit. Offer lid graft, over lifted add
to your list all mind prevail, share your own.

For Tom

Do relent so do borrow for, ever infringe you
whether allow close up in redempt so. For do
to give over why for cue rested, for done along
drove besides must give for. Severance risk it
make ado turn-out, relative familiar else invoke
assist ever for over please did explode, is calm.

Swift heart so to be reached, hand back sewn
by its near cleft firstly implored relict, on over
ours by still water so to rent, fabric agitate by
and low. For usual mean to tend, out to use
in refuge placement did so want, so to back
from tearing store reflect over for ever inflected.

However dear done for this, remedy full assume
what's known all in pocket irrigate, did you would
for love's transit gone to my ground near both in
yours, hand over mine. So close so warm no next
fallacy refer tonic or search, define for where this
much rising, hope in full attend are there or are.

Onwards resent once over no yet despite fit token
redeem fitting ever more stick, for up reset to reckon
in hand in part dear satisfy, replenish lease overt
by given streams and current folded. Soon too for
gratify, brim over plainly moreover, inspect dear heart
passing swell, felt patched, fill to all loyal found.

Index of Titles or First Lines

EU DECLARATION OF GPSR CONFORMITY

Books published by Bloodaxe Books are identified by the EAN/ISBN printed above our address on the copyright page. This digital reprint was manufactured by Lightning Source at the printing works indicated in their code. This declaration of conformity is issued under the sole responsibility of the publisher, the object of declaration being each individual book produced in conformity with the relevant EU harmonisation legislation with no known hazards or warnings, and is made on behalf of Bloodaxe Books Ltd on 1 May 2026 by Neil Astley, Managing Director, editor@bloodaxebooks.com.

www.ingramcontent.com/pod-product-compliance
Lightning Source LLC
LaVergne TN
LVHW051224070526
838200LV00057B/4599